Poet in the Fortress

ALSO BY THOMAS AITKEN, JR.

A Foreign Policy for American Business, 1962

Poet in the Fortress
THE STORY OF LUIS MUÑOZ MARÍN

by Thomas Aitken, Jr.

AN NAL — WORLD BOOK

Published by The New American Library

To my mother, Marion, and my wife, Barbara

ACKNOWLEDGMENTS

Most acknowledgments end where they should begin: with mention of the writer's patient wife. In this case, Barbara Aitken took the role of research director and collaborator in the project and joins me in thanking many willing helpers, too few of whom can be listed here.

Teodoro Moscoso lent early encouragement, and Ismaro Velásquez, then on Sontheimer & Runkle's public relations staff, aided our first probes. Governor Luis Muñoz Marín and his wife, Inés, submitted to lengthy interviews with their usual good grace. Governor Muñoz Marín has granted permission for the reprinting of selections from his Godkin Lectures and the poems "Umbrella," "Death," and "At the Stake." Of the Fortaleza staff, Heriberto Alonso and Charles Zimmerman were particularly helpful.

Valuable assistance was granted by the University of Puerto Rico. Dr. Rodolfo Rivera, library chief; Emilio Colón, head of the Colección Puertorriqueña; Professor Thomas Mathews of the Institute of Caribbean Studies; and historians Lidio Cruz Monclova and José A. Gautier gave of their time and knowledge.

The San Juan Star, with its incisive columns by A. W. Maldonado and the perceptive interpretations of editor William Dorvillier, was a rich source of material.

Talks with writers, teachers, politicians, and private citizens filled many crevices in the story's pattern. All are remembered gratefully. Space limits the list to Earl Parker Hanson, José Trías-Monge, Marco Rigeau, Mayoress Felisa Rincón de Gautier, Samuel Quiñones, Antonio Fernós-Isern, Raul Gándara, Ed Rosskam, Gunter Hett, Don José Alegría, and Gustavo Agraít.

Arabel Porter and Victor Weybright were comforting editorial guides, patient, good-humored, discerning.

Friendly hands offered more photographs than we could use. We are indebted to the Fortaleza's photographer, Fernando Colorado; *The San Juan Star* and Gunter Hett; the New York office of the Economic Development Administration of the Commonwealth of Puerto Rico; the island's Institute of Culture and Department of Education.

CONTENTS

INTRODUCTION:

The Paradox of Puerto Rico

THE STORY OF Puerto Rico is a study in opposites, surprises, and inconsistencies. The island itself, a green gem set in an unusually placid sea, basking in an average yearly temperature of about seventy-five degrees, has been repeatedly devastated by some of the most violent onslaughts in the history of hurricanes. A compact area of only 3,435 square miles, it contains both dry scrub and a jungle-covered mountain watered by nearly perpetual rain. Its people are crowded into a density index of some seven hundred per square mile —more than Japan's and about equal to what the United States would have if everyone in the world were put within its borders; yet Puerto Rico's citizens still challenge Malthus with one of the world's highest rates of population increase, and improve their standard of living while doing so.

Puerto Rico's political history has evolved in a series of surprises. The island first turned its back on history in the early nineteenth century; while most other Spanish colonies in the New World struck for independence, Puerto Rico decided to stay with Spain. In 1898, just as Puerto Rico had gained autonomy under the Spanish flag, an ironic turn of fate immediately placed the island in American hands, nullifying her short-lived freedom for fifty-four years, even changing her name to "Porto Rico," following the American pronunciation. In 1940, after decades of fruitless effort to obtain a grant of self-government from the United States, Puerto Ricans declared that their political status was a secondary issue; more important was the problem of obtaining a decent living for their sick and starving people. In 1952, secure in the belief that they had developed a successful approach to their economic difficulties, they returned to the question of their political status and proposed a formula for which there is neither provision nor prohibition in the Constitution of the United States. Puerto Rico became a commonwealth, a "Free Associated State," and the validity of the definition has been under assault ever since. Finally, in August, 1963, after some sixty-six years of association with Puerto Rico, the United States Congress saw the necessity to set up a thirteen-man commission to spend eighteen months to study and report on the island's political status—an issue still entangled with complexities and contradictions.

Puerto Rico's economic history in recent years has been similarly at variance with familiar patterns. In the decade of the 1940's the Puerto Rican government bought out landholders, broke up estates, took over public utilities and public services, and went into the manufacturing business. It was creating a socialistic state under the American flag.

In the fifties the government reversed this trend, selling its factories to private industry, and the administration undertook an intense program of aid and encouragement to private business.

In the sixties Puerto Rican leaders have reaffirmed a belief that material progress should be tempered by the spiritual needs of their people and have revived the discussion about the allocation of capital and goods between the private and the public sectors of their people.

Possibly this tendency toward the unexpected can be laid to the heterogeneous nature of the Puerto Rican himself, as derived from his forebears. Many of the first Europeans to settle in Puerto Rico were emigrants from other islands that, although nominally governed by great states, quietly preserved a core of independence: the Balearics, Corsica, the Canary Islands. In Puerto Rico they encountered the Arawaks, a peaceful but stubborn tribe of Indians more inclined to suicide or flight than submission to the new Spanish masters. The more antisocial newcomers joined the Indians in the hills. Later, runaway Negro slaves trekked to the hideaways. Here was produced the Puerto Rican *jíbaro*, the quiet, stolid hillman who came to know his own mind and trust few others.

Fading into the pages of Puerto Rican history are a succession of Spanish governors, followed by American administrators, none of whom have left their mark. In the memories of living Puerto Ricans, there have been only two leaders on the island: Luis Muñoz Rivera and his son, Luis Muñoz Marín. It was the father who struggled to obtain Spain's grant of autonomy for Puerto Rico, then saw liberty vanish under the American flag. It was the son who revived the struggle and devised a new formula for Puerto Rican freedom.

In the forefront of Puerto Rican public life is Luis Muñoz Marín, on whom so much of the island's recent development hinges. In him are combined many opposites: poetry and politics, toughness and tenderheartedness, idealism and practicality, the colossal energy of the doer and the contemplative nature of the thinker.

Behind him are the Puerto Rican people, in whom the flair for the unexpected takes many forms.

This is a people whose fanatics attempted the assassination of their governor and of the President of the United States in 1950 and whose patriots led all the states of the Union in voluntary enlistment for service in the Korean War.

This is a people who fled to the United States in a great surge during the 1950's and now are returning to their island in almost equal numbers.

This is a people whose taxi drivers seem cold-bloodedly to maim pedestrians on the streets, yet give a passenger a free ride because they may like the way he names his destination.

It is a people proud of the American-style freeways that lead a dizzy race out of its capital city, but dedicated to preserving as a monument to its Spanish heritage the confusion of narrow streets and crumbling edifices of the capital itself.

This is a people whose favorite sport is baseball and whose cultural hero is a Spanish cellist.

This is a people who are rarely called Americans by their fellow citizens in the United States and are rarely called Latins by their blood cousins in South America, yet who often serve as a bridge between the two.

This is a people whose island, once known as "the poorhouse of the Caribbean," is now described as "the showcase of the Americas."

These are the people who once elected, and have five times re-elected, Luis Muñoz Marín, formerly a poet and journalist, to lead them to a novel solution of one of the most intricate economic problems of our times. Elements of that solution are being used by many developing countries around the world. Its pattern forms the basis for the policies of the Alliance for Progress.

This is the story of the poet, kind, gentle—and contrary—who took over the fortress of the governor.

Poet in the Fortress

ONE

A Party at the Fortress

I<small>T WAS STILL DARK</small> when the old man stepped onto the road to San Juan, carrying the nine grapefruit appended to a single branch. The old man had never seen anything so remarkable. This was certainly a phenomenon worth presenting to El Vate at the inauguration.

San Juan was eighteen miles away, and the inauguration of the governor was six hours off. But the old man shuffling along the road recalled that in seventy-one years he had often walked the distance in four to five hours. The first times there had been no road for miles from his hut; later, only a cleared stretch of dirt padded with dust or clogged with mud in the rain. Now the way was paved. And the nine grapefruit and the starched spotlessness of the old man's white shirt and pale-blue trousers would better survive a walk than a ride with the boisterous holiday crowd on a bus. He could use the forty-five cents in his pocket for a cup of coffee and a ride home.

The darkness did not trouble the old man. Dawn would come before he reached strange territory. He knew when he passed a neighbor's mango tree, another's tiny grove of papayas. He recognized the sniff of a mongrel that had started for him with a growl. He grinned as he heard Paco's rooster clearing his throat for the morning song; the wailing of Gabriela's baby drifted from a shack outlined in the starlight.

As he came to the bend in the road, the old man heard the door of the bar and grocery store creak open. Antonio came to the doorway, stretched, then called out to him, "Hey, Pedro, you little old man, where are you going at this hour?"

"To San Juan. I'm going to give these grapefruit to Muñoz at the inauguration."

Antonio laughed. "You silly old fool. El Vate is going to be busy today becoming our first Puerto Rican governor. I mean, the first one elected by us. You'll never get near him. Say, what is that? Nine on a branch?"

"Nine on a branch," old Pedro said. "Even Don Luis Muñoz Marín has never seen anything like it."

Antonio rubbed one of the grapefruit gently. "No, I guess not," he said. He looked up suddenly. "Here comes the bus, Pedro. Let me help you on."

The old man shook his head. "Let it go. I am going to walk."

The bus roared by, its load of passengers shouting and singing. Two cars came immediately after.

Antonio stared. "That bus is all the way from Ponce. They haven't slept all night." The old man was walking away.

"Careful, old man!" Antonio called after him. "The road will be full of cars—from all over the island. This is a big day."

The old man never felt lonely on the road. There was a hut and a friend under nearly every tree or cloistered in every grove. In Puerto Rico there were always people everywhere. He remembered that Muñoz had said there were too many, that families were too big, and that when they had more money, they would have fewer children because it was that way in other countries. Pedro had felt guilty about his fifteen children and all the grandchildren. But he did not understand why there would be fewer children when everyone had more money. This mystified him, though he understood most of the things Muñoz said.

He understood when Muñoz said not to sell the vote any more, because then Pedro could vote for the Popular party to do the things he wanted, and the government would belong to him, and if it did not keep its promises, Pedro could vote the next time for another party. Pedro had not heard this from Muñoz directly, but from friends who had been there when Muñoz stopped his old car at the store one day and explained it to some people standing on the roadside. And when Pedro later found that his hours in the canefields were shorter and his wages increased, he became convinced that his one vote for the Popular party actually counted.

He could understand too when Muñoz said it didn't matter whether Puerto Rico was a state or a colony or independent because every man who was sick or starving was a slave. Of course it was more important to be well and have something to eat. Nine of his children had been buried in little white boxes. The old man remembered an argument about all this one Sunday at the bar. One of the young fellows back from the war said Muñoz was a turncoat for saying this because he used to be for independence and now he was just for himself. The old man had wanted to fight him, but the young fellow laughed and pushed him back in his chair, saying, "You're too old to fight me, Pedro, and it's lucky for you." Pedro had sat there, humiliated, with tears of fury burning in his eyes. The others just laughed. Someone clapped him on the shoulder and said that he was not to worry, that he was more a man than the young soldier, who didn't have any women or children.

He could understand Muñoz too when he said that everyone must work hard so that there would be money for hospitals and schools, and free lunches for hungry children, and factories with good wages. But now, even as he tried, Pedro was too old to work harder.

The sky was now a gray curtain hiding the tropic sunrise. In a few moments the gray veil would be whisked aside and the glory of a pale-blue sky with rich pink-bordered clouds would be shot with the first rays of gold. The moment came. Pedro felt the early heat of day and saw his shadow at his feet.

There were other walkers on the road. And more cars speeding by. There were cries to Pedro of "What have you got there, old man? There's no marketplace today!" To each one Pedro smiled and said, "These are for El Vate."

The noises, the children skipping by, the young people marching ahead, all the cars and buses, all the cries of gaiety blended into the heat and the shadows on the road. When the sweat began to drop into the old man's eyes, it all became dreamlike. He recalled other big days—some like this one, some different.

It had been different the day in 1888 when Pedro, as a boy, had walked into town with his father to watch the installation of a new Spanish governor. He had been frightened when the mounted Spanish soldiers flashed their swords at the crowds to make way for the governor's grand carriage. He had been more terrified and excited later, when his father had a fight with a Spaniard. Pedro and his father had been forced to hide in the canefields that night.

Then there was the day in 1897 when the other Muñoz, Don Luis Muñoz Rivera, father of El Vate, had come back from Spain with an agreement for the island to rule itself. Muñoz Rivera, who had been called "El León" ("The Lion"), was a big, handsome man with a fierce moustache and lots of tumbling black hair. Like his son Muñoz Marín, who was called "El Vate" ("The Bard"), Muñoz Rivera was a poet, and adored by the people. But El León had relied more upon his pen, whereas El Vate, like a troubadour, went into the countryside and told the people stories to illustrate his ideas. So they came to love him as a friend as well as a leader.

The old man saw some flags being carried on the road, the American flag and the Puerto Rican flag with one star. And they reminded him of another day, in 1898, a year after El León's pact with Spain. Then American soldiers had trudged along the road to San Juan, looking hot and tired and disgruntled even while people cheered because they thought the soldiers were bringing more freedom to the island than even Muñoz Rivera had won from Spain.

Now the flags were right beside the old man, a crowd was around him, and a bus stopped. The crowd pushed aboard, shoving the old man with it. Desperately he held the branch with the nine grapefruit still on it as high as he could, while the crowd jostled him toward the middle of the bus.

"What have you got there, old man?" someone shouted as the bus lurched forward.

"These are for the governor, for El Vate."

Two young men in a seat near him laughed and yelled, "Eat them yourself! You'll never get near Muñoz."

Then a big man with his stomach hanging over his belt leaned over the youths and shouted, "He's got nine! You haven't even got two! Get up and let him sit by the window and protect his present for the governor."

The two young fellows grinned sheepishly as the crowd cheered and laughed and yelled, "You don't even have two!" They rose and old Pedro slumped into the seat by the window, holding the branch before him.

He fell into a doze and was awakened suddenly when the bus stopped, and he heard the driver call, "Everybody out! I can't go any farther!"

The old man soon found himself on foot, walking and stumbling through the Parque Muñoz Rivera, then on the *avenida* of the same name, the *avenida* that skirted the cliff overlooking the ocean. As he felt the mass of countrymen around him, he suddenly grew panicky. Would he reach the Capitolio? Would El Vate still be there? He heard cheers and music ahead, getting louder as he pressed forward, holding the branch before him.

Then he found himself pressed against a tree, looking across an avenue where a great parade was marching. Beyond was a hill of people crowned by a stand in front of the Capitolio. In the stand was Luis Muñoz Marín. Next to him was his wife, Doña Inés, and all around them, in white suits and white dresses, the great people who had come from the United States and other countries and from the great haciendas of Puerto Rico to see El Vate become governor. Now a float was in the parade with a sign, "January 2, 1949—Muñoz Marín, Our Own First Governor." Then some gun carriers came with signs on them. One carried a banner, "Jalda Arriba" (Up the Hill), the slogan of the Popular party. The crowd cheered.

Pedro pushed toward the street. Some people made way. Suddenly he was free, and he ran across the street. There was laughter and applause and more cheering. Then the old man, still holding the branch high, was in the other crowd, pushing his way up the hill until he could move no more. Despairingly, he looked up at the stand. He thought Muñoz was looking back at him. He could see El Vate throw down a cigarette and wave at a policeman nearby. Then Pedro lost sight of Muñoz. Some moments later two policemen were at the old man's sides. He became afraid. He had not meant to cause trouble, only to give the grapefruit.

The policemen pulled him through the crowd, up, up, pushing, joggling, pulling. He was standing in front of El Vate! Right before him was Muñoz, standing tall, his face glistening with perspiration, his thick black hair damp, his large dark eyes looking at old Pedro with kindness and a glint of humor; but his mouth was serious under the wilting moustache.

"What do you want, old man?" Muñoz was saying in the soft, compassionate voice that Pedro remembered from radio speeches.

Old Pedro thrust the branch with the nine grapefruit before him. "Just to give you this."

Muñoz took the branch, appraised it. "Nine on one branch," he commented, "and fine fruit. Did you grow them, old man?"

Pedro nodded happily. All about him there was silence; the crowd's noises had dimmed.

Muñoz put out his hand. "I thank you," he said. "I thank you for the grapefruit, but even more do I thank you for the spirit that brought you here." And he shook the old man's hand as the crowd cheered again. Muñoz turned to the policemen.

"Escort him to the lawn in back of the stand, where he can sit down and watch and hear the ceremony," he requested.

The old man sank gratefully onto the grass. But he stirred himself and stood up when El Vate, whom people had once laughed at as nothing but a young poet with wild ideas, began to speak.

Pedro listened as Muñoz Marín, in his rumpled white suit, extended his hand to the crowd and said, "I have just taken an oath to serve the people of Puerto Rico in the office that I have assumed today. Let it be understood as sincerity, and not a lack of humility, when I say that it was not necessary for me to do so. With an oath or without it, the forces of my conscience have sought to make my life an oath of service to my people. In the government or out of it, there is this obligation for everyone who sees ways of serving and who feels that he has the strength to do so."

The crowd cheered and old Pedro applauded. Yes, they would all serve Puerto Rico!

As Muñoz continued, the old man lost some of the words. His eyes wandered over the scene of the multitude below the Capitol. He saw some children, lost, crying for their parents, but everyone else was silent in the fierce sun. There was another sign on a tree with "January 2, 1949—Muñoz, Our Governor." Pedro looked again toward Don Luis Muñoz Marín and heard him say: "I believe that ours is a people that does not need juridical definitions as an aid to spiritual welfare. . . . To find its way out of obsolete colonialism, it does not feel compelled to recur to obsolescent nationalism." The new governor then told how Puerto Rico would have to find new solutions to the problem of her political status because the old ideas no longer suited the new world. And he told again how hard Puerto Ricans would have to work to build their country.

Finally, as if he were talking to Pedro, he lowered his voice and said: "Neither do I wish to end without the expression of my most profound respect for the common man of Puerto Rico who has known how, beset by hardship and suffering, to establish with his vote a government that has not offered to provide him sweets or marvels but to lead him honestly along the difficult uphill road."

As the roar of the crowd replaced the intimate tones of El Vate, the mass began to break up and move in all directions. Old Pedro saw Muñoz stand waving, then move away, probably to his new home in the Fortaleza, the fortress of the Spaniards, the home of the governors.

Pedro started down the hill. A small boy looked at him and asked, "Where are you going, old man?"

"To Rio Piedras," said Pedro.

"How?"

Pedro smiled. He did not want to talk. He did not want to forget anything that had happened. He shrugged. "That depends on me," he said.

While Pedro and others made their way home and the new governor went to the Fortaleza, the reporters rushed back to their newspaper offices to file the day's story before the start of the evening festivities.

The reports, varying only in style and detail, said all citizens of Puerto Rico—those who had voted for the opposition candidate, Judge Martín Travieso, who propounded statehood for the island; and those who had voted for Francisco Susoni, the independence candidate; as well as the sixty-two percent who had balloted for Luis Muñoz Marín—all were joined in pride at welcoming the first Puerto Rican elected to the governorship.

The articles told of the notables who had come to the inauguration: Fred Crawford, the American congressional representative who had sponsored the bill for the election; Oscar Chapman of the Department of the Interior, representing the President; the minister of state of Guatemala, who had lost his seat and his temper in the crowd; representatives of governments and states; leaders of the minority parties; the mayoress of San Juan, Doña Felisa Rincón; Jaime Benítez, chancellor of the University of Puerto Rico; Ramos Antonini and Samuel Quiñones, leaders of the island House and Senate; and many others.

A few reports attempted the story of the man who had just taken office. They mentioned his father, Luis Muñoz Rivera, as the island's first great patriot, then briefly sketched the new governor's youth as a poet and writer before he came to Puerto Rican politics, ostensibly to lead his people to independence. Some professed astonishment at the political acumen of a man who had been able to turn openly against his first political standard and still hold the loyalty of the mass of voters. A few cited as another proof of Muñoz's flexibility the recent decision of his party to abjure government control of the effort to achieve economic stability in favor of full support for private enterprise. They implied that the hero of the day, despite the brilliance of his leadership and the charm of his nonconformity, had put himself on trial.

As reporters filed these stories, the hero was facing his first official battle—the reception at the Fortaleza, for which five thousand invitations had been issued. The host was struggling with a black tie, with which he was ill-acquainted. Muñoz's language at the moment was neither poetic nor transcendental. It was dimmed to only a sputter when Jesús Piñero, the old friend who had preceded him in the governorship as an interim appointive executive, offered him a black snap-on.

"Thank God—or thank Jesús, in this case," muttered Muñoz. "Pardon the irreverence, but you know how I hate all neckties." Then he laughed, looking at Piñero, and said, "This makes up for you telling me to invite Trujillo."

Piñero nodded. "I still say—he is the head of the Dominican Republic, and a neighbor."

"And I still say that for me there wouldn't be any inauguration if that dictator were to come."

The dialogue was ended by the governor's wife, Inés Mendoza, who called out that guests were already arriving. Indeed they were coming by every land route in San Juan. Sunset had fallen, and the streams of pedestrians, most of whose cars had been blocked far from the Fortaleza, were winding through the festively decorated streets of the oldest city under the American flag. Over the cobblestones tramped the horde, passing the Triana building, named for Rodrigo de Triana, who first spotted land from the crow's nest of Columbus' vessel; walking by the Cathedral, where so many Spanish rulers had worshiped; filing past the Casa Blanca, the sixteenth-century fortress home built for Ponce de León's family; gathering in the Plaza de Armas, where the city hall looked over the public square; finally converging on the Fortaleza, the fortress palace of the rulers of Puerto Rico.

As they marched into the grounds, the guests perceived in the light of garden lanterns the fiery blossoms on flamboyant trees and the profusion of orchids glowing through the hanging foliage. Through an archway they could see the governor and Inés receiving arrivals in the large patio, partly surrounded by Spanish colonnades and draped with the miniature lily blossoms of *azucena* vines. Palms, ferns, red hibiscus, purple bougainvillea, and gold, trumpeted *canaria* filled out the tapestry of the gardens.

Soon all but the lights and flowers overhead were hidden by the throng. The scent of flowers, even the heavy fragrance of *dama de la noche,* was overcome by the perfumes of gala-gowned ladies and the bland odor of rum and Scotch highballs.

The chirp of birds that had greeted the first visitors was lost in the hubbub of a thousand voices. Of the orchestrated sounds of the small native bands, only the beat of Caribbean rhythms throbbed unsmothered by the chattering cacophony.

Soon Muñoz and Inés escaped to one of the secretarial offices, abandoning the palace to the crowd. Guests streamed through the ancient throne room with its Genoa-marble floors and mahogany paneled walls, the Hall of Mirrors, even the garden suite and the upstairs veranda that overlooked the entrance to San Juan Bay. The old lady they found quietly and happily enjoying the affair was Doña Amalia, the governor's mother. Perhaps she was remembering how her husband, Luis Muñoz Rivera, had also been, for a short time, the administrator of the island. Finally the crowd discovered Muñoz's hiding place, and the line of well-wishers formed again.

When the drinks, the sandwiches, the music, and the energies of a crowd that had been celebrating for a week ran out simultaneously at two o'clock in the morning, the Fortaleza began to disgorge its human burden. High heels clicked again on the streets outside. Among them padded the sandals of the peasants the governor had invited from every village on the island.

As they left the lights of the Fortaleza glowing in the Puerto

Rican night, the last departing stragglers heard a desperate cry from
the palace: "A toothbrush! Just a toothbrush, that's all! This place
isn't a home; it's a museum!"

Within the Fortaleza, while the scurried search for the toothbrush
of the new governor of Puerto Rico occupied Inés and the daughters,
the governor himself found his first moment of solitude on the veranda facing the bay. He lit perhaps his hundredth cigarette of the
day and with its smoke drew deeply on the night air. I will be, he
thought, the first man to sleep here whose responsibility is first to
the people of Puerto Rico.

Behind the thought was a realization of the trust the people had
deposited in him and in his declarations that their spirits could
achieve freedom only when the shackles of sickness, hunger, and in-
ability to find work had been removed. This would be done, but
there was the wonder, in a lingering anguish, as to whether the
spirit would still be there when the bellies were full. Another Muñoz,
his father, had been as warmly acclaimed on a night as glowing and
fragrant as this one as he demanded that the free expression of human dignity be placed ahead of all other aspirations, as if this, and
no other, were the problem of this island in the Caribbean Sea.

TWO

The Restless Colony

LUIS MUÑOZ MARÍN was born on February 18, 1898, just ten days after his father was named Premier of the first autonomous Puerto Rican cabinet and only three days after the American warship *Maine* was blown up in the harbor of Havana. In retrospect the convergence of these three events seems prophetically significant. But to Puerto Ricans, at the time only one of the happenings appeared to be of unusual consequence. Completely overshadowing the islanders' interest in the arrival of a son in the new Premier's household or their shock at the latest violent episode on the troubled neighboring island of Cuba, where the bloody rebellion against Spain was now in its third year, was their jubilant realization that Puerto Rico, after centuries of uncertain colonial status, was now to enjoy self-government at last.

This great prize had been won, almost single-handedly it seemed, by Muñoz Rivera himself. No one could forget Don Luis' years of debates with opposing Puerto Rican political leaders who had either wished to ape the Cubans in their struggle for outright independence from Spain or preferred to remain snugly under the blanket of the motherland. Muñoz Rivera had insisted that the island could gain her political identity without losing her association with the parent power. In 1896 he had traveled to Spain and negotiated a pact with Práxedes Mateo Sagasta, leader of the then out-of-power Spanish Liberal party, which promised to accomplish just that if the Liberals should win office. And in 1897, when the Spanish Liberals by a stroke of fate did come to power, they had honored the Pact of Sagasta.

The pact not only reasserted Spanish citizenship for Puerto Ricans. It also granted them the right to elect their own two-party parliament, which would legislate freely over all affairs of the island that did not enter the jurisdiction of the Spanish national government. Puerto Rico would have a voice and a vote in the administration of the home government through elected representatives to the Spanish House, the Cortes. And the island's right to participate in trade treaties affecting her interests was guaranteed by Spain. An appointive Spanish governor-general would continue in office, but his prerogatives were limited to matters affecting Spain. Should he propose any executive action, it could be carried out only by approval of a member of the Puerto Rican cabinet. And all these terms and conditions were written into a constitution for Puerto Rico that could be amended only on the initiative of the Puerto Rican legislature.

Puerto Rico's new status was consecrated by an election on February 8, 1898, which gave Muñoz Rivera's Liberals a majority. El León, everyone agreed, had reached the height of his career. And Puerto Rico had reached the climax of its patient quest for unblemished autonomy. The triumphs, in each case, had been long in the making.

Full realization that it was a colony had not emerged in Puerto Rico until the cry against Spanish rule spread throughout Latin America early in the nineteenth century. In Mexico Manuel Hidalgo, the priest; in Argentina, Chile, Peru, Colombia, and Venezuela the men on horseback, San Martín, O'Higgins, Sucre, and Bolívar; and in Brazil the forces that sequestered Portugal's house of Braganza—all spread the clamor for independence. Only the islands of the Caribbean remained with Spain, but within them the stirrings of discontent began. Of this group only Puerto Rico, except for one abortive uprising, never took up arms against the Spanish. Puerto Rico developed the technique of struggle into the practice of negotiation, a method it has never abandoned, a pursuit in which its leaders have become expert.

The sunny islands of the Caribbean were originally distinct from Spain's mainland colonies in that they were primarily strategic outposts rather than targets for plunder. At first, of course, the Spaniards had hoped they too secreted golden treasure. Columbus landed on Puerto Rico on November 19, 1493. The dispute about his site of debarkation on the island has never been resolved. Today, Governor Muñoz Marín skillfully eludes it by saying of the classic statue of Columbus with arms outstretched that wherever it is placed on the island, it is saying, "He landed over there."

One of the discoverer's young officers, Ponce de León, pleased with what he saw, obtained Crown permission to return with his wife and son to Puerto Rico as first governor of the island.

Except for a short-lived revolt among the native Arawak Indians, his governorship was a peaceful one; however, court politics and rumors of gold followed Ponce de León, eventually forcing him to yield his place to Diego Colón, a son of Columbus. Ponce sailed to Florida, supposedly in search of the Fountain of Youth, to set a precedent many travelers have since followed.

The colony was still a neglected outpost when the Puerto Rican streams had run out of gold. Then, a loan from the Spanish government in 1536 helped the island, encouraging it to the cultivation of sugar. Sugar brought the slaves from Africa because there were too few Indians to cut the cane. By 1550 some fifteen thousand Negro slaves were toiling in Puerto Rican canefields.

Puerto Rico was now still further away from the wealthy viceroyalties of the South American mainland. Its pattern of life as a holding of Spain for the next four centuries was already formed.

Rather than a source of wealth like the gold-encrusted colonies of northern South America or the land-rich regions of the southern viceroyalties, Puerto Rico in the years that followed became an economic charge upon Spain.

Since there was nothing to conquer and no booty to be won, Puerto Rico was eventually free of arms, and family quarrels were conducted with the pen.

Since it was an island open to a quarrelsome sea, it was often subject to attack and even more often received the exiles from strife-torn neighbors—principally the French from Haiti, Martinique, and Louisiana and the Spanish loyalists from Cuba and Venezuela.

Administrators from Spain became, in Puerto Rico, as self-seeking as they were in Peru or Mexico, but with less to gain. But the Puerto Ricans, instead of seeking vengeance with the sword, eventually went to headquarters in Madrid to arrange their removal. This resulted in a gentleness of nature and a stubbornness of spirit.

Spain fostered the outpost as a strategic gateway to the mainland, just as centuries later the Americans would view it as a bastion for the Panama Canal. Its defenses were based on the Fortaleza and El Morro in San Juan, with construction of the former begun in 1533, the latter in 1539.

Before the century ended the forts proved their value, driving off the assault of Sir Francis Drake in 1595 with a shot into the captain's cabin that quickly convinced him that there were good gunners ashore. Another thrust by a Dutch squadron in 1625 was nearly successful when the sailors entered the city of San Juan; but the fortress held, and the invaders returned to the high seas.

Meanwhile, as the European demand for sugar increased the value of arable land in the coastal regions, Puerto Rico developed a plantation society. Withdrawing from the forced labor of the steaming plantations were the few remaining Indians, the Negro slaves who could steal away, and the unendowed Spaniards who sought a living rather than a struggle. They strayed into the hills, each to his plot of subsistence farming, each to his hut, with his woman and his children and later his small herd of cattle. The man of the hills, Spanish, Negro, or Indian, meshed in a society that developed an unaggressive assuredness, a skepticism about the strutters of San Juan, the capital, with their posturing imitation of Spanish social patterns. He became the *jíbaro*.

The fortunes of the island depended mainly on occurrences outside—a recurring irritant in its history. The break of the American colonies with England stimulated Puerto Rican agricultural exports as the British cut the shipping routes between the States and the British West Indies. Irritated at the intrusion of Puerto Rico as a source of rum, sugar, and honey, England offered to trade Gibraltar for the island. The Spanish government was not interested.

Finally the British made their last effort to take the island by force, sending Sir Ralph Abercromby, who had just taken Trinidad easily, to accomplish the mission in 1797. For the first time the people of Puerto Rico joined their armed Spanish guard in action, with some twenty thousand farm workers streaming into San Juan to battle the invader. After a month of struggle Abercromby gave up the project.

Reeling under the blows of Napoleon's soldiers and the far-off demands of their American colonies for independence, the Spanish people, who had established a fugitive government in Cádiz outside the French zone, gratefully invited loyal Puerto Rico to elect a representative to the Cortes of Cádiz. By decree Puerto Rico was declared a part of the Spanish nation, its inhabitants to enjoy equal Spanish citizenship.

Ramón Power Giralt, young, handsome, gifted as a writer and speaker, was elected to the post of deputy by the newly forming liberal element of island politics. He arrived in Cádiz in June of 1810 with a set of instructions provided by his emergent and somewhat excited constituency. They expressed Puerto Rico's complete adherence to the Spanish nation, while demanding immediate reform of the island government, which they qualified as despotic, arbitrary, and tyrannical.

Power's instructions also included a number of quite specific recommendations to an already harassed home government: the establishment of a university on the island, with emphasis on the humanities and sciences; the establishment of hospitals and infirmaries; and the formation of a vocational school to correct delinquency for both sexes, because "preventive laws are far more effective than punitive ones." New roads, land reform, tax reform, and trade concessions were all mentioned in Power's instructions, and also included was a demand that Puerto Ricans be given preferential rights to government jobs on the island.

That the Spanish accepted this blast of demands without exasperation was a tribute to the charm and oratorical powers of Sr. Power Giralt. They may have realized too that the Puerto Ricans were delivering a cargo of pent-up social philosophy extracted from the new French and American political thought. The Cortes acceded to much that Power Giralt requested, trimming some of the powers of the Spanish governor on the island, lifting most remaining trade restrictions, and giving impulse to the awakening economic development of Puerto Rico for the coming decades of the century.

The population, which had been estimated at 155,400 in 1800, exceeded 500,000 by 1850. Trade multiplied in dollar value. Goods sold in 1815 totaled $1,382,046; by 1850 the export level was up to $11,099,349. Although sugar was the island's leading export, the increasing European demand for coffee soon encouraged a new class of growers in the hilly interior of the island; with them there was a new type of land worker, poorer, more closely tied to the soil, almost a serf on the new coffee plantations.

With new money on the island, a social life bloomed that was closely molded to Spain, to European literature, art, and drama. More families were able to send their sons to Spanish universities. Many of them stayed for extended periods, forming a generation of Puerto Ricans in the homeland.

The activity that gained most momentum was politics. Ramón Power Giralt had died of yellow fever in Spain in 1813 at the age of thirty-eight. But the taste for participation in political affairs, vitally influencing Puerto Rican lives, which came with his performance in Cádiz, was never to be forgotten. The word, in writing and speech, was now and forever to be a political weapon, and it soon divided the Puerto Ricans into groupings separated by their attitudes about the island's relationship with Spain and the administration of the island itself. The liberals sought more freedom for the island to run its own affairs and wanted social reforms; the conservatives tended toward continuation of Spanish colonial rule and closer island association with the homeland. With time, the liberals, who would find in Luis Muñoz Rivera their next great leader, became Autonomists and the conservatives became Assimilists.

Born in the hill town of Barranquitas on November 6, 1859, Luis Muñoz Rivera was son of the leading citizen and one-time local mayor, and grandson of a loyalist Spanish officer who had come to the island from Venezuela. His parents gave him the classic small-town education of private schools and tutors. He was trained to go into his father's business, Muñoz and Negrón, a trading post. But the boy in his teens proclaimed his desire to be a poet.

His father scoffed at the idea: "Look," he said one day, holding up an issue of the Ponce newspaper, "if you could write a poem like this, perhaps you could become a poet someday."

"Yes, Papa," said Luis. The poem was his own, written under a pseudonym.

The son's ideas were those of a rising generation in Puerto Rico. He took the liberal side against his father's conservatism. And he took it with considerable vehemence, to the point that once the mayor of Barranquitas—not his father—sent a warning to the governor: "Here I want and have need of more police vigilance because in this district there is a very rebellious person."

The rebellious person dedicated more passion to his poetry and his politics than to his father's business. In his early twenties he had already aroused interest in literary circles. With increasing frequency his works appeared in the Ponce periodical published by a Sr. Ramón Marín. Finally Muñoz Rivera made his appearance in the office of the publisher, drawn to the man who was producing the island's only honestly independent newspaper. The young man was fascinated by Ramón Marín, a figure of courage and talent, a playwright whose two plays produced in the small town of Ponce late in the nineteenth century returned the incredible profit of two thousand dollars. Marín also conducted a private school. Many of his patrons paid him in slaves, and Marín, antislavery apostle, set them all free.

Muñoz Rivera became extraordinarily familiar with the hilly road between Barranquitas and Ponce. He was still a partner in the house of Muñoz and Negrón, but his verse was becoming a poetry of purpose. He wrote of it in words like these:

> I was not born to emit the notes
> Of the nightingale in the city enslaved;
> I am going to the rough and unknown regions;
> At the end, arriving with broken wings;
> But, at the end, I know, I will arrive.

As Muñoz Rivera wrote in his eulogy of his father, "I came to my thirtieth year in Barranquitas." His own preparation to enter the public life of his country, his decision to make a move that would separate him from home, was a leisurely process despite the fire that early lit his poetry and essays. But it was a period to watch the many changes in Puerto Rican life and in that of the Spanish regime on which it was based.

From 1868, when Luis was nine years old, until he formally entered Puerto Rican politics, Spain went through a provisional government, a liberal monarchy with the Italian king. This was the First Republic and the return of the Bourbons. On the island there had occurred Puerto Rico's first and only violent rebellion, called the Grito de Lares, an uprising in a hill town led by a Venezuelan, Manuel Rojas, and an American, Mathias Bruckman. The rebellion was more a labor protest than a political upheaval, being principally a demonstration against the "work carnets" that laborers were forced to carry. It was suppressed quickly and had no significance at the time, but it remained on the record for the island's nationalists to refer to as a symbol under the American occupation some sixty and more years later. Also vital in its effect on the island's way of life was the abolition of slavery in 1873.

The winds of freedom were blowing with rising briskness in the southern part of the island. It was primarily Ramón Marín who encouraged the young man, in 1883, to join the Liberal party in Ponce. Leader of the Liberal party was Baldorioty de Castro, who brought Muñoz Rivera to the attention of other party leaders in 1887, when the group founded the Autonomist party, openly espousing self-government along dominion lines, fashioned after the Canadian pattern.

In the view of the Spanish governor, Romualdo Palacio, this was rebellion and must be repressed with force. Military law was declared, party leaders were jailed, and Spanish soldiers galloped about the island using detention and torture to impose the governor's law. Protests to Madrid obtained the governor's removal, but the will of the party was broken. Only a few leaders, the "rebellious person" among them, clamored for its continued resistence.

Three years later Luis Muñoz Rivera renounced his partnership in his father's business, again took the road to Ponce, and there established his own newspaper, *La Democracia.* Two years later, in 1893, he married Amalia, the daughter of Ramón Marín.

Muñoz Rivera's first editorials in *La Democracia* revealed the empiricist that had thrived unperceived in the garb of a poet. He attacked the injustices and inequalities of the Spanish administration on the island itself, addressing himself to causes close to the daily lives of his readers. In the councils of the party he protested against any outright campaign for complete self-government and argued for affiliation of the party with one of the leading parties in Spain:

> Let us not dedicate ourselves to useless battles and the striving after goals impossible to attain. There are spirits who seek the most beautiful of illusions. Can they be realized? Then let us follow the lighted star. Is there no manner of bringing these people to the practical way? Then let us tie our desires to the impositions of reason, not wasting our valor on conflicts of fantasy.

We are men of our century, eminently positivist in the noble and generous sense of the word; this is not the epoch for generating dreams and building vain mirages.

Platonism has no destination in our times.

Party veterans restrained the younger leader for five years. Finally he went to Spain alone in 1895, purportedly to convalesce from a near breakdown. But illness had never displayed more vigor in Madrid and the other cities of Spain. His letters, editorials, and dispatches from Spain during this five-month period there have filled a volume of some ninety-four thousand words.

He attended political meetings. He studied the parties contending for leadership of the Spanish people. He analyzed their prospects and the policies of their leaders to determine which party could be negotiated with to obtain the maximum of autonomy for Puerto Rico.

He found time for the theater, bullfights, night-long harangues on art, women, politics, and wine. He delighted in embarrassing the old guard in Puerto Rico with reports sent back to *La Democracia*, relating the hideous crimes noted in the Spanish newspapers. And he was constantly disturbed by the bloody Cuban revolution because he feared that it would steel Spanish attitudes against the autonomist goals of his own party in Puerto Rico.

". . . The Cuban war is for us a vast and unlooked-for disappointment," he wrote. "Puerto Rico, loyal and always reasonable, will bear the nightmare of Caesarism. There the windows are broken. Here we will pay the bill. . . ."

Muñoz Rivera's stay in Spain gave him the weapon he needed to win leadership of the Autonomists in Puerto Rico. When he returned he was the man who had been there. He was the man who had come to know personally the Spanish leaders. In 1896 he convinced the party that it should send a commission to Spain to negotiate the fullest possible measure of self-government. The wing led by Rosendo Matienzo Cintrón withdrew its opposition. Muñoz Rivera and two other members were named to the commission.

They landed in Spain in July, 1896. The scene at the dock must have been somewhat mournful, for not one representative of the Spanish government, headed by the conservative Don Antonio Cánovas de Castillo, was there to meet the hopeful Puerto Ricans; nor was their arrival noticed by any contending Spanish party. The mind of Spain was on Cuba. These forlorn travelers were only an annoyance. But they set their paths for Madrid, where Spanish politicians appointed minor emissaries to distract them from their purpose.

Muñoz Rivera had become acquainted with these tactics the year before. Alone, he set off, leaving the commission behind him. Finally, on a beach at a southern vacation resort, he tracked down Práxedes Mateo Sagasta, chief of the Liberal party and a man in whose integrity and political prospects the well-informed Muñoz Rivera had great faith.

Sagasta was wary of the young man. He wanted to know if the other members of the commission would accede to any agreement he should make with Don Luis. Muñoz Rivera stated boldly that the majority of Puerto Ricans were with him. Then Sagasta leaned toward him and said, "Tell me. What will you do if I refuse to come to an agreement with you?"

Muñoz Rivera reflected a moment. In New York the Cuban Revolutionary Committee was actively seeking support. The group had already written to Don Luis suggesting that the Puerto Ricans throw in their lot with Cuba. Arms could be found for militant action against the Spaniards in Puerto Rico. "If we cannot find a basis for agreement," answered Don Luis, "I will be forced to return to Puerto Rico by way of New York."

Sagasta stiffened, but his adversary was not to be faced down at this moment. This was the hour toward which Muñoz Rivera had directed his political years. The two men sat back and continued their discussions.

When Don Luis returned to Madrid, the other members of the commission were still caught up in protocol and in efforts to come to terms with the conservative Cánovas, who was attempting to put off the entire mission with stop-gap legislative concessions. Don Luis had an agreement. The commission had only arguments.

Signed in Madrid in January, 1897, the Pact of Sagasta was submitted to the Liberal party in San Juan in February, and won a majority. In August of the same year a Spanish anarchist assassinated Cánovas. As Don Luis had predicted, Sagasta's Liberals were called to power; and in November, 1897, Práxedes Sagasta complied with his word to the young Puerto Rican who had harangued him on the beach in southern Spain. Don Luis Muñoz Rivera had won self-government for his people, who soon named him their first Premier.

But even before the first assembly of the Puerto Rican parliament was convoked, on July 17, 1898, the island's fate was once again being shaped by outside forces.

Echoes of the explosion that rocked the American battleship *Maine* were being heard around the world. In April the United States declared war on Spain. By mid-July, less than three months later, Commodore George Dewey had taken Manila, the United States had claimed Guam, American troops were triumphant in Cuba. And General Nelson Appleton Miles, commander in chief of the American army, now directing operations in Cuba, was engaged in correspondence with Washington about secret plans to take Puerto Rico before the Spanish might terminate their lost war.

THREE

Legacy of a Poet

MADRID WAS indeed ready to make peace and had asked France to mediate, hoping to reach an agreement before the United States should lay hands on every available scrap of offshore Spanish territory. The French government on July 21 asked her ambassador to Washington, M. Cambon, to present the Spanish request for peace. It arrived on July 22, but General Miles was already on the waters on his way to Puerto Rico from Cuba. Ambassador Cambon, unable to decipher the Spanish request, was informed the code was in the Austrian Embassy. The Austrian ambassador was out of town. When he returned, four days later, it was too late.

On the afternoon of July 25 the populace of Guánica, Puerto Rico, had excitedly watched General Miles's impressive bulk hefted onto its shore. He was followed by soldiers and sailors numbering some three thousand. As the soldiers set up camp back of the beach, the people of Guánica approached timidly. A few of the younger or more bibulous spirits expressed their hospitality in cheering, grinning, and making friendly gestures. The Americans waved at them, but with little enthusiasm. Many were sick with malaria, yellow fever, and dysentery. All were exhausted by the cattle-boat conditions on the transports that brought them from Cuba. And all were steaming in the woolen uniforms that the U. S. Army had issued them for tropical combat.

Their general was in an exhilarated mood. Nelson Miles, fifty-eight-year-old warrior from New England, had begun his fighting career as a volunteer in the Civil War and continued in army service in the fifteen-year struggles with hostile Indian tribes west of the

Mississippi. He was not a politician or a student of world affairs. He was a soldier. He also saw himself as a liberator; and he judged Puerto Rico, since the island was under the Spanish regime that had so brutally sought to suppress the Cuban rebellion, to be in need of the ministry of arms that had freed Cuba.

General Miles had overlooked War Department orders to land at Fajardo, on the end of the island, where the navy would direct the operation. He later explained that he had chosen a strategy that would reduce bloodshed, but many authorities suspected that he wanted Puerto Rico to be an army rather than a navy conquest to assure army command after it was taken. On the first question he need not have been concerned. The Spanish garrisons knew that the war had been lost in the Philippines and in Cuba, and they had no intention of dying for the last and poorest island in their shrunken empire. They adhered to the now legendary order of their General Rivera, who is said to have declared, "If there are a lot of Americans, run; if there are a few, hide; if there are none, engage in battle."

General Miles must have spent his time thoughtfully while resting in Guánica, because three days later, when he joined General James Wilson's unopposed landing in Ponce, he issued a remarkable proclamation:

To the Inhabitants of Puerto Rico:

In the prosecution of a war against the Spanish Crown, the people of the United States, inspired by the cause of liberty, justice, and humanity, have sent their armed forces to occupy the island of Puerto Rico. We have come to this country wrapped in the flag of liberty, spurred by the honorable purpose of pursuing the enemies of our country and of yours, and to destroy or capture all those who present armed resistance. We offer you the protecting arm of a nation of free citizens, whose power rests fundamentally in the sovereignty of justice and humanitarian principles. Therefore, the first effects of this occupation will be to liberate the Puerto Ricans from the political relationships which had previously been imposed upon them and to receive, we trust, Puerto Rico's enthusiastic acceptance of the government of the United States. The principal objective of the American military forces will be to put an end to the armed authority of Spain and give to the people of this beautiful island the greatest measure of liberty that may be compatible with military occupation. We have not come to do battle with the people of this country, who for centuries have been victims of oppression, but to offer you protection of your persons and your possessions, to stimulate prosperity and grant you the rights and benefits offered by the liberal institutions of our system of government. . . . This is not a war of destruction. Our purpose is to grant all those who may come under the control of our military and naval forces the advantages and benefits of civilization.

Nelson A. Miles

Major General, Commander of the Military Forces of the United States of America

The people of Puerto Rico did not look beyond General Miles's words for other meanings. Most of them probably never heard or read his proclamation. The United States was said to be a great democracy that was ruled by the consent of its people. It had won this right in its own revolution little more than a hundred years ago. Its troops must be carrying the flag of freedom as they marched across the island.

The soldiers had fanned out in three directions from Ponce, with San Juan as their eventual meeting place. The next month they were there. They had lost more men from disease than combat.

Farmers stayed in the fields and waved at the passing troops without leaving their work. In village squares where the soldiers bivouacked, the townspeople continued their evening promenades, carefully skirting the brown tents and smiling with friendly interest at the Americans. Language prevented any further communication except the one usually established in darkened areas by the bolder of both sexes. The soldiers rarely arrived in or left a populated sector without cheers of welcome or farewell. They, as soldiers always, were the silent spokesmen of their country.

Meanwhile the words of General Miles, published in the Puerto Rican and world press, were already being taken by informed readers as naïve or sinister. On and off the island it was judged in certain circles that the United States had pushed its way into the war with Spain. The Americans had been inflamed by the cause of the Cuban revolutionaries, but the fuel for that fire was the "expansionist" mood

of the electorate that had put President McKinley into office. Mc-
Kinley himself was a hesitant conqueror. He headed a parade that
he would dearly like to disband. But its ranks were made up of
those who sought to try the strength of the United States against a
European major power and who believed that America should join
in the worldwide colonial pattern being formed by the Western
nations. Cuba was their opportunity. So they also landed in the
Philippines. And they demanded Guam.

In Washington Puerto Rico was seen as the gateway to the Caribbean, a fortress to guard American interests on the shores and islands
of northern South America and Central America, an insurance that
later development of a canal through the Panamanian isthmus
would be undisturbed by other inquisitive powers. General Miles's
orders to leave Cuba for Puerto Rico on July 21 had been marked
"urgent."

Most Americans knew little more of Puerto Rico than did General Miles. They did not realize that the forces of their government
were undergoing the ridiculous exercise of freeing a people to whom
the Spanish government had just granted a nearly full measure of
liberty and autonomy, more than they would enjoy during the next
half century of American rule.

Why, then, did the Puerto Ricans so joyously greet the new conquerors? Why did they make American flags to wave at the Yankee
soldiers? What did their *"Vivas"* mean?

Luis Muñoz Rivera, sitting silently in the office of the secretariat
of the government of Puerto Rico, puzzled over the reaction of his
people. Perhaps they feared that Spain, outraged at her loss of Cuba,
would destroy the liberties she had so recently granted Puerto Rico.
Often over the centuries of Puerto Rico's bondage to Spain the
mother country had struck down her colony's efforts to achieve self-
government when other Spanish colonies had tried her patience. But
Muñoz Rivera knew also how much Puerto Rico would lose with a
transfer of sovereignty in the same year that she had established,
after ten years of difficult negotiations, almost complete freedom for
her people.

Puerto Rico was not a tropical island isolated from the benefits of
a civilization that General Miles had said would light its way to a
better life. Puerto Rico was not a colony whose urgings for self-
expression were trampled under by garrisons of Spanish soldiers.

Puerto Rico was an autonomous province of Spain. Now it was invaded by a foreign power.

Muñoz Rivera heard the cheers of his people as they greeted the invaders in the streets outside his shaded office. It was not only the destruction of the edifice that he and his compatriots had wrought that sounded bitterly in his hearing. In the shouts of the populace he detected the undertone of an imminent disillusion that would one day bring dejection. He wondered who, on that day, would put his people on their feet again.

But now the cheers revealed the elation of a people already imagining new benefits. In their relationship to the United States, they could see themselves sharing the prosperity of its sturdy people. As Americans they would enjoy an economic democracy free from the inhibiting influences of Spanish masters. This attitude was later analyzed by an eminent Puerto Rican spokesman, who wrote, ". . . not only did the people of Puerto Rico expect to retain, under United States sovereignty, all political authority that Spain had relinquished to them as an autonomous state in 1897, but they looked forward to added freedom, if for no other reason than that the change of political allegiance meant a change from a monarchical system to a republican democratic regime." * This was the rationale of hope, not of Muñoz Rivera's pessimism.

When the American command assumed control, Don Luis beat a personal, although temporary, retreat to Barranquitas, hillside town of his birth. Some family servants were still in the family home his father had left behind, and they were much more interested in the baby boy that the *patrón* and Doña Amalia brought back with them than in any dislocations of the government.

Little Luis Muñoz Marín was now seven months old, and the servants sought and obtained permission to take the child down the slopes to the center of the village, where he could be displayed to the townspeople.

Up on the hill, standing on the broad, open veranda of the Spanish home, Don Luis could see the servants thread their way down the narrow dirt road carrying his young son. Then, just by raising his gaze a bit, he could look over the nearby hills shaded by coffee trees,

* Antonio Fernós-Isern, "From Colony to Commonwealth," *The Annals of the American Academy of Political and Social Science* (Philadelphia, January, 1953).

past the neighboring green valley and its jumble of palms and mango and banana groves studded with flowering trees and hanging orchids, on to the edge of the island and the deep blue water washing its shores. This was a familiar vista of his external world; to his inner eye another picture was equally clear.

This was the inner image that drew him to his mahogany-paneled study one day to write the poem "Sisyphus." The lines retold the Greek myth of the Corinthian king who, because of an offense to Zeus, was condemned after death to the eternal and hopeless effort to push a gigantic rock up to the crest of a craggy mountain. It has been a theme for the ages. Homer wrote the story eight hundred years before the birth of Christ. Albert Camus, depressed by the fall of France and its occupation by the Germans in World War II, would also write *Le Mythe de Sisyphe* in 1942, declaring that there is no punishment more bitter than hopeless effort, but that effort alone is enough to fill the spirit of man.

Muñoz Rivera brought a change into the Sisyphus story. In the classic tale the rock keeps slipping back to the abyss just as the hero's success seems near; in the Puerto Rican poem, Sisyphus actually places the boulder on the crest of the hill. He stands there, covered with dirt, blood, and sweat, the high air cooling his fevered body, the adulation of the admiring onlookers ringing in his ears, when a thunderclap, a bolt of lightning, and a terrible gust of wind shake the hilltop and topple the rock to the flatland where he had first shaken it loose. Sisyphus, his shoulders bowed, is ready to follow it to the bottom of the hill to resume his eternal labor. This, for Muñoz Rivera, father of Luis Muñoz Marín, was the story of Puerto Rico; this, for Puerto Rico, was the story of Muñoz Rivera.

The Puerto Rico that the United States won in 1898 was urged by three drives that beset many or most groups, nations, and individuals: fear of isolation, positively defined as desire for association; the search for dignity and identity, coupled with urgings for independence; the struggle for physical well-being. These motivating forces have equally impelled the most powerful nations, and they are strongly apparent in the efforts of newly emerging countries to achieve an orientation to today's world. Among individuals as well as political groupings, neuroses have set in when any one of the

three needs—association, identity, or well-being—has either overbal-
anced the other two by becoming predominant or has disappeared
from the trinity.

With Muñoz Rivera the leader of the struggle for identity, another islander represented the forces of association. Perhaps it was
inevitable that the American liaison with the political body of Puerto
Rico should be established through this man. He had sought the first
opportunity for contact with the Americans in May when a U.S.
naval vessel had appeared off the port of San Juan to lob some
warning shells at the capital.

Dr. José Celso Barbosa had then manned the oars of a small skiff
and approached the ship. When he returned to port, he was the Puerto
Rican representative of the International Red Cross. This title he
had added to the more weighty one of chief of the party in opposition to Muñoz Rivera's Autonomistas, as they were then called. As
Celso Barbosa rowed back to the shores of San Juan, despite the
perspiration that rolled down his darkly colored face and the steam
that fogged his glasses, he felt that his star was rising. He was specu-
lating how he would soon change his party's name to the Republican
party, to parallel the one in power in Washington. He had opposed
the separation from Spain. Puerto Rico, even with a measure of
autonomy, should never risk being cast adrift by the mother country.
But during the course of his education he had come to know the
United States and to wish that this republic could hold in Puerto
Rico's history the place that had been Spain's.

The son of a Negro doctor and a refugee Venezuelan mother,
Celso Barbosa had received his early education mostly from tutors.
Benefactors, impressed with the youth's ceaseless absorption of
knowledge, found the means to send him to the University of Baltimore. There he soon mastered English, and studying in a new language, captured all undergraduate honors. He went on to New York,
studied medicine, and continued at the University of Michigan. He
graduated from Ann Arbor in 1880 and returned to Puerto Rico to
specialize in children's medicine.

His memories of the United States were rich with the kindness of
its people, the wealth of its educational facilities, the progress of its
society, the freedom of its political structure. When the Americans
came to Puerto Rico, the future took on a new and brighter light.

He was ready to work with them, and since he spoke their language and knew their country, they were ready to accept him as representative of their new territory.

The naval bombardment in May, 1898, that hurried Celso Barbosa into his rowboat to meet the visitors from the north also fired a shell through the window of a jail cell occupied by a twenty-six-year-old Spanish carpenter named Santiago Iglesias Pantín.

Iglesias, a labor leader (in those days the term was "labor agitator"), was as familiar to his jailers as the stones of the old building. His involvement with labor's struggle for better treatment had begun when he was a twelve-year-old carpenter's apprentice in Coruña, Spain, where in a riot against the monarchy he had climbed the barricades, fortunately to be rescued by his mother before the mounted police could reach him. Two years later, alone, he was on a ship bound for Cuba, where he dodged Spanish authorities while he incited the Cuban workers to rebellion. In 1896 he had come to Puerto Rico, where again he made more trouble for the establishment than cabinets for his customers.

The Spanish wasted little time finding jail accommodations for Santiago Iglesias, and even under the tolerant secretariat of Muñoz Rivera he was serving his term when the Americans arrived. But his leadership of the Puerto Rican worker had been immediate. He was now the spearhead of the third political current in the United States's new island territory, the group that cared only incidentally about independence or political association but was vibrantly concerned with a decent life for the toilers of Puerto Rico. Santiago Iglesias had heard and read of the American democracy and its newly stirring labor movement, and his spirits, too, rose with the sight of the Stars and Stripes.

Muñoz Rivera, Celso Barbosa, and Santiago Iglesias were the three men who stood at the head of the three streams of Puerto Rican thought that met the American invasion. The causes they symbolized would some day meet in the career of Luiz Muñoz Marín.

It was a reflection of something intrinsically American that the invaders, even while following the new and exciting course of empire, should take notice of the needs that Santiago Iglesias sought to satisfy through militant labor action. Even as the first U.S. governor almost automatically followed the Spanish example by again clapping the labor leader into prison, he was filing reports on the poor state of Iglesias' followers.

Muñoz Rivera, in his few short months as administrator of the autonomous government under Spain, had achieved notable gains for the island but they did not show. He had freed Puerto Rico from crown taxes, stamp taxes, license taxes, fees for judicial action, and probably most important, taxes on fish sold on the island. He had eliminated some one and a half million dollars from the islanders' tax burden in a few months.

But American reports revealed only poverty and backwardness in this new tropical possession of the United States. Like most quick studies, they averaged the exceptions out of the picture. The population was variously estimated at from nine hundred thousand to one million. Of either total, eighty percent were said to be illiterate. There were only five hundred schools and only eight percent of the school-age children attended them. There were no universities. These figures could not show Puerto Rico's cultural accomplishments. Of the educated few, most had studied at universities in Spain or, like Muñoz Rivera, received rich educations under the guidance of tutors. A local literary tradition had been based on indigenous themes rather than the pale imitation of Europe so characteristic of authorship in many other Latin-American countries and in large part on the United States's Eastern seaboard. True, it had a Rousseau-like flavor, but its spine was the island and the man who lived in its hills. Zeno Gandía, José de Diego, Miguel Guerra Mondragón, Lola Rodríguez de Tió, and other writers of prose and poetry were its leaders. Painters, less original, were following Francisco Oller, one of whose works now hangs in the Louvre. Musicians, taking their inspiration from Caribbean themes, were moving toward the Puerto Rican development of the *danza,* whose leading exponents have since been Juan Morel Campos and Jesús Sanromá.

Economically the statistics were equally unimpressive. Agricultural production accounted for ninety percent of the island's exports, and the total was minimal. Six out of ten Puerto Ricans were gainfully employed in agriculture, yet only twenty-one percent of the entire area was under cultivation. With the population barely over a third of its present figure, there were thirteen hundred persons per planted square mile. Only forty percent of the cultivated land was used to produce edibles. Another forty percent was devoted to coffee, fifteen percent to sugarcane, and an overlap of fourteen percent was used for growing bananas. Cattle were pastured on much of the uncultivated land, enough for home supply and some export.

The difference between urban and rural populations was as wide as in most countries, including the United States, as the nineteenth century approached its close. The largest city, San Juan, housed about thirty thousand people. There were eighteen towns with more than twenty-five hundred citizens each—and there were the beaches, countryside, and the hills. The only railroad ran 154 miles around the coastal plain planted to sugar. The remainder of the island was joined by 160 miles of roads that often were more obstructive than useful, particularly during seasonal rains.

Importers flourished. They were concentrated in San Juan and Ponce. With little bank credit available, they financed most of their own purchases and added scandalously high interest rates to the price of goods they distributed.

Disease was more prevalent in the small towns and the country, although San Juan was scarred by maladies. The capital's streets seemed literally to crawl with crippled victims.

Statistics are almost meaningless in describing the miserable state of public health. Dysentery, hookworm, and venereal diseases were prevalent. Malaria and yellow fever were endemic; smallpox swept the island in waves. U. S. Army doctors reported primitive sanitary conditions as the primary cause of diseases; later, medical students attributed most ailments to poverty and its combination of malnutrition and filth.

This was the Puerto Rican panorama as the Americans first saw it. The impression persevered. It was distorted, but it was the scarred face of Puerto Rico that first turned toward the invaders of the nearly unknown island. In retrospect, that first impression of the physical life of a newly encountered people seems to parallel the views that have since shaped Western attitudes to other emerging peoples and that threaten to muddle our understanding of them. Whether African, Asian, or Latin American, the face of a people may be colored, dirty, or scarred as it appears on dusty roads, parched fields, jungles, or crowded city streets. This is not a nation, its history, its culture, its spirit, or its aspirations.

By order of the new American administrator, General John R. Brooke, Luis Muñoz Rivera had been confirmed as the leading voice of government on the island of Puerto Rico. General Brooke had replaced Nelson Miles. Now he announced that the island should continue to govern itself under the Puerto Rican constitution, which had been negotiated with Spain. Luis Muñoz Rivera, secretary of the government—also known as Premier—should continue to preside, with his cabinet, over his people. There was only one proviso: that all laws be compatible with the constitution of the United States.

Muñoz Rivera's spirits rose with the possibility that the measure of sovereignty his people had wrested from Spain would be honored by the new possessors of the territory. But his optimism did not completely overcome his doubts. The American army was still there, seemingly everywhere. There was a new culture to deal with and a new language.

Soon there was another new general. When General Brooke was appointed military governor of Cuba after a few months in Puerto Rico, his successor, General Guy V. Henry, who had a military disdain for civilians, especially recently conquered civilians, aroused further misgivings. On December 19 General Henry called a general assembly of the island parliament, its cabinet, and its "Premier" to announce that he would favor elections under universal suffrage only when his country should deem the Puerto Ricans prepared for such political responsibility.

Enraged at the insult to his countrymen, Muñoz Rivera submitted his resignation. His cabinet followed suit, and General Henry was free to name his own government.

The general had another surprise for the Puerto Ricans. Since the cabinet posts were vacant, the general declared, the cabinet format would be abandoned also, with the major government sections administered by his appointees. Thus, in effect, General Henry voided the constitution of Puerto Rico and the autonomy that Spain had granted the island through the Pact of Sagasta.

The writer of "Sisyphus" was in the abyss, and the rock of his hopes had been hurled into the chasm. Certainly it was a time for Don Luis to ask himself the question What can I do now?

The answer was as futile as it was automatic. Don Luis founded another newspaper, *El Territorio*. Almost as soon as he had published the first edition, it was apparent that the power of his editorial style in Spanish would have no effect on the Americans; and he now had nothing to say to his disheartened compatriots. So he agreed readily when, early in 1899, the landowners asked him to represent them in Washington to reopen the export trade that the military had blocked.

It was a desperation mission. Crops were rotting in Puerto Rico, with the Spanish market closed and the American one not yet available. But the venture was doomed to failure. President McKinley was too absorbed with other matters to give much attention to the complaints of a mettlesome new territory. He was little disposed to attend the arguments of an island politician who was already reputed to be a troublemaker; and neither the President nor his advisers quite knew what to do about Puerto Rico, the insurgent Filipinos, or the exotic Cubans—all legacies of the Spanish-American War.

Don Luis was not surprised. He had expected little. Meanwhile he was probing for a view of the future, for an understanding of the Americans, for a breach through which he could later thrust the logic of an appeal that would reclaim the dignity of his people.

He found that the brawling young giant of a nation had many facets that led his searching intelligence and sensitivity to visualize new possibilities. He took heart from the rough sense of American justice, the unyielding belief in equality that demanded a like opportunity for all and granted concessions to none, even the weak. He sensed that at the end of the century the United States was bursting with a sense of power, presaging a new role in the affairs of the world.

Muñoz Rivera's attunement to politics helped him analyze the forces shaping American society and its government. The Republican administration tended to represent the American sources of wealth, the new industries, the large farms. It spoke for their drive toward prosperity within the country and their tendency toward empire outside the borders. The Democratic group represented labor, small businesses, many small farmers. It looked with disfavor on the obligations connected with the new territorial acquisitions, was concerned with the morality of the colonial system. Many workers were uncommitted, moving from one party to another, swayed principally by new leaders seeking to weld them into a union movement seeking gains through direct, nonpolitical action.

Muñoz Rivera saw that Celso Barbosa's party in Puerto Rico might establish contact with the American Republicans. Celso Barbosa spoke English. He was already proclaiming a desire to join Puerto Rico with the United States, eventually as a state. The Americans were attracted to him. They viewed his attitude as friendly and loyal.

Muñoz Rivera wondered too whether Santiago Iglesias, in his efforts to bring together the workers of Puerto Rico, might seek the guidance of the American labor leaders and Socialist party. Iglesias was in the midst of the island's disorders now, inciting sugar workers to strike for higher wages, trying to forge a labor unit to confront employers and the authorities, attempting to maintain his own freedom for sufficiently prolonged periods to work for his socialist ideals. Muñoz himself had jailed Iglesias only a year ago. He personally had told him that he was an evil influence in Puerto Rico, that he was a foreigner and should return to his native Spain. Now Muñoz observed similar activities in labor's ranks in the United States, but he understood them as little as he did Santiago Iglesias. The workers and their activities did nothing to further political ends, in Don Luis' view. The overriding goal, he believed, should be to achieve dignity and identity for the individual and for the society in which he lived. Working conditions were not a factor to obstruct or further that cause. He did not realize that during these crucial years Santiago Iglesias would do more to attract the attention of the American people to the plight of Puerto Rico through his obstreperous battle for labor's rights than Don Luis would accomplish in the columns of his periodicals or the forums of politics. Nor did he comprehend that on their different courses he and Santiago Iglesias were, in a sense, struggling for the same objective, the freedom of the Puerto Rican spirit, he through the political struggle for dignity, Iglesias through open combat for decent living conditions. These two men, who would never understand each other, who would often lock horns like bulls in battle, who would always be political adversaries, would come to harbor a hidden respect only for each other's sincerity and courage. And their distinct philosophies would one day fuse into the concepts of Luis Muñoz Marín, Don Luis' son, destined to be the first Puerto Rican to be elected to the governorship of his island.

After five months in the United States Muñoz Rivera returned to Puerto Rico to confront again the dismal picture of economic retrogression and political despondency. On August 15, 1899, General George W. Davis, who had replaced General Henry and encountered a people in ferment, had announced the further elimination of civil control; henceforth all government departments would be administered by his military appointees.

Muñoz Rivera, however, had discovered in the United States that not all Americans were in the army; eventually the conquerors would run out of generals. While waiting for that day, Don Luis started another newspaper, the *Diario de Puerto Rico,* and in writing of the Americans in Puerto Rico, he seemed to contrast them with many he had met in the United States: "Reality does not correspond to the dream; the fabulous benefits have not occurred; the rapid progress is not visible; the democratic freedoms have not appeared; . . . the liberty for which Washington and Lafayette struggled remains on the continent without reaching the colony. We endure an absolutist type of government that disappeared in Europe with Louis XIV and Ferdinand VII; we dreamed of the law and the sword appeared."

Santiago Iglesias, feeling the same distress, translated his concern into the anxieties of the workers: ". . . Degrading and reactionary orders had been put into effect by the military, advised by our own vested interests. The Puerto Rican workers saw with bitter sadness and desperation that many of the governmental practices, despotic and antihumanitarian, that had been condemned by even the Spanish government were now newly imposed with the consent of the American general." *

The separate protests of Don Luis and Santiago Iglesias were unavailing. Against them stood the landowners, the same body that had asked Muñoz to represent it in Washington. The Americans chose to take the landowners' views as representative of the island's interests.

* Santiago Iglesias Pantín, *Luchas Emancipadoras* (San Juan: Cantero Fernández, 1929).

Many planters already believed that statehood for Puerto Rico was possible and advisable. Accordingly, the old island political parties were reorganized and renamed.

The opposition to Muñoz Rivera, under the leadership of Celso Barbosa, formally announced its leanings under the Republican banner. In October, 1899, Don Luis arrayed his team of Autonomists under the new name of Federals. On the surface both parties held to the same tenets. Both espoused statehood.

For Muñoz Rivera this was one of the political shifts that were later decried as opportunistic. His objective was to establish a political footing equal with the Republicans for bargaining toward a more autonomous situation. He was also influenced by a concept of the United States that has been drastically altered—federalism. His writings referred to the United States as "they," not "it." He saw the nation as a grouping of sovereign states rather than a centralized government, and his view was apparent in his gramamatical usages. He visualized gaining for Puerto Rico the sovereignty of an American state in terms of self-government, caring less for congressional representation and seeing little hope for it.

Shortly after Muñoz Rivera's party had taken shape, President McKinley staved off further immediate protest by sending a commission to Puerto Rico to study labor and social conditions. This year-end survey in 1899 reported misery throughout the island: workers followed a ten-to-eleven-hour work day for slave wages, child labor was common practice, unemployment was widespread, and out of a population of nearly a million people some seven hundred thousand were without shoes. The last item was one that could be understood quickly. Demands for corrective action arose from all sectors of the American public.

Congress' answer was the Foraker Act, passed on April 12, 1900. The senator whose name identified the bill was Joseph Benson Foraker, former Republican governor of Ohio, party leader, and able constitutional lawyer. A colorful figure, athlete, Civil War veteran, dramatic public character known for his sensationalism as "Fire Alarm" Foraker, his entanglement in later political scandal left a final residue of scorn on the law that established civil government in Puerto Rico.

The bill was notable for its representation of the two dissonant characteristics of American policy during the first half of the twenti-eth century: economic generosity and political insensitivity. In deal-ings with many Latin-American nations, with Asians, with Africans, and occasionally with Europeans, the United States has often been disappointed that its monetary openhandedness has not been appreci-ated. We have been surprised at the bitterness that our accompany-ing political myopia has caused. We have thought that monetary generosity to a poor and proud people—and the pride of poverty is more sensitive than that of wealth—gave us the right also to dictate the structure of its government, to preach the rules of its public morality. After half a century we learned that we were being accused of purchasing loyalty rather than sincerely aiding people in need.

The Foraker Act, duly studied, pondered, and analyzed before its passage in Congress, was a classic example. Even the most intensely dedicated Puerto Rican bent on independence, as was Muñoz Ri-vera in the depths of his spirit, admitted the fairness if not the per-fection of the Foraker Act's economic provisions. It amounted to a declaration of economic union between the United States and Puerto Rico.

Puerto Rico was to share the U.S. market and its tariff system. A common currency was proclaimed. All Puerto Rican duties collected in trade with other nations were to revert to the insular treasury. The island was to be free of United States taxes and was to use its own tax revenues to support its own administrative needs. Furthermore, as a result of protests placed by Matienzo Cintrón and Muñoz Ri-vera against American interests that were already buying up land from desperate island farmers, a limit of five hundred acres was placed on the legal ownership of property by corporations.

The act opened doors to profitable trade and to development of the island by its own and American interests. It granted Puerto Rico free access to the world's fastest-growing market and offered opportu-nities to American investors that could help build the fortunes of the island.

In its political structure, however, it demonstrated the naïvete of its authors by supposing that its guarantee of the Bill of Rights to Puerto Ricans would also protect its people from economic exploita-tion—when many Americans in their own land were finding that this guarantee was no solution for their own economic problems.

Politically, following the British colonial pattern, the act provided

for civil government with the governor, judges, auditor, commissioner of education, and all department heads appointed by Washington or its designated American authorities. Puerto Ricans were to
be allowed to elect representatives to an insular House of Representatives, but the senior legislative body, an executive council of
eleven members—six to be American—was to be named by the governor. These were political appointees, unrelated to the background
of the island. Mostly they were residents newly in business in Puerto
Rico. Muñoz Rivera never ceased raging against this frustration of
all Puerto Rican political initiative.

Finally, the act was directed to "the people of Puerto Rico," leaving the island's inhabitants, for the first time since Columbus landed
on the island, without citizenship of any sort. The declaration of
the American Congress that the United States wished only to deal
on fair and equal terms in economic matters was blemished by its
statement that the contract was being granted to a people unable to
manage their own affairs or to claim any nationality.

As such, the act was one of the more important divisive factors in
Puerto Rico's subsequent political history. On the one hand, a
sector of the populace began cynically to join the American investors
in the acquisition of huge profits. Another sector was spurred to seek
outright independence by any means. And it fell to Muñoz Rivera
to try to bring these two factions together on the grounds of human
dignity.

He faced the task without dismay. "We won with Spain, which
was the prototype of musty tradition," he wrote. "Why not triumph
with the United States, which are the beacon of a radiant tradition,
of a democratic tradition?"

FOUR

Sisyphus

O<small>N MAY 1</small>, 1900, the Foraker Act became law, and the government of Puerto Rico passed from the hands of American generals into the hands of American civilians. The first civilian governor, Charles Herbert Allen, was a reluctant governor. President McKinley had exercised almost the utmost in persuasion to convince Allen that he should give up his post as undersecretary of the navy to accept the governorship of Puerto Rico. Mr. Allen was about to spend some of the busiest and perhaps the most distressing months of his life.

In the United States Democrats and Republicans were engaging in a Presidential campaign. The incumbent, President McKinley, in a side reference to Puerto Rico, stated that "I have not thought it prudent to put into the hands of employees elected by the people the government of all the island, because I doubt that their abilities, in politics or from experience, would be sufficient for the immediate exercise of so high a grade of self-government. . . ."

The platform of the Democratic party declared that "We assert that no nation can long endure half republic and half empire, and we warn the American people that imperialism abroad will lead quickly and inevitably to despotism at home." The warning was disregarded, but Muñoz Rivera saw it as prophetic. He placed the hopes of his Federalists, as the former Autonomistas were now known, on the Democrats. On the island the new Governor Allen, a Republican, was soon working with Muñoz Rivera's opposition.

The Foraker Act proviso establishing a common currency and replacing the Puerto Rican peso with the U.S. dollar was causing great hardship. The peso had been worth sixty cents. Employers considered it opportune, therefore, to reduce wages numerically by forty percent. Merchants, on the other hand, seeing no reason to adjust prices, eagerly accepted the forty-percent increase in the value of goods on hand and on order. In one stroke, real wages and most savings had been drastically cut. The already desperate workers, led by Santiago Iglesias, went out on the streets. Several times a week police action led to riots.

The island's Republican party, supported by insular capital, took the side of authority. With police consent they assaulted Santiago Iglesias' followers on the streets; protected by law, they slandered them in the press. Although Don Luis had previously shown his antipathy for Santiago Iglesias, his sense of justice led him to assail the persecution levied against the labor leader by the island's Republicans and the Americans. Gleefully, then, the Republicans publicly accused Muñoz Rivera of a political alliance with the Socialists and other "agitators." He was stung into restating his position in his *Diario de Puerto Rico:*

> We have said it and we repeat it; we are neither with nor against the Socialists. Although we consider their propaganda premature, we do not see it as illegal, and even less do we believe that they should be persecuted with blood and fire. Time and reality are the elements that will demonstrate the scope or the inanity of their thesis. . . .
>
> But we are today, as we were yesterday, as we will be always, on the side of the persecuted. . . . We do not care whether the oppressed, the deprived, the persecuted is Federalist or Socialist; we will not even ask if he is a Republican. . . .
>
> Therefore, because the Socialists have been cruelly attacked, because they have been jailed for we know not what imaginary crimes, because they are assaulted savagely and with implacable hatred, we put ourselves at their sides, and we protest the outrage. . . .

Throughout the hot summer of Governor Allen's first year, Muñoz Rivera's attacks wore on the nerves of the administration and of his political foes. Throughout the island, tempers were rising feverishly. The summer sun seemed unbearable and relentless, the nights steamy and still. Flies by day and mosquitoes by night invaded even the porticos of the Fortaleza; and only a short distance away, the stench of garbage on the streets of San Juan was more malodorous than ever. Hugging the buildings for their shade, beggars and idlers stunk like the manure steaming in the streets. Their sunken eyes probed passersby for pity and burned with envy of those whom fortune had obviously touched with grace. The blight of hatred was falling over the island, while the editorials of Muñoz Rivera continued to rail against the evil of its evidence, against the use of power to still the voice of protest.

Finally, in September, Muñoz Rivera pierced the skin of authority in protesting the mayor's treatment of two companion Federalists named Rubio and Figueras. The mayor, Manuel Egozcue, a Republican, was the municipal voice of the governor. He had ordered a month's sentence of forced labor on the prisoners, demanding that they be required to clean the streets of San Juan in public view. The victims refused and were placed in solitary confinement on bread and water.

The protest that Don Luis' *Diario* published was a scalding criticism of the regime and the Republicans who cooperated with it. Entitled "A Pack of Hounds on the Prowl," its censure was so impelling—"vituperative," the governor later called it—that throughout San Juan guns were quietly taken from their hiding places. The faces of men were clouded, menacing. Word immediately reached Don Luis to warn him of impending danger. Moustache bristling, eyes glowering, muscles tightened on his neck, the publisher bent to the preparation of the next day's *Diario*.

The streets of San Juan slept. It was the noonday siesta of September 14. From different parts of the city men converged stealthily on the building that housed the *Diario*. At a signal, they crashed through its wooden door and into the shop behind the offices. By the time Muñoz Rivera and some of his staff had arrived to throw out the last of the intruders, the shop and some presses and type fonts were all but destroyed.

Much has been written about Governor Allen's indifference to this disturbance, even a claim that he rebuked the American Army command for ordering out soldiers to end it. The *Diario* appeared to be eliminated from the San Juan scene.

It was bruised, it was badly wounded, but the *Diario* was not dead. To the amazement of the town, it appeared the next day, a skimpy edition with little news and very few advertisements; but on its front page, repeated to the last word, was the editorial that had provoked the attack. And seated at his desk, with a pistol in a drawer, was the publisher and editor, Don Luis Muñoz Rivera.

The next day an anonymous leaflet was scattered in the city's streets. It excoriated Muñoz Rivera and called for vengeance against his published insults. Friends advised Don Luis to leave town for a while. Other Federalists asked the governor to provide protection. Neither man had ears for such advice. The next day, September 17, the *Diario* again published the editorial.

An expectant citizenry awaited the next move. It was obvious that "The Lion" was as fearless as ever, but this time he faced a desperate foe, one made brave by assurance of official support. The blow fell quickly. On the night of September 18 about a hundred men broke into and destroyed the offices and shops of the *Diario*, then assaulted the home of its editor. Don Luis chose to defend his family. With a few friends, his own burly shoulders, and some pistol shots into the air, he cleared his home of the intruders.

The next day he moved his family to safer quarters in the nearby town of Caguas. There he soon reestablished his old newspaper, *La Democracia.*

But Don Luis was disturbed. His wife saw it in his long, brooding silences. His son sensed it as he crawled against the solid legs. Don Luis was shaken because his adversaries this time were his countrymen. They were not Spaniards. They were not Americans. They were the people he was fighting for, and divided among themselves, they were involved in increasingly violent quarrels. This, thought Muñoz Rivera, was something like civil war. Worse, this was a demonstration of the weakness the Americans had attributed to his people—their political instability, their immaturity.

He had never withdrawn from a fight in his life, and he never would. But now he realized that he was challenging the wrong adversary. He must leave. He must exile himself and his family. Muñoz Rivera would pit himself against the real opponent at the real source of power: the Congress of the United States. And with his departure perhaps his own countrymen could settle their differences in peace.

On November 15, 1900, he formally resigned his leadership of the Federal party.

Early in 1901 Don Luis, his wife, Amalia, and the boy, Luis Muñoz Marín, were in New York.

The Puerto Ricans were reversing the American invasion of their island. And they were carrying their own weapons. Santiago Iglesias came to the United States in February, 1901, to see the famous labor leader Samuel Gompers and be presented by him to President McKinley. While in the United States he put his unflagging energies to winning the support of organized American labor for his new labor federation in Puerto Rico. Meanwhile he earned his living as a cabinetmaker in New York.

Luis Muñoz Rivera had set up his armory in the same city. He established the *Puerto Rico Herald* on the city's West Side, letting fly his attacks on evil and evildoers in Puerto Rico and Washington. The newspaper was published in English. Following their different methods, Don Luis and Iglesias were making an impact.

The brashness of starting a periodical in a strange language, publishing it behind the enemy lines, and directing its message to a vast and indifferent public coincided with the challenging figure Don Luis presented on the New York scene. Don Juanesque in appearance and somewhat so by inclination, he soon gathered adherents, American and Puerto Rican, and began a relationship with the United States that would last for the rest of his life. He would learn its language and one day impress its Congress with his eloquence. He would learn its predilections, understand its ideals, analyze its prejudices, and direct his own fight back up the hill by weaving through these obstacles rather than trying to tear them aside.

At this point, however, his efforts to deal with Puerto Rico's new masters, the Americans, often seemed futile. This struggle with Spain had been a quarrel within the family. It was conducted in a language common to all, the customs, mores, pleasures, and penance shared by Spain and its recalcitrant island. You could talk to a Spaniard and know when he lied or when his word was a pledge. You could write a poem and know it would be read in Madrid. The irony of your bitter editorials would not be lost on the Spanish parliament. In Cádiz or Barcelona or Valencia or the capital, you

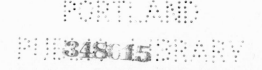

could walk the streets, sit in a café, read the newspaper, sense the mood of the motherland toward your cause, and debate with your adversaries because you were of their blood. And the culture that your people were developing was an outgrowth and an extension of Madrid's rich treasure.

But now, with the Americans, you were lost. Your new masters spoke another language, wore their clothing differently, treated their women in strange ways, could not read your newspapers And if, someday, you became one of them, you would be nothing. Muñoz Rivera wrote of this to a close friend on the island.

"In the future," his letter started, "there will be abundance, physical well-being, a richness of fruits and metals; but there will be no country. And, if there is, it will belong to Americans and their sons and grandsons. In half a century it will be a stain to wear a name of Spanish structure."

Later Muñoz Rivera would change this opinion. But even now the new striking power of his New York newspaper made itself felt when Santiago Iglesias returned to Puerto Rico late in 1901. Almost immediately after disembarking on the island's shores, Iglesias was thrown into jail again, charged with violation of a Spanish law proscribing as a crime any public effort to bring about increases in wages. When, in December, Iglesias was sentenced to three years, four months, and seven days of imprisonment, the *Puerto Rico Herald* exposed the barbarity of the decree and was quickly followed in its outcry by American labor organs and the American press. The public was shocked that its representatives in Puerto Rico were fostering the continued imposition of Spanish law in an American colony. The scandal reached the White House. The next year the courts, pressured by Theodore Roosevelt, now President, revoked the sentence; the use of Spanish law in Puerto Rico was banned forever.

Muñoz Rivera's word still carried in Puerto Rico also, for *La Democracia* continued to be published, and in it were his letters from the United States. And in 1902 a new collection of his poems was published in a volume called *Tropicales*. Meanwhile he saw that his absence from the island was not solving the issue of political fratricide there. He observed that economic exploitation was increasing. The influx of major American investors in sugar and tobacco

lands was creating new combinations of concentrated wealth that continued to hold down wages in an atmosphere of desperate unemployment.

One of his old associates in Puerto Rico was also reaching new conclusions. Rosendo Matienzo Cintrón, lawyer, writer, speaker, teacher, and politician, was preparing another shift in his political direction. Matienzo Cintrón, six years older than Don Luis, had joined his party in 1896 and had served with him on the famous mission to Sagasta. He had broken with Luis Muñoz Rivera when the Americans came to the island and was now working within the ranks of Celso Barbosa's Republicans. But he had come to despair of any progress as long as the island's parties continued to battle against each other rather than the Americans. He began to call for political unity on the island.

Wary of direct contact and the possibility of rebuff, Matienzo Cintrón and Muñoz Rivera observed each other with some circumspection. The courtship of these two bold and outspoken men was strangely timid. Their public statements were almost like the dropping of handkerchiefs and roses. But Matienzo Cintrón remained a member of the Republican party, and Don Luis was still listed with the Federals.

It was apparent to friends and family that Don Luis was falling into periods of strange distraction. These were not moods of melancholy. Immersed in them, he looked like a chess player before an imaginary board. It was at such a moment that Doña Amalia found him with the letter from Matienzo Cintrón.

"He suggests I go back to the island," explained Don Luis.

Doña Amalia's eyebrows rose.

"But I have no money for the trip," said Don Luis flatly, and he answered the letter in that vein.

Money was accumulated to bring Luis Muñoz Rivera back to the island, where he soon entered into the kind of clandestine manipulation that Puerto Rican politicians so much enjoy. It was necessary to keep the Federalist celebrity away from Matienzo Cintrón, or the Republicans might become unduly alarmed about the plans of the two men to combine in an effort to bring together all Puerto Rican parties.

Months of negotiation went by. The election year of 1904 came

on, and finally the stage was set for an open declaration of love on
the part of Muñoz Rivera and Matienzo Cintrón. The two salty
party leaders relished the drama of the idea. More, they recalled
how once, some seven years ago, it was Matienzo Cintrón who,
giving up his opposition, helped put Don Luis in a position to seek
Sagasta in Spain. Now Muñoz Rivera was working for Cintrón's
project for unity.

Muñoz Rivera now called a meeting of the Federalist party at the
Hotel Olimpo. On February 18, 1904, the meeting opened. Muñoz
Rivera declared that the cause of Puerto Rico superseded the interest
of the party and asked that the Federal party be disbanded. All
participants knew their lines, and the motion was passed by acclaim.
The next day the same group loudly approved another motion, proposed by Muñoz Rivera and seconded by José de Diego, to establish
the Unionist party of Puerto Rico.

Immediately a committee was appointed to rush from the Hotel
Olimpo with an invitation to Rosendo Matienzo Cintrón and his
closest lieutenants in the Republican party, asking their adherence
to the new banner. To no one's surprise, they accepted. Only hours
later, Cintrón, flanked by his followers, marched down the center
aisle of the meeting to the stage as the assembled audience rose in
a delirious ovation. The embrace of Cintrón and Muñoz Rivera was
discussed in many a San Juan café into the late hours of that exciting night.

The people of Puerto Rico heard the call of the leaders who had
stood together in their struggle with Spain before the Americans
came to the island. Now, under a new American governor, Beek-
man Winthrop, who warned local judges and the police that he
would not tolerate the abuses that had stifled opposition to the Republicans in 1902, the people again joined Luis Muñoz Rivera in a
new effort to move the rock of Sisyphus to the hilltop. The vote was
89,713 for the Unionistas de Puerto Rico and 54,092 for the Re-
publicanos.

From the balcony of his home near the Plaza de Armas in San
Juan, Don Luis heard the acclaim of his followers. Beside him was
his son, Luis, now six years old, who would be close to him throughout the coming struggle, in San Juan, in New York, in Washington.
The boy would watch the drama of "Sisyphus," which one day he
himself would reenact.

Election returns took more time in 1904. The boy, Luis, understood little but sensed a great deal. He had no thought of why he was allowed to stay up so late this night, but felt that the occasion was not an ordinary fiesta.

Young Luis had never before seen the messengers who were now calling numbers up to his father, seated stolidly on the balcony over the Plaza de Armas. Nor had he seen such a crowd as this on the square below. There were not only many more people than ever before; they acted differently from any gathering his six years could recall.

The noises of the crowd changed from muffled routine to a lighter, more suspenseful tone, spattered now with little cries of excitement. The even, scuffing footfalls that mark the usual rhythm of indolent pacing in tropic heat seemed to break their threnody with heel-tap staccatos and the rising beat of new groups thrusting through San Juan's narrow streets to the plaza.

Laughter and some shrillness came into the tone of the growing crowd's orchestration. Some words spilled loudly out of the soft roar. "Unionistas. Don Luis. Luis Muñoz Rivera!" The speakers of the new word "Unionistas," and also the old name "Luis Muñoz Rivera," looked at the man on the balcony as they called his name.

He moved only to accept an occasional small cup of coffee from one of the women who periodically darted out onto the balcony. She seemed to be everywhere, yet constantly near Don Luis. This was his wife, Doña Amalia, lively, quick, and sure. Flickers of light flashed on her black hair and softly lit the ivory cheeks that were part of her famous beauty. She was always beside Don Luis; even when she moved away with one of the guests, her gaze continued to cherish him.

Clinging to his father, almost too small to be seen, the small boy, Luis Muñoz Marín, was enthralled at the sight on the plaza below. Nearly everyone in San Juan must be there, jostling awkwardly everywhere on the cobblestone streets, on the plaza's dirt paths, over the grass, clustering under the trees, and on the other side, under the great arches of the Ayuntamiento, the white-stone headquarters of the municipality. The gleam of perspiration shone on the faces of the men who watched the balcony of the Muñoz Rivera home.

Their black hair glistened even in the shadows. There was a soft breeze blowing on the boy, but below, the heat was rumpling the men's white clothing while large sweat stains spread over their backs. Only a few women were there, standing on the sidewalks, pressed back against the buildings of the four sides of the plaza. Many looked like black shadows against white walls; a few were more daring, in yellow and pink.

The boy turned as a man bent over his father and said, "Don Luis, you will have to speak to them soon."

Muñoz Rivera shook his head. "It is you, Don Tulio Llarínaga, who is being elected resident commissioner to the United States!"

The other man laughed. "I will go to Washington for the Unionist party. I will talk to the Yankee Congress if they will listen. But these people"—he shook his head toward the crowd below—"these will not go home tonight with only a few words from me, or even from Don Matienzo Cintrón. You must speak to them, Don Luis."

The conversation was interrupted by a great shout from the crowd. Above it a strong voice called, "Tonight, a new party! Tonight, a hero from before! We salute them both." And as the cheer rose, the boy looked quickly at his father. A hero? Soldiers were heroes. Kings were heroes. Muñoz Rivera slowly turned his gaze on the boy as a smile broke the severity of his bushy-browed, ruggedly handsome face.

The men nearest the balcony saw the smile and began to call for a speech, and at last Don Luis rose to address them. The lines of a poem were coming into his mind, the lines of "Sisyphus." "This is the symbol of unending strife . . . of foolish glory, never truly won, and pain, eternal as the earth . . . this is the story of the poet's life." His deep dark eyes were set in the mold of anguish and determination, a tenderness mixed with unflagging hope. For the struggle was not over.

The Unionist victory had occurred under American supervision; but the political divisions of the Spanish era still persisted: the haunting desire for association posed against the struggle for identity; the fear of isolation in conflict with the groping for dignity that has ever plagued the steps of nations new and old. The issue could not yet be faced clearly, for it was mired in a swamp of human misery that made both dignity and association farcical for the island's masses. Even under the best American effort since 1898, the

Foraker Act, only the proven literate or those who owned property had been allowed to vote. Santiago Iglesias had not even a part in the contest of 1904, nor did his followers. With all the nobility of their Spanish descent, the Puerto Ricans, including Don Luis Muñoz Rivera, had, like Don Quixote, been fighting the wrong enemy. One day the son of Muñoz Rivera would say this in words that would reach the citizens of the island.

FIVE

Death of the Lion

FROM THE NIGHT that young Luis heard the multitude in the Plaza de Armas acclaim his father's return to active politics, the rhythms of his life accelerated frenetically. On any afternoon the boy, coming home from school, might find his father gathered with other leaders of the Unionist party discussing political strategy. Night after night, when Luis was in bed, the meetings would continue downstairs in the front of the house, the voices rumbling as those of adults do in the ears of the young—the steady, low roar, often punctuated with exclamations and insistent outbursts that must have sounded very fierce, occasionally terrifying.

At other times the house was silent. Don Luis would be traveling about the island or would be in the *Democracia* office. Then those who came to the door seeking him would leave quiet messages with Doña Amalia. The times were exciting, even if the six-year-old was not sure why.

Don Luis was anxious for a period of reflection about the strategy for eventual removal of the black insult of the Foraker Act, its saddling of Puerto Rico with a foreign government, its denomination of Puerto Ricans as "the people of Puerto Rico" and the citizens of no land on earth.

The violent denunciations of the Foraker Act, when it prescribed Puerto Rico's system of government, were too emotional to be informative. Its effect on the island's political life and the birth of a new hostility to the United States were to outlive even the corrective action that Muñoz Rivera would finally sponsor.

Since the Act retained full executive powers in the hands of Washington appointees, the legislative efforts of the Puerto Rican people were consistently negated. One such exercise in futility was the effort to control the grab of sugar lands that was being spearheaded by American capital at the turn of the century. The provision for a five-hundred-acre limitation on the ownership of land by agricultural corporations was an attempt to equate property rights with human rights, but it had been flouted by the very parties it attempted to control. Their indifference to this restriction was, of course, permitted by successive administrations in Puerto Rico and in Washington. The result eventually created a situation reminiscent of the Spanish land-grant system with all its inequities.

In a few years more than half of the best agricultural land of the tiny island, with one of the most dense populations of the world, was owned by four absentee sugar corporations whose local governmental influence kept taxes and wages down and would-be strikers within "law and order." In many ways a big sugar corporation was a state within a state. Thus the benefits of economic union with the United States were largely lost to the people of the island.

In the election year of 1904 Samuel Gompers, leader of American labor, visited Puerto Rico and made a report on what he saw:

> . . . I have seen men working in the sugar mills of Puerto Rico fifteen and sixteen hours for forty cents a day. I have seen men toiling in the sugar fields virtually dragging themselves through fifteen hours a day for forty or forty-five cents. Some of the millers of sugar have installed a system of stores as obligatory supply centers for these working men, working men working fifteen to sixteen hours for forty to forty-five cents a day, paid in stamps representing cash redeemable only in these company stores. The people in these villages have no other funds than these stamps. . . . So the workers are compelled to live bonded to the earth like the ancient serfs under the rule of their masters and at the disposition of any of those rulers who might want to expel them and destroy their huts. . . . In my trip through Puerto Rico, I saw more idle men and more without work, not idle by choice, but because there was no work, than I have ever seen in my life among people of equal numbers. . . . I have never seen so many human beings showing so clearly the signs of malnutrition, nor so many women and

children with the marks of hunger in their faces. No, never
have I seen such an accumulation of misery in one people, and
understand that I know something of this mother earth. . . .
I have been asked occasionally whether the condition of the
Puerto Rican people is better or worse than it was under the
Spanish government, and I understand the question and must
reply in this way: That, having seen the misery and the poverty
and the utter impossibility of workers' homes that might permit
decent, modest, and comfortable family relationships and knowing the terrible fact that every month there is an average of
450 to 800 deaths from anemia or, in other words, misery, or,
rather, starvation (and consumption), I declare to you ladies
and gentlemen that it matters little to me under whose laws or
administration the conditions are better or worse. What I do
know, and affirm, is that the conditions existent in Puerto Rico
today reflect no honor or credit upon our country.

Opposition took varying forms. Under Celso Barbosa, the Republicans eventually sought equality through statehood. The effort to develop a crusade for independence rallied under the banner of José de
Diego, another Unionist leader. As yet unrevealed was the determination of Luis Muñoz Rivera to obtain the type of autonomy he
had wrenched from Spain, and in much the same way.

Paralleling his technique of the 1890's—rallying public opinion
behind him by exposing the administrative injustices and incompetence that were immediately visible and comprehensible to the people on the island—Don Luis in 1905 published a series of editorials,
this time about Americans, entitled "The Failure."

For a poet, he had become a master of the editorial use of statistics.
Devastatingly, he pointed out that the island government budget
under the Americans equaled the 4.4 million pesos the Spanish had
spent in 1897, but without expenses for a five-thousand-man garrison
or the former contributions to the church. By refusing a needed loan,
raising taxes in some sectors, ignoring the requests of the Puerto Rican House of Delegates, building roads at double the old costs, and
leaving eighty-five percent of the school-age population without
schools, the Americans absorbed the budget in payment of high salaries to United States bureaucrats in the island government.

In six years, Don Luis declared, half the appointive offices had been given to Americans, 626 of them on top salaries. Education cost the island government $15 per student per year, against $13 in New York state; $6 million was needed for schools, not the $850,000 presently allocated.

The defective civil administration under the Foraker Act was contravening its objective; it was "de-Americanizing Puerto Rico."

The editorials were effective. In the 1906 elections the Unionist party moved into a majority position and this time young Luis saw his father acclaimed as a delegate to the Cámara (House of Delegates).

The Lion was emerging from his lair. In early 1908 his roar was heard in one of his greatest speeches before the Puerto Rican House. His first words were for the Americans. Even his sarcasm did not dim his attitude of respect for ability and good intentions, but he quickly moved to a demand for human equality:

> I accept intervention; what I do not accept is its superiority. I applaud the Americans for the network of roads that they have built with the island's money. I applaud them ardently for the schools that they maintain, with the enormous credits voted by this House and also for the progress of the island. On these two points, they are doing a good job. . . . I tender to them my approval, I endorse them, I encourage them. But this House will not permit for one day more that anyone should trample upon us. There, up north, they judge themselves superior to the rest of the world. Indeed possibly they really are. They are giving humanity a giant push; they are modifying methods, broadening ideas, realizing a progress that no one denies nor disputes; let it be recognized and let it glorify them. No Puerto Rican did or ever will—nor would it be allowed—dispute the supremacy of policy or administration in Wisconsin, Rhode Island, or Massachusetts. And here, in our land, we will not allow anyone to put himself over us. . . .

The master politician then spoke for everyone: statehooders, independence-seekers, and believers in associate autonomy, but he carefully placed priorities on political action. He revealed his objective, and with it, as he had with Spain, the threat that might follow denial:

If it were possible to open the heart of every Puerto Rican, and if it were possible to see the collective soul of the million beings who inhabit this forgotten rock, we would see there written, in indelible letters, the word "independence." . . .

Our duty is to ask, to demand, to insist that the status of Puerto Rico be resolved in the manner of a state in association with the other states, in the manner of clear autonomy in association with the other American colonies . . . and if, finally, we lose all hope, we exhaust the last recourse . . . we will ask independence for Puerto Rico.

Repercussions were almost immediate. More Puerto Ricans were appointed to government jobs, and their salary levels were raised. Pressing its new initiative, the Puerto Rican House refused to approve the next year's budget, which was imposed over its veto, and it appointed a commission of three, headed by Luis Muñoz Rivera, to see President Taft in an effort to achieve modification of the Foraker Act. They were turned down brusquely. Muñoz Rivera reported that "Taft roared like a lion wounded by the hunter's arrow." Although Don Luis lost the roaring match, it may have helped the Unionists win the 1910 elections, 100,634 to the Republicans' 58,572, with Don Luis balloted to the post of resident commissioner to Washington, which was his residence for the remaining years of his life.

Now young Luis was twelve years old. The English he had learned as a child in New York came back to him quickly when he reentered the American school system in Washington. He was tall for his age, and the great brown eyes that women were to observe fondly and writers to describe at length were already his most distinguishing feature.

Don Luis, in a strangling effort, succeeded that first year in mastering English, at the age of fifty-one. This was vital to him in fulfilling the office of resident commissioner created by the Foraker Act. He was the elected representative in Washington of the Puerto Rican people. Certified by the Puerto Rican administration, he was presented to the State Department and the Congress as an observer.

In 1904 the House had voluntarily granted its privileges, except for voting, to the Puerto Rican official. Beyond this point the influence of the commissioner depended upon the ability and prestige of the man in office. He could talk individually with members of the Congress in the Capitol or elsewhere. He could, and did, bring them to his home and find them at social affairs. In this sense the commissioner literally had to make his job. He was charged with the responsibility for making known in Congress the feelings of his constituents, and he was expected to report back to the island on the sentiments of Congress in matters affecting Puerto Rico.

Muñoz Rivera was accepted in Congress as truly representative of Puerto Rico. His personal history soon became known in sectors important to the island. He was invited to sit with the Interior and Insular Affairs committees of the House, also the Committee on Armed Services and on Agriculture. To an observant son like Luis the activity of the dedicated commissioner was a living lesson in politics. To the Americans it was a demonstration of Puerto Rican intellectual competence. The big Puerto Rican with the majestic bearing of an aristocrat won the full respect of his congressional cohorts.

They came to appreciate his honesty, his bluntness, and his reasonable ability to avoid head-on collisions. And many recognized that, like all of them, he was fighting a constant rear-guard battle with his constituents and political opponents in Puerto Rico.

The leader of the Unionist party was José de Diego in name, but now in reality it was Muñoz Rivera. And changes in the American political picture were driving Don Luis to frenzied efforts to control the extremists in his party.

Woodrow Wilson was elected President of the United States in 1912. This was the man who told Congress in his first message: ". . . we can fulfill our obligations for a generous justice toward the people of Puerto Rico, giving them the full and ordinary rights and privileges ceded to our own citizens on our own territory. . . ."

Was this another Práxedes Sagasta? Were the Democrats of the United States to reproduce the story of the Liberals of Spain? Muñoz Rivera prepared for such an eventuality. He had only a few years left. Unknown to Don Luis, a cancer was waiting to spell out the last years of his life. From the sensitive viewpoint of his fourteen years, young Luis watched his father move into the last great effort.

The cool doctrinaire thinking of the American professor whom the people had made President was not easily accessible to Puerto Rico's ardent resident commissioner. Muñoz Rivera sensed an area of warmth and compatibility behind the glacial atmosphere of the White House, but reaching it was an agonizing experience. His spirit may have faltered at times, but he did reach the American President at last, and must have convinced him that his sincerity matched Wilson's devotion to his own aims.

Wilson advised him about the policy the Unionist party should represent, as the island's majority group, in order to obtain White House endorsement for an improvement in Puerto Rico's status. Don Luis would have to achieve the removal from his party's platform of its demand for independence. To do this it would be necessary to overcome the party's official leader, José de Diego, revered on the island for his lifelong consecration to this goal.

Muñoz Rivera desperately attempted to avert De Diego's opposition. "Here, in the United States," he wrote in a frantic letter, "independence propaganda produces a terrible reaction against the Unionist party." But De Diego insisted that a change in the party policy could be considered only at a full party convention.

The convention was held at the Miramar Theater in San Juan, beginning on October 24, 1915. It was joined in a turbulent atmosphere. A third Unionist wing, under Martín Travieso, was trying to move toward statehood. The Republicans were stirring up the populace by pointing out the deep divisions within the Unionist ranks. And outside of both parties Santiago Iglesias, disgusted with repeated failures to obtain attention to the plight of the workers, was forming the Socialist party of Puerto Rico to enter the 1916 election.

The confrontation of De Diego and Muñoz Rivera, veterans of the struggle against Spain and against the United States, and in their hearts joined by the deep desire for freedom on their island, was tragedy on the scale of the Greek stage, for both were drawn by forces beyond their individual wills and each suffered secretly for the other. The outcome was a political victory for Muñoz Rivera— and perhaps another scar upon his heart. By acclaim, the platform was amended to a demand for self-government, with independence mentioned as a matter for consideration at a future convention. Muñoz Rivera returned to Washington with the support of his party, the endorsement of the new governor, Arthur Yager, and the approval of Woodrow Wilson. José de Diego, abandoning Puerto Rico irrevocably, departed for Spain.

Luis Muñoz Rivera had committed himself to a bitter task. He had no assurance of the possible decision of Congress or of its terms. He knew he would have no second chance to amend a failure. He had fought against his own secret longings and those of his people.

"I was a separatist in the dawn of my youth," he told a friend. "I continue to be a separatist as I enter the doorway to old age. I do not renounce my ideal. But if we are to constitute a sovereign people, we will do it through a law voted in the Capitol in Washington. This law will not be achieved by eloquent speeches, nor hymns to the race, nor the appeals of senile monarchists and young Iberian republicans. It will be obtained by convincing the Congress that in truth we are worthy of being free."

As he set himself to the task of so persuading Congress, it became increasingly apparent that the law to be offered, although a great improvement over the Foraker Act, would be a disappointment. The outlines of its main features emerged during the debates of 1916. It would grant the Puerto Ricans United States citizenship and a popularly elected two-house legislature; but the island's governor, the supreme court, the auditor, and the commissioners of education, labor, health, and agriculture would be Washington appointees, the Cabinet would be appointed by the President (four members) and the governor (two members), and the governor would have a veto over the legislature. Suffrage would still be limited to literates and property holders.

Muñoz Rivera wanted the same rights as an American state, which he knew was impossible. He carried the battle from the Insular Affairs Committee to the floor of Congress. He cajoled congressmen in corridors, at dinners, wherever he could find them. He reminded Congress that under Spain the governor's powers permitted him to "reign but not rule" and that the cabinet had been Puerto Rican and had held power of approval over the governor, that the island administration had been in Puerto Rican hands, and Puerto Rico had been granted representation in the Spanish parliament.

The bill went to Congress with only a shabby change: that the legislature could appeal to the President of the United States over his governor's vote. It also would permit Puerto Rican individuals to refuse American citizenship, in which case they would continue to have none.

While Muñoz Rivera was collecting his failing strength for the final onslaught, his son was at Georgetown University, showing

small interest in his studies but revealing a great propensity to repeat his father's early saga. He was writing short stories, essays, and
poetry. And, as his father had done in his younger days, he was seeing the Puerto Rican problem with the eyes of a new generation.

Luis Muñoz Marín recalls midnight conversations with his father
about the troubling currents of thought that then, as with all gen-
erations, were creating doubts about the wisdom of ancestors and
parents. Socialism was the intellectual magnet for curious and caring
youth, the possible new approach to equity in a world where the
unrestrained exercise of power was overlooking a valley of distress.
Muñoz Rivera, mellowed, always a humanitarian in his own way,
listened to young Luis' questions, sitting by the living-room couch
on which the boy slept and joining in verbal examination of them
before taking his own last problem into the darkness of the adjoin-
ing bedroom for the night. No one else heard or was interested in
the boy's views at the time. The spotlight was on the shaggy, lion-
like head of Muñoz Rivera.

Now speaking in the House in perfect English, Don Luis made
his last great appeal on May 5, 1916. He did not want statehood,
but he sought rights equal to that status. Growing old almost before
their eyes, he delivered to Congress an appeal that was successful in
gaining universal male suffrage on the island and that was prophetic
of the partial response it would receive more than twenty years
later:

> Give us now that field of experiment which we ask of you,
> that we may demonstrate that it is easy for us to constitute a
> stable republican government with all possible guarantees for all
> possible interests. And afterwards, when you acquire the cer-
> tainty that you can found in Puerto Rico a republic like that
> founded in Cuba and in Panama, like the one you will found at
> some future day in the Philippines, give us our independence
> and you will stand before humanity as the greatest of the great,
> that which neither Greece nor Rome nor England ever were, a
> great creator of new nationalities and a great liberator of op-
> pressed peoples.

Congress was moved, but Luis Muñoz Rivera this time was speaking at the wrong moment in history. The bill, with no further

changes, was written into final form. Although it fell far short of Muñoz Rivera's aspirations, the Jones Act, as it came to be called, was a great step in the direction of dignity and even of identity for the Puerto Ricans. It offered them a citizenship, and it granted them the right to vote for their own legislators. But as an example of legislative artisanship, it was a poor product. By making the legislature responsible to the Puerto Rican electorate, and the executive, judicial, and administrative sectors answerable to Washington, it guaranteed discontent, injustice, continuing dispute, and incompetence in government.

Muñoz Rivera, saddened and sick, returned to the island with his family in September, 1916. With assurance that the Jones Act would be passed early the next year as it was, on March 2, 1917, the island postponed its elections accordingly. But Don Luis had no strength left for the struggle. They soon left Barranquitas for the San Juan home of an old friend, Eduardo Giorgetti, prominent in the Unionist party.

Muñoz Rivera must have known he was dying and that he might not survive the operation being planned for him. One night friends talked with him at his bedside, and one assured him, "Don Luis, the people of Puerto Rico are all with you."

"Then," said Don Luis, "this is a good time to die."

The next morning, November 15, 1916, Muñoz Rivera had gone to "the silence and the repose."

Of his father's death, Luis Muñoz Marín, now nearly nineteen, wrote:

> . . . I would be a giant to embrace the mountains that he contemplated in his boyhood, the mountains for which he struggled from his youth onward, the mountains that shelter his countrymen, the *jíbaro*, and that now entomb his body. . . . a giant to hold close all the Puerto Ricans who guard forever in their noble hearts the sacred memory of my father. . . . a giant to complete the work of Luis Muñoz Rivera. . . .

But the boy was not yet a giant. The years of proof were before him, the long years until the people of Puerto Rico should deem him ready to take up the task of Sisyphus.

SIX

The Iconoclasts

O NE NIGHT in 1922, in an apartment on the West Side of New
York, two men were blowing smoke in each other's faces and trying
for something to say. Their difficulty was that they were old friends
among strangers. They had arrived only minutes ago. The one who
knew nearly everyone else in the room had brought the other to
one of the Sunday nights of Mr. and Mrs. Luis Muñoz Marín.
At these soirees, well known among a coterie of writers, explorers,
teachers, talkers, and commentators on the world scene, only two
rules were in force. No one was invited; people just came. And no
one was permitted to read his own or any other poetry aloud.

The newcomer, after a deep pull on his cigar, asked his knowing
friend, "Where is the host?"

"Over there. The tall, dark, young fellow."

"The one with the haunted eyes and lots of black hair?"

The friend of Muñoz Marín paused. "People do talk about his
eyes. I'm not sure I would call them haunted; I tend to define them
as—searching."

"All right," said the man with the cigar. "Who is the Latin type
he's talking to? They're certainly going at it."

For a moment the two men watched Luis Muñoz Marín and his
friend wave their hands as they engaged in an obviously spirited
conversation.

"He's a Venezuelan, an exile. They're probably plotting the overthrow of Juan Vicente Gómez, the dictator of Venezuela. Luis is
pretty emotional about it."

As though he had heard them, Luis suddenly turned; then, with the Venezuelan trailing him, he hurried, hands outstretched, to receive the two most recent guests. Now he was smiling with the pleasure of adding two new talkers to the small apartment's hubbub. In a brief exchange the guests learned that Muñoz Marín had been attempting to convince his friend that desperate action in Venezuela now would be fruitless. A revolt should be preceded by careful preparation of the working classes.

Luis had the year before attended the American Federation of Labor convention in Portland, Oregon, as a delegate accompanying Santiago Iglesias, founder of the labor union's branch in Puerto Rico. There he had introduced a resolution calling for moral support of the development of democracy in Venezuela and everywhere in the American hemisphere. He could not say whether his intense interest in Venezuela arose from its proximity to Puerto Rico, from his ancestors' residence there before they came to Puerto Rico, or from the country's suffering under the cruelest of the South American dictators. He felt that the latter cause was predominant.

With a smile and a wave of his hand, Luis left the men and made his way across the room to his wife, Muna Lee. They had been married three years and had one child, Luis, who was now wailing alone in another room. Muna Lee was small, dark-haired, extraordinarily vital, perceptive, quick of movement, and understanding. She had been born in Mississippi, three years before Luis and the Americans arrived in Puerto Rico. Her studies had taken her through Blue Mountain College, the University of Oklahoma, and the University of Mississippi. Muna was a poet and generally conceded to be a good one. In 1915, four years before meeting Luis, she had won *Poetry* magazine's lyric prize. Now she was writing "Sea Change" and was translating Spanish-American poetry for a coming anthology issue of *Poetry*.

Luis too was writing poetry for publication. He and Muna Lee had gathered about them a group of literary spirits who came regularly to the Sunday night parties; Horace and Marya Gregory, Marya Zaturenska, Sara Teasdale, Constance Lindsay Skinner, Vachel Lindsay, and William Rose Benét. Adding color to the group were the painter Zuloaga and, occasionally, Juan Belmonte, Spain's famous bullfighter. Constance Lindsay Skinner was often co-hostess for the parties. Her tastes ran to explorers: George Hubert (later Sir Hubert) Wilkins, Vilhjalmur Stefansson, and the Lomen brothers, from

Alaska. The talk turned easily from the Left Bank to the South
Pole to Venezuela to the Fabian Society and then to Puerto Rico.

The mind and heart of Luis Muñoz Marín was making much
that same circuit as he joined the American thinkers tossing on the
seas of the twenties. He had been cast adrift by his father's death,
cut loose from his steady crusade for the political dignity of Puerto
Rico to taste at nineteen the failure of his father's heroism. His father had given the people of Puerto Rico the Jones Act and a per-
sistent hope for determination of their own political affairs. He had
also left his family about four hundred dollars.

Eduardo Giorgetti, in whose home Muñoz Rivera had died, arranged with a group of friends to buy a house for the widow, Doña
Amalia, and to establish the offices of the newspaper *La Democracia*
in the residence on a rental basis that would guarantee her an income.

Luis returned to Washington, worked for a short time as secretary
to the resident commissioner who succeeded his father, Sr. Félix
Córdova Dávila, then went to Puerto Rico for a few months. Soon
he was back in the United States, where he met the young American
poet whom he married in 1919. Luis' own poems were following the
trajectory of his undirected spirit. One, a series of short poems under
the title "Queries," was published by *Poetry:*

    1. "Umbrellas"
       Tell me,
       Umbrella-mongers
       When has an umbrella ever
       Kept the rains and the mist from entering a heart and
          shaping it with dreams?
       When has it kept the rain and the mist
       From entering a heart and breaking it?
    2. "A Death"
       One more husk never again to blur beauty
          in passing;
       One more husk gone to feed the roots of
          the gathering spring;
       One more world of hunger and memory
       Gone to feed the roots of the gathering spring.

3. "At the Stake"
    How can I take you seriously, martyr?
    Did I not once surprise the bottom of my soul
    In the act of enjoying hugely
    The renunciation of the surface of my soul?

Then the theme of his own island would recur, amidst the explorers, the writers, the painters; even in the subway from the upper West Side to Greenwich Village and back; even as newspapers hailed the Hoover Relief Commission, care of the war-torn countries of Europe; even as a new surge of industrial greatness swelled across America and new riches were being accumulated by many of the countries of South America, and as the mass of Puerto Ricans slumped deeper into despondent poverty. Luis turned back to his island, writing "Pamphlet": *

I have broken the rainbow
against my heart
as one breaks a useless sword against a knee
I have blown the clouds of rose color and blood color
beyond the farthest horizons.
I have drowned my dreams
in order to glut the dreams that sleep for me in the veins
of men who sweated and wept and raged
to season my coffee . . .

The dreams that sleep in breasts stifled by tuberculosis
    (A little air, a little sunshine)
  the dreams that dream in stomachs strangled by hunger
    (A bit of bread, a bit of white bread)
  the dream of bare feet
    (Fewer stones on the road, Lord, fewer broken bottles)
  the dream of calloused hands
    (Moss . . . clean cambric . . . things smooth,
      soft, soothing)
    The dream of trampled hearts
      (Love . . . life . . . life)

* Dudley Fitts, ed., *Anthology of Contemporary Latin-American Poetry.* Norfolk, Conn.: New Directions, 1942. Reprinted by permission of New Directions.

Those years were full of talk, of endless verbal exploration, of a never-ending examination of the Puerto Rican issue to which Muñoz Rivera had dedicated his life and to which Muñoz Marín, in the eyes of some unfriendly contemporaries, seemed indifferent. Friends said that he was undergoing a process of redefining the problem, that the parting from his father's program was painful for him.

Muñoz had eagerly absorbed the ideas of New York's "free thinkers" and read the moderately stated social principles proposed in John Spargo's *Applied Socialism*. Disturbing in its contrast to these concepts was the new shape of Puerto Rico's Unionist party after Muñoz Rivera's death. Its leadership had fallen to Antonio Barceló, who used the banner of independence to attract votes while accepting the financial support of large landholders primarily interested in holding down wages and taxes. Thus, almost inevitably, Muñoz Marín's thoughts and speculation had turned to his father's one-time adversary, Santiago Iglesias, whose Socialist party was now in the thick of Puerto Rican politics. In 1917 it had registered 24,468 votes and had elected Santiago Iglesias to the Puerto Rican Senate. This was the first election held under the Jones Act, which Iglesias had strongly supported.

On an important visit to San Juan in 1920, when Luis and Muna's son was born, Luis carried with him a check from his family doctor in New York, Dr. Julio Henna, a self-exiled Puerto Rican who favored independence and had years ago left the island in disgust with the American administration. The check was for the purpose of helping the Socialist party newspaper of Santiago Iglesias. Muñoz accordingly delivered it and told Iglesias he would like to join his party.

The old warrior, remembering the years of combat with Luis Muñoz Rivera, glowered at young Luis and asked him if he were certain that he wanted to make this affiliation. The young man assured him that he was. "Well, then," said Iglesias, "come with me tomorrow and see what we do."

The next day Iglesias took Muñoz Marín to the eastern end of the island, where they visited an encampment of idle and troubled sugar workers. Iglesias spoke to the strikers, assuring them of support and urging them to hold fast to their demands. Impulsively, Luis found himself on the stump, giving them oratorical proof of his own endorsement.

Iglesias accepted Luis, but the young man soon lost his enthusiasm for the Puerto Rican Socialists. Iglesias was now the last of the Puerto Rican leaders of Muñoz Rivera's period. José de Diego was in Spain. José Celso Barbosa, leader of the Republican party, had just died. Iglesias was still working for labor, but to the idealistic young Muñoz it seemed that he was being entangled in the network of island politics. In his attempt to create political power that would support his original goals, he was being diverted from them. Dignified by public office, endorsed by the powerful American Federation of Labor, he was no longer the street fighter who had spent so much time in Spanish, Cuban, and Puerto Rican jails.

Now he was seeking more votes for the Socialist party. He had already allowed this new cause to obscure the primary one, having unsuccessfully proposed a coalition with the Republican party, whose members opposed every principle for which Iglesias had always fought. However, on one concept the two parties understood each other. They both espoused statehood for Puerto Rico.

Muñoz was in full disagreement with Iglesias' belief in statehood. His father's goal of autonomy was, in Luis, bulging into a desire for outright independence, and his impetuous spirit did not harmonize well with compromise at that time. He parted from Santiago Iglesias before 1924. Meanwhile, it is not difficult to understand how stodgy the old Spanish carpenter who led the Socialists may have appeared to Luis when compared to the Sunday night crowd. However, Santiago Iglesias survived the disagreement, stayed in his post as Puerto Rican senator. In 1924 his party was strengthened by the adherence of a dissident group of Republicans.

By 1932 the entire Republican party was allied with the Socialists, and Santiago Iglesias was elected resident commissioner to Washington, a post he held until his death, in 1939. He had become the dean of Puerto Rican politics and was internationally known in labor circles.

To Muñoz Marín Santiago Iglesias displayed a record of three achievements: he started the labor movement in Puerto Rico; he launched the Socialist party with no concern for the island's political status, only for its workers' economic welfare; he tried to persuade the masses not to sell their votes. But there was one idea that the labor leader did not leave with Muñoz—socialism. This was to come from his associations in New York and from the sphere of Nemesio

Canales, a Puerto Rican lawyer turned writer who was the hub of a circle of *bon vivants* on the island.

Prophets have often sought revelation in solitude; Luis was now seeking his in people. Curiously, he was moving between one group of American thinkers and another quite different set of observers in Puerto Rico; but in both coteries he was drawn to men of similar tendencies in their concern for humanity and their scorn for the trappings of society.

In the United States Luis became a friend of Edwin Markham and with his permission did the definitive Spanish translation of his "Man with the Hoe." He admired Edgar Lee Masters, Vachel Lindsay, and Carl Sandburg and wrote essays on their work that appeared in *Quasimodo,* a magazine published by Nemesio Canales.

And now, whenever Luis visited Puerto Rico, he joined Canales and his friends in night-long talks. The group also included Luis Lloréns Torres, a poet who had been a law partner of Canales until both men had decided that writing in poverty was more rewarding than a prosperous plodding from their office to the court of law. Others were Benítez Flores, Palés Matos, De Diego Padró, all listed in the annals of Puerto Rican literature. With them Luis used to meet at the end of the day at La Mallorquina in the center of San Juan, and while a tireless and listening waiter would keep their glasses full, they would discourse on the absurdities and evils of their day. Of the group, Nemesio Canales made a lasting impression on young Luis. Canales was a Fabian socialist. He introduced Muñoz Marín to the world of Shaw, Sidney Webb, H. G. Wells, and Graham Wallas, with Conrad and Ibsen thrown in for seasoning.

Canales' trenchant ideas were a restorative after young Muñoz's disappointing alliance with Iglesias. And soon the heady atmosphere of the Fabian socialists had won young Luis away from the socialism of the horny-handed reformer.

Probably many more people have adhered to the principles of the Fabian Society unknowingly than those who espoused them with full conscience. Like most socialist concepts, Fabianism, founded in England in 1884, recognized the necessity of a democratic political structure for its survival. It differed from other political movements in that it did not lay down a doctrine. The Fabian empiricists believed that facts carried their own proof more quickly than conflicts over theories could. They would be much more concerned with getting a slum cleared than in joining a discussion over the rights of slum dwellers to better conditions. The job done would win new adherents to the Fabian idea of social reform. Whereas Bernard Shaw, the Webbs, and later Clement Attlee knew they were Fabians, intellectuals in New York, San Juan, or Paris might be Fabians without knowing it. Among them were Muñoz Marín's companions, notably Nemesio Canales.

Canales was twenty years older than Muñoz Marín, having been born in 1878 in the small town of Jayuya. His parents were moderately wealthy, and when his father insisted that Nemesio study medicine, he required him to attend Spain's University of Saragossa. The American invasion in 1898 rescued Canales, who was called back by his father and permitted to enter the University of Baltimore to study law. He learned English during his first year of studies, later emerging as an honor student. Back in Puerto Rico, in the city of Ponce, he became a partner in the highly successful law office of López, Tord, Toro, and Canales.

He was attracted to Muñoz Rivera's Unionist party and became one of its delegates to the lower house. He soon made a reputation as an orator, one of his favorite causes being women's suffrage. His own comment on both attributes was somewhat disdainful. "I have said already in every possible tone," he declared, "that I have no vocation or aptitude for oratory; that every speech costs me such an effort that it almost makes me lose my reason and even my life; that I only serve to be silent; and that with all good will I would amputate my tongue and remain mute if it were not, from time to time, that I feel a great need to murmur something, something deep and vague of the soul, into the avid ear of some charming woman."

In 1912 Canales started a Ponce newspaper, the next year a magazine, and two years later the satiric magazine *Juan Bobo* ("Silly John"). In 1918 he decided that law was interfering with his writing, and he abandoned the practice. He traveled in South America, becoming an outstanding figure in academic and literary circles with his lectures and writing.

Muñoz Marín, reared in an atmosphere of dedicated struggle, was clutching the wings of Parnassus when he met Canales. Here was a man who used the figures and forms of art to scoff at the pretensions of men while shedding a tear for their foibles. Here was a writer who could describe himself as "a small man with a fat face, irregular and dull," who could "forgive my father for the ugly crime that he committed by naming me Nemesio," and who could deride his own writing by saying, "I have always put so much curiosity and emotion into the innumerable things that compose the spectacle of life that, frankly, I have never had time in studying grammar to go beyond the conjugations."

In San Juan and in New York, young Luis delighted in Canales' company, in his ideas, and in his refusal to conform to rigid social patterns. Muñoz Marín has often enjoyed recalling the effect on Canales' young son of the derisive discussions that were carried on between his father and whatever guests may have joined the many philosophic evenings. Muñoz discovered something of this the day he asked the child of six years what he would like to accomplish when he became a man. "I want to be a moneyed bourgeois," said the boy, who knew this meant having comforts his family was denied.

But it was precisely this type of label that Canales scorned and by so doing left with Muñoz Marín something of his distaste for formal classification of people or adherence to political dogma as such.

Muñoz Marín kept a briefcase into which he dropped notes about Nemesio Canales for a book he wanted to write about him. When he became more absorbed in the other people of Puerto Rico, he lost the briefcase; but he did not lose his admiration for Canales.

Nemesio Canales died of a heart attack in 1923. Ailing and poor in San Juan, he had seen the end coming and wished to see the wife and son he had left in New York. It was a stroke of Latin kindness that led Antonio Barceló, leader of the Unionist party, who had often felt the barb of Canales' writings, to invent for him a mission to Washington to discuss an economic problem. He boarded ship with Santiago Iglesias, who fulfilled the unhappy duty of radioing on to New York the news of Canales' death at sea.

The year before, Canales had been removed from his position in the island Department of Justice for publishing in *La Semana*, his latest political weekly, an article by Alfonso Lastra Chárriez entitled "I Accuse," directed against the American governor E. Montgomery Reily, President Harding's appointee. The article caused a great stir in Puerto Rico and some notice in the United States, where it was reprinted in *The Nation*. Although not the author of the essay, Nemesio Canales accepted the governor's reprisal.

Governor Reily was attracting to Puerto Rico some of the same kind of attention that the "Harding gang" was to draw to various areas of the United States. And he had stirred a hornet's nest with his efforts to root out of the Puerto Rican government all Unionists or others who sought the island's independence. Since the Unionists were the majority party, they were profoundly disturbed by Reily's attack on their political privileges.

The same year that Canales' journal carried Chárriez's spirited outburst against Reily, an editorial in *The New York Times* noted:

> Representatives of the Unionist party of Puerto* Rico have arrived in Washington on Dec. 1 to demand the removal of the governor, E. Montgomery Reily of Kansas City, who was appointed by the President last spring. They charge maladministration in office by arbitrarily removing judges and court officials without trial. They say Governor Reily took with him from Kansas City six politicians whom he appointed to responsible positions in the island. . . . The extraordinary number of Americans in government jobs in Puerto Rico since Governor Reily's advent caused the Senate on Dec. 7 to adopt a resolution calling for a list giving the number and names of Americans employed by the Government of Puerto Rico. . . .
>
> Governor Reily himself arrived in the United States on the steamer *Tanamo*, which entered New York harbor on Nov. 20 with fire in her hold and sank at the pier the next day. Members of the Governor's party charged that the fire was the result of a plot against his life. . . .

Into the tempest now strode Muñoz Marín, now twenty-four, with an article on January 4, 1922, in *The New Republic* that impressed a number of readers with its maturity. Entitled "A Ninety-Eight Percent American in Puerto Rico," it began:

* Editor's note: The American press used the spelling "Porto Rico" until 1932, when the Spanish "Puerto Rico" was recognized. The latter usage is followed throughout this book.

Some time ago the governor of Puerto Rico, Mr. E. Montgomery Reily, arrived at the port of New York in a burning ship. The fire had started the day following the ship's departure from San Juan with its precious cargo, and the rumor is abroad that the calamity was not a mere accident but had been caused by an infernal machine of some sort secreted in the bowels of the vessel by a fervent Puerto Rican patriot with the intention of sending Mr. Reily to the bottom of the sea. . . .

After ridiculing the reports that had made headlines in American and some Puerto Rican newspapers, Muñoz lent them his own interpretation:

. . . But rumors express desires when they do not express facts or fears. What, then, is the basis of this desire on the part of the majority of the natives to eliminate Mr. Reily, if not from the world at least from their island?

If observers were looking for similarities to the style of Muñoz Rivera or differences from the rhetoric of the old Spaniard-fighter, they may have been amused by reading another attack on a governor of the island, and they also would have observed a new quality: humor, a sardonic ability to weigh the islanders as well as their oppressors, an irony that should have been a warning that Muñoz Marín would never subject himself to the political party leaders then in Puerto Rico or ally himself permanently with them.

He went on to discuss party differences and to describe Reily's reaction to the Unionists' eventual desire for independence as "just as impossible for him to conceive why on earth there were men who actually wished to quit American citizenship as it is for the average Puerto Rican to conceive why there are men who do not wish to be citizens of Puerto Rico."

The article ends in a summary of Reily's ruthlessness toward the Unionists and his favoring of the minority parties, stating that, "This ruthlessness and this benevolence, existing side by side in the same personality, are astonishing. Already, judicious men acquainted with the postwar psychology and the postwar lingo of the United States are saying that whether he likes it or not, this paradoxical bourbon-liberal is but a 'ninety-eight percent American.' "

The governor was replaced shortly by Horace Mann Towner,

formerly a member of the House Committee on Insular Affairs and an administrator who worked harmoniously with the Puerto Ricans. But Reily's damage had been done. He had lent encouragement to a political spirit more concerned with party than with island development. As the Unionists, Republicans, and Socialists began to bargain over votes and trade concessions, ideals gave way to deals, while the objectives of identity, association, and welfare faded with the promises made by party leaders. The compromise the Unionists soon made with their first goal of eventual independence spurted an irate group out of the organization to form the Nationalist party, espousing outright independence and violent means for attaining it.

This group was representative neither of workers nor of the wealthy, but of the middle class and student intellectuals, many of whom had been angered by the discriminatory treatment they had received as soldiers during the war. Among them was a slender, passionate young Harvard graduate named Albizu Campos. Later, as president of the party, he directed attempts on the life of the President of the United States and that of Luis Muñoz Marín, governor of Puerto Rico.

Albizu Campos was the illegitimate son of a white Spaniard and a mestiza who was Basque, Indian, and Negro. He inherited his mother's coloring. Campos' wealthy father sent him to Harvard, and when the First World War broke out he registered for the draft in Cambridge but asked for assignment from Puerto Rico in the belief that there no color line would exist. The army created its own barrier and Campos was assigned to a Negro regiment as an enlisted man. Later he was transferred to officer's training camp. He emerged from the war a first lieutenant and a passionate enemy of the United States.

Now a group reaction to the residue of Reily's administration gave Campos an opportunity to launch his fiery and bloody career. Urging him on was Laura Meneses, the Peruvian girl he had met while she was studying chemistry at Radcliffe, a woman whose rebellious intensity led her years later into the camp of Fidel Castro, whom she has served as associate of the Cuban delegation to the United Nations.

This was not a movement that could attract Muñoz. It had no consuming appeal to his intelligence or his sense of humanity. Although he may have understood the frustration that goaded Campos and his

associates, Muñoz was already acquiring the uncanny capacity for
the long view that has since impressed admirers. Certainly nothing
the Nationalists offered could serve the island's needs or further its
interests. Their program contained no provisions for development,
no remedy for the island's ills. In this the Nationalists were little
worse off than the established political parties, and Muñoz was fortunate in being more interested in his writing than in the prospect
of joining the political scene. But his instincts were already reaching
into a future that he may have divined intuitively.

Amidst the unappealing atmosphere of Puerto Rican politics, it
was the man whom the politicians were disregarding who touched
Muñoz's sensibilities. This was the *jíbaro,* essentially the working man
of the hill country, although the term has been applied to the worker
in all parts of the island.

The *jíbaro* was implied in Muñoz's early poetry, emerging in his
prose as Muñoz began to sell articles to American magazines. One
of these essays, in *The Nation,* April 8, 1925, was titled "Puerto
Rico: The American Colony." It contained Muñoz's romantic description of the man to whose fortunes he would one day join his
own:

> . . . These forsaken *jíbaros,* pale, frequently blond, always
> poverty-stricken, form the most consistently unmixed body of
> Europeans on the island. Whenever the hookworm permits, they
> are more active physically and mentally than the people of the
> coast. And yet their ideals are of leisure, whereas the ideals of
> the coast (not necessarily the practice) are becoming those of
> activity and go-getting. Here the shade of the guava tree still
> suggests the hammock; the moon calls out the singer and his
> *tiple.* Troubadours compete with songs for the love of barefoot
> girls, though machetes are thought good enough to cut to de-
> cisions, often within the limitations of a gentlemanly code.
>
> The *jíbaros* are infantile, passionate, shrewd in their simple
> dealings, susceptible to religious quackery, and manage to carry
> a surprisingly heavy load of generosity along with their poverty.
> They have frequently been imposed upon by the outside world
> and have developed a naïve armor of suspiciousness that enrages
> the politicians and rural confidence men who try to prey upon
> them. . . .

The article is even more interesting for its revelation of the forces in conflict within Muñoz. He was becoming more and more magnetized by the idea of independence as a premise for dignity and identity. He could hardly, at this early stage of his life, have tolerated his father's patient willingness to espouse a statehood status on the basis that it might give Puerto Ricans a sovereignty equal to that of the American states.

Young Luis could see as clearly as anyone else that Puerto Rico was poverty-stricken and that much of Latin America was enjoying a postwar upsurge, lifting many of its countries to unprecedented prosperity. He commented sardonically on this, writing: "Perhaps the sharpest difference between Puerto Rican development and that of the rest of Latin America lies in the fact that there has never been a serious movement for Puerto Rican independence. Such political expression of a feeling for independence as we may have had came—some say strangely and some say naturally—under the American regime." Then, prophetically, Muñoz was to add: "But the sentiment for independence is real enough among young fellows and the common people, and it only waits to be organized by a politician with some poetry in his make-up."

Stimulating this growing conviction within Muñoz, yet warning him of its consequences, was an increasing sense of economic reality. He had described the Puerto Rican economy as providing all the after-dinner benefits "without the dinner," and now he proceeded briefly to analyze the island's coffee, sugar, and tobacco industries. He stated:

Twenty-three years ago there were scattered over the island several hundred more or less primitive mills that turned out a round 69,000 tons of sugar annually. In 1920 there were half a hundred modern factories, belonging for the most part to large absentee corporations, turning out six times that number of tons. That is the open glory of the colonists. Profit has been known to surpass one hundred percent per annum, and a very large share of it leaves the island never to return. That is the secret glory of the colonists. And even this ghastly spectacle of wealth drained from a starving population into the richest country on earth is sanctimoniously entitled in the official reports "a favorable trade balance. . . ."

. . . The tobacco industry is entirely under the tutelage of the American tobacco trust, and coffee-growing, the last refuge of the falling middle class, suffers from the fact that to the great coffee-drinking people of the United States all coffees taste alike!

The article made clear to *The Nation*'s readers that Puerto Rico was not a happy American colony. It was a people more oriented to Latin America; more interested in Venezuela's effort to rid herself of the tyrant Gómez than in the next United States election; more concerned with the idea of an Antillean Republic of Cuba, Santo Domingo, and Puerto Rico than the results of the World Series; more perturbed about buying its food at prices it could pay—free from American tariff controls—than in selling sugar to and for American industries.

Muñoz had by now become known to many readers of the American press. He was writing for H. L. Mencken's *Baltimore Sun*, selling two or three articles a month for twenty-five dollars each, beginning to do some book reviews for the New York *Herald Tribune*, appearing occasionally in *Smart Set* and *The American Mercury* as well as *The Nation*, and writing regularly for *La Democracia* in Puerto Rico.

Adrift in the fabulous twenties of the United States, married to a brilliant American woman at the start of her career, living among the skeptics of an opulent world while his own country was suffering the humiliation of poverty, disassociation, and political oppression, Muñoz might well have gone over the edge. Unfriendly commentators have claimed that he became a "bohemian," that his nights of talk and drink and general rousting about New York or San Juan were a careless whiling away of his time. But his articles, his poems, and his statements show a sensitive, driven young man in a world bedeviled by doubts.

In the jungle of the twenties, it was perhaps miraculous that the tall and handsome son of Puerto Rico's greatest public figure, bereft of money or position, never lost sight of his island home and the tragedy that was stifling the lives of so many of her "pale men of the mountains."

SEVEN

The Ferment

W<small>ELL MIGHT</small> Luis Muñoz Marín's thoughts have been disordered when he returned to Puerto Rico in 1926. He had left New York with Muna Lee, Luisito, and now a tiny daughter, Munita, to accept the editorship of *La Democracia*. The newspaper his father had founded was now an organ of the Unionist party, its publication a responsibility of Antonio Barceló, who had inherited the party from Muñoz Rivera. He had offered the editorship to Muñoz Marín on the basis that he, Barceló, would hold the privilege of separately expressing his own opinions in the daily. This was a concession to the different political attitudes the two men might hold, with perhaps an unexpressed hope on the part of Barceló that an association with the son of the founder of the party and of the journal would strengthen both.

The two men must have approached this relationship with some reservations. Barceló was a merchant politician who traded for votes as he bought and sold dry goods. He was of Muñoz Rivera's generation and under the leader's direction had been a faithful party worker. His failure to understand the philosophy of Muñoz Rivera's leadership became evident after the resident commissioner had died. The long step-by-step trek toward island self-government that Muñoz Rivera had visualized became a sharp search for political leadership under Antonio Barceló. Barceló wavered between the theses of outright independence and statehood, judging them more for their appeal to voters than their values as goals.

Although Barceló could quickly appreciate the potential political attraction of Luis Muñoz Marín, he must have known of his recent

socialist sympathies, of his writings, of his free-thinking companions, and of his complete personal independence, untarnished by
compromise and negotiation.

The arrangement was doomed at the start. During the year that
Luis and Muna were in Puerto Rico, *La Democracia* reflected the
attitudes of both Barceló and Luis, as arranged, and said little.
Muna Lee worked at the University of Puerto Rico, her major task
being the teaching of poetry. In 1927 the Muñoz Marín family was
back in New York. Now Luis renewed the career he really loved,
writing for magazines and newspapers, collecting ten dollars a
month from *La Democracia* for articles, regular amounts from the
Baltimore Sun, and odd payments from other publications. They
moved to Teaneck, New Jersey, but disliked suburban life and returned to New York's West Side. They heard and read the limited
public discussions of the Puerto Rican situation in defense of the
American contribution or critical of its failings.

The case for the United States had validity until it was placed
against the island's needs. The budget for government and public
services during the thirty-year American administration had risen
from $1.5 million to over $12 million a year. For health services, it
had risen from zero to over a million dollars; 1,035 schools had been
built. An island with no roads to the interior had been given a network of some 1,300 kilometers. Deaths per thousand had fallen
from 26.39 to 22.43, not an impressive gain. But births per thousand
had risen from 28.99 to 40.55, a frightening increase. The net increase in population per year went up from 2.60 per thousand to
18.12.

The Brookings Institute report, started in 1928 and published in
1930, showed Puerto Rico's population going up from less than a
million to nearly a million and a half, whereas the British West
Indies, nearby, was gaining only three hundred thousand over its
much larger 1901 figure of one and a half million. Brookings' reason
why Puerto Rico added to her population twice as fast as the West
Indies was its faster economic development. However, the report
stated that the Puerto Rican population had outrun its means of
subsistence.

Supporting this comment was the Brookings study of living conditions. Over fifty percent of the rural population was housed with
two to five persons to a room, in shacks with no plumbing or light.

Rural wages were seventy-five cents a day for sugar workers, fifty cents for coffee laborers, and eight cents an hour for fruit pickers. Up to forty percent of school children also did piecework at home; family incomes, counting unemployment periods, came to a median of $250 to $275 a year. Of economically productive families, most were spending ninety-four percent of their incomes for food. Most of the home piecework was in the tobacco and garment-worker trades. Unemployment was in the neighborhood of twenty-seven percent.

The consequent effect of poverty and malnutrition on health was shown by figures placing diarrhea and enteritis as the major causes of death by disease—21.8 percent; tuberculosis 12.1 percent; malaria 6.2 percent; uncinariasis, or hookworm, only 1.6 percent, but a major threat to survival because of its weakening effects. All these diseases are of germ or parasitic origin. The tuberculosis rate was much above that for any "other civilized country" recorded. Uncinariasis was debilitating, according to Governor Towner's 1925 report, ninety percent of the rural population and fifty percent of the urban population.

Despite the provision of buildings for education, eighty-four percent of the rural schoolchildren did not continue their schooling after the third grade; seventy-four percent of the adult rural population was still illiterate. Poverty was the pressure that spurted the children out of school and to some sort of job or effort at home. In the schools studied, one or more of the children were found to have left their homes with no breakfast; forty-two percent had had coffee only, and this black, without sugar or milk. The report bore so strongly on rural conditions because sixty-seven percent of the population was based in or depended upon the island's agricultural economy.

It was clear that sugar, which had been doubled in its production per acre by American investment and management, was now largely under American absentee control. The total crop had increased from seventy thousand tons a year to eight hundred thousand. More than half of the acreage and the crop was managed now by four companies, largely American-owned. Meanwhile the Puerto Rican-American Tobacco Company had gained control of the tobacco crop and cigar business. The coastline railroad was owned outright by Americans, as was the shipping facility. Because lands planted to

sugar and tobacco yielded more in cash than those in coffee or subsistence food, the latter were converted or being abandoned. Their
inhabitants came to the coast seeking work, many ending their days
in the huts spawned by the city slums that scarred Muñoz Marín's
picture of his island home. He had but to remember San Juan's
beggars and watch New York's millionaires and read the reports to
suppose that the latter were living on the flesh of the former.

It was natural enough for the impressionable young man to arrive
at the conclusion that the independence that his father had held
back as a final goal should be sought now. It must have seemed reasonable that the profits that American companies were returning to
the continent should be held on the island to build decent lives for
its citizens. It must have seemed right that ragged children begging
from American sailors should instead wear clean clothes, go to
school, and solicit no one. It must have seemed logical that the forty
thousand women working for pennies a day to embroider for New
York garment makers could earn dollars at the same work for island
exporters. But it did not seem right that he should hate the nation
that exploited his people, because he had never learned to hate. He
had learned to think. And he had thought in order to learn. But
nothing he had thought and nothing he could learn could deter
him from the emotionally inspired belief that the dignity of his people and their well-being would best be joined in their own hands.
Had he not been influenced by (1) not having a platform from
which to speak, (2) having a wife, Muna Lee, whose keen mind
modulated excesses of the spirit, (3) exposure to Fabian thought,
which believed in a decent job done now rather than a crusade
launched against history, (4) the subconscious but abiding memory
of his father's unswerving but patient march; had he not had those
influences working upon him, Muñoz Marín might not have been
far separated from the man who later swore to have his life.

This was Albizu Campos, leading the small but fiercely protesting
Nationalist party. While Luis was back in New York, Campos in
1928 took his own cause to Latin America. A fiery speaker, he was
violently denouncing the American oppression of his "enslaved people." No one has been able to measure the damage that Albizu
Campos caused the United States in Latin America. The picture of
an apparently emaciated young firebrand from a starving American
island possession, seeking support from his Hispanic cousins in a

crusade for freedom, could only have been recalled in dark colors when South American politicians later sought plaudits by attacking the United States. His Peruvian wife, inflamed as was Albizu Campos, aided his access to the Marxist APRA group in Peru and its small branch in Mexico. Marxism later wore away from the Apristas, but hatred gained on Albizu Campos.

Meanwhile Mr. and Mrs. Muñoz Marín, deep in their writing and their edging toward the careers that awaited them, journeyed to Havana in 1928 to the Sixth Pan-American Conference, more of a cultural than a political gathering. Muna Lee, skilled writer and scholar, was one of the conference's key speakers. Luis was a translator and became noted mostly for his efforts to badger a dilatory executive group into paying him and his cohorts the meager sums promised them. Both were successful, Muna as a brilliant speaker, Muñoz as a good-natured negotiator.

It was in 1928 too that Puerto Rico was assaulted by "the worst hurricane of the century." The Puerto Ricans gave the appellations of saints to their hurricanes. This tropical cyclone was named San Felipe, and it raged over the island on September 13, driving to their knees an already miserable people. Three hundred dead were counted, as well as many more injured. Destruction was evaluated at fifty million dollars, over four times the cost of insular government functions for the fiscal year.

Statistics can never describe the effect of a hurricane on a concentration of undefended people. The demonic howling of winds that sound like a thousand mad devils, the crashing of trees and telephone poles, the dousing of all light like a candle gleefully blown out by a laughing fiend, the isolation of huddled wretches as telephones go dead and transportation ceases and the streets become a shrieking battlefield, the passing hours of continuous fury, until a benign sun rises to shine on the wreckage of an island—this is a drama that cannot be told in numbers. But it can change the lives of the human beings who survive it.

Throughout the island, wretchedness like that in the slums named La Perla and El Fanguito was aggravated by the storm's wreckage. In every town where a patch of slum had been staked upon unwanted ground—and this meant in every town—the sweep of destruction had flattened the area of tiny homes. On the smaller scale of an occasional two or three huts within shouting distance on a hillside, there had been the figures of thin men and women and children crawling through the brush to find each other—and nothing more. La Perla and El Fanguito had grown out of poverty and unemployment. They were filled with families exiled from the subsistence lands that had been turned to the good cash sugar crop. They were crowded with the bodies of men whose few months in the canefields left them idle the rest of the year, to survive somehow in San Juan. Now they would be joined by the cousins who had stayed in the hills to tend the coffee crop that was already a declining export.

Since the American occupation, coffee had fallen from a leading place in the island's economy. Americans could buy coffee more cheaply from Brazil and Colombia and Guatemala, and they did not appreciate the rich flavor of the Puerto Rican bean. Europe's imports from Puerto Rico also tended downward as Puerto Rico was woven into the isolation of the American economy. Now San Felipe, with one gust, finished the story of coffee in Puerto Rico. The coffee workers and their families would now migrate to the coast, looking for work in the sugar fields, where unemployment was already a way of life, and would swell the ghettos of La Perla and El Fanguito in San Juan.

Meanwhile the entire island, wondering how it would recover from this blow, went about recovering by picking up the wreckage.

If the island was uncertain about its source of assistance, it was because of the impact of two leading American personalities who had nothing in common.

One was Charles Lindbergh, America's hero of the twenties, who had first flown the Atlantic. He had come to Puerto Rico as a step in his triumphal tour of South America. Lindbergh was young, modest, and daring, and because the French had gone mad over the lone flyer who landed in a single-engine plane near Paris, Latin America was ready to give him her heart. In Puerto Rico, in early 1928, crowds clustered about the young man, and officials bustled to offer the highest honors. But the political leaders of Puerto Rico also joined in a resolution, which they presented to the colonel for transmission to the President. This was a request for an outright grant of independence, tagged with a charge that the United States was responsible for Puerto Rico's economic state.

Lindbergh, as requested, delivered the message, upon his return, to President Calvin Coolidge, a tart New Englander who saw in it neither humor nor reason. His answer was a lengthy and bitter letter to the patient Governor Horace Mann Towner, who withheld it until the University of Puerto Rico finished celebrating its twenty-fifth anniversary that year.

The usually taciturn President began by stating that the United States had never undertaken the obligation to make Puerto Rico independent. He then repeated the description of the Puerto Rican country worker written thirty years previously by the island's own scholar, Dr. Cayetano Coll y Toste:

. . . only a laborer, the son of our fields, one of the most unfortunate beings in the world, with pale face, bare feet, lean body, ragged clothing, and feverish look, he walks indifferently, with the shadows of ignorance in his eyes, dreaming of the cockfights, the shuffle of the cards, or the prize in the provincial lottery.

No, it is not possible that the tropical zone produces such organic anemia. This lethargy of body and soul is the offspring of moral and physical vices that drag down the spirit and lead peasants to such state of social degradation. . . .

Coolidge went on to recount the benefits that American occupation had brought to this miserable creature. And, finally, in a flourish of Back Bay statesmanship, he concluded with a patronizing admission:

There is no disposition in America, and certainly not on my part, to discourage any reasonable aspirations of the people of Puerto Rico. The island has so improved and its people so progressed in the last generation as to justify high hopes for the future.

Puerto Rico was stunned by the American President's insult. Its effort to answer was muffled in the complex rhetoric of political leaders, all as outmoded as their adversary. The voice of Muñoz Rivera could no longer be the island's clear statement of its cause. And as a free-lance journalist in New York, Muñoz Marín could only writhe and speak for himself. And who would listen? This was the world of the *boulevardier* Mayor Jimmy Walker of New York; of America's tennis darling, Helen Wills; of Al Jolson, the Jazz Singer; of Walter Chrysler, new tycoon in a great, burgeoning business; of Owen D. Young, preparing the plan that would alleviate Europe's postwar debt; and in India, of Mahatma Gandhi, quietly and resolutely planning his country's march toward nationhood. Who would hear the outcry of Muñoz Marín's protest against a slur upon his suffering colleagues on an island in the Caribbean Sea?

Through the lightheaded atmosphere of the bubbling twenties, however, was advancing another storm that would, through misery, induce Americans to hear again the groans and whimpers and protests of others. It struck its first glancing blows early in 1929, after the stock market had been undergoing a series of warning gyrations. But the first bolt was not enough to reach the people. The market even recovered and rose again as speculators who had not yet made their fortunes saw a new opportunity. Even the academicians said that only paper profits had been lost, and those only by the imprudent. The capital wealth of the nation was untouched. A businessman was now President. Herbert Hoover would carry the nation to a new plateau, even after the assault of market action on his first year in the White House.

Muñoz Marín, at this keenly observant time of his life, found the scene and the cast of characters changing even faster than he could adjust his views. Until this time his sights had been leveled on an island of scarcity in a blue sea and a nation of abundance bounded by an envious world. Now that island was in distress and that nation was being rocked by a threat it could not understand, a menace it still relegated to the financial pages. Muñoz was still presenting the case of Puerto Rico in repetitive terms. In an article for *The American Mercury*, in February, 1929, he had again described the inequity of American domination of his island.

The anguish of Muñoz was more complex than his father's, for Muñoz Rivera had been able, in a straightforward way, to strive for self-government under Spanish rule, with no distress over cultural conflicts and with the comfort of association, distant though it be, with a world power of like background. Young Luis could only foresee the annihilation of dignity and of any opportunity for decent living under the American flag, with no gain from the island's continued association with an alien culture. His choice of independence for his people was a commitment, then, to cultural isolation, for Spain was gone.

In the same article, he touched on the "contamination" of American ways, writing:

> Puerto Rican politicians may now be publicly accused of keeping mistresses. The charge doesn't come near defeating them, but evidently there is some suggestion in the atmosphere that makes it seem relevant. Twenty years ago it would have seemed preposterous to advance such an argument as in any way affecting a man's fitness for office.
>
> The indications are that we may soon find ourselves adopting a subtly feminized point of view as unsatisfactory to both men and women as the one now prevailing in the United States. The change, in spite of the stupid simplicity of our traditional mores, would seem to be for the worse. We were groping toward adjustment; now we are drifting toward equality.

In this essay, entitled "The Sad Case of Puerto Rico," Muñoz allowed his gaze to wander over a broad section of the tropic landscape. He discussed education, the university, and the attitude of the students who, he claimed, were intellectually and emotionally attached to the Hispanic past of their fathers. And he credited the university staff for respecting the value of Puerto Rico's Iberian culture. The prophetic tone of his comment was probably accidental, but reference to it now makes it no less applicable to the new countries who have gained a dominant voice in the United Nations.

> . . . saving a culture, even an inferior one, from becoming the monkey of another, even a superior one, is a good in itself. And in the present case it is by no means certain that the heritage shared by Puerto Rico is to be unfavorably compared with the heritage to which the blind forces of production and exchange now seek to hook it up.

Finally he approached the unapproachable, the mixing of cultures that has since occurred, not only in Puerto Rico, and that has been resisted, not only in Puerto Rico, and that is still occurring because transportation and communications are creating a cultural osmosis from Tokyo to Addis Ababa. He asked the question about the island's cultural future:

> . . . Will the island retain its historical personality? An unqualified answer . . . would necessarily fall short of the possibilities. Perhaps a more absurd fate is in store for us. Perhaps we are destined to be neither Puerto Ricans nor Americans, but merely puppets of a mongrel state of mind, susceptible to American thinking and proud of Latin thought, subservient to American living and worshipful of the ancestral way of life. Perhaps we are to discuss Cervantes and eat pork and beans in the Child's restaurant that must be opened sooner or later. Perhaps we will try not to let mother catch us reading the picturesque verses of Quevedo. Perhaps we are going to a singularly fantastic and painless hell in our own sweet way. Perhaps all this is nothing but a foretaste of Pan-Americanism.

Perhaps Muñoz Marín, at thirty-one, was becoming one of the prophets of his time.

In 1929 the depression seized the United States, and Theodore Roosevelt, Jr., became governor of Puerto Rico. Both had lessons for the absorbent mind of Luis Muñoz Marín. There is no evidence that Luis understood the significance of the October crash of the stock market any better than anyone else. Its somber aftermath was, however, spread before him, as the young Puerto Rican and his young family continued to live in New York. They saw the lines of jobless forming at the entrance gates of factories. They saw begging increase on the streets. They watched the index price of stocks sink from 190 to a sluggard settling at 50. They saw the lines of worry deepen on the faces of friends who could not hope for replacement of the jobs they had lost. They could read the advertisements offering foreclosed real estate bargains for sale. They heard of the bank failures, which finally came to number five thousand and which wiped out the savings of thousands of honest people. They could listen to the news exposures of unsavory financial dealings laid bare by the crash. They could watch a nation that had been riding a cloud of unabashed materialism sink into a stupor of bewilderment, while rage seethed below its surface. Before them was proof that sovereignty and independence did not assure a man his wages for work or put a full meal on his family's dinner table. Muñoz Marín and Muna Lee were people of extraordinary intellect and fine sensitivity. Like others, they could not interpret the depression, but it left an impact upon them that was not forgotten. Its meaning became apparent in the later thinking of Muñoz Marín.

The life of the Muñoz Marín family did not change drastically. They were already poor and they only became a bit poorer. Muna Lee became increasingly active in public affairs, with emphasis on Latin America. She was a director of national activities of the National Woman's Party, honorary president of the Social League of Suffragettes of Cuba, and director of the Bureau of Public Relations and Information of the Inter-American Commission of Women of the Pan-American Union.

Muñoz was still writing for a variety of publications. Theodore Roosevelt's performance in Puerto Rico was giving him a new theme. The son of the former American President had become a colonel in the American forces in World War I and had founded the American Legion in 1919. Appointment to the governorship was President Herbert Hoover's recognition of the younger Roosevelt's political influence and public spirit.

Roosevelt tried to act as though Puerto Rico were a state and talked as though it should one day become a dominion. To the extent permitted, his officeholders were Puerto Ricans. His remedial action in Puerto Rico combined social reform with economic innovation. Muñoz Marín wrote enthusiastically about the new type of governor in an article titled "T.R.—P.R.," published by *World's Work* in July, 1931. "He is by way of solving Puerto Rico," Muñoz proclaimed.

He used the article as a vehicle again to expound on the ills besetting the island, and he revealed a new sense of economics in analyzing them. Going beyond the now familiar complaint about low wages, he discussed ill health as a result of economic maladjustment, taking his readers also through a brief exposition of the problem of uneven land ownership and poor distribution of Puerto Rico's limited wealth. He then lauded the new governor for his program of

land purchase for homesteading and the establishment of vocational
rural schools, farm bureaus, and a bureau of commerce to attract industries to the island.

"A country with a population such as Puerto Rico is called upon
to support," commented Muñoz, "cannot subsist decently without
industrial development."

If ever Muñoz had been the wisecracking bohemian that his detractors have labeled him, it was apparent that the years in depression-ridden New York were rapidly maturing him as a writer and a
thinker. It was interesting to observers to remark a new optimism in
statements such as, "Puerto Rico can, in fact, become the workshop
of the Caribbean," and such an appreciation of Roosevelt's "common-
sense, cautious means, calculated to arouse the minimum of opposition," and his declaration that Roosevelt "realized that first of all the
results of a badly organized social state must be alleviated. All
sources of aid must be tapped—the government of Puerto Rico, the
private Puerto Rican purse, American philanthropic institutions, the
federal government. In the course of this campaign Governor Roosevelt has probably presented the case of Puerto Rico to the American
people, both in its immediate and far-reaching aspects, more completely than any other American or Puerto Rican has done in the
past thirty years."

Muñoz's acclaim of the governor was duplicated on the island.
Roosevelt made an immediate hit by using some two hundred words
of Spanish in his inaugural address and directing his remarks to the
economic and social problems of Puerto Rico rather than its political
status. His wife, dancing with Unionist party leader Antonio Barceló at the inaugural ball, was equally well received. Roosevelt immediately distrusted the reports ready for him at the Fortaleza and
went out on an inspection of the island, mostly on horseback. In
articles for the New York press he reported the misery he saw on
these excursions. From Congress, which had appropriated $8,150,000
to alleviate the hurricane damage, Roosevelt extracted another
$3,000,000 for small farm loans.

He was critical of waste and sloppy administration, citing as
examples a lavishly built hospital for the insane, a sanitarium for tu-
bercular patients that had only 247 beds when sufferers were numbering 40,000, the majestic marble capitol building under construc-

tion, and a jail with mosaic doors imported from Spain. "This," he reported, "was being finished by convicts, and once, when some of them working on it ran away to the nearest village and got very drunk, the warden punished them by refusing to let them back into the jail." Roosevelt also commented scornfully on a panacea proposed in which canaries would be given to the poor, who would teach them to sing the *"The Star-Spangled Banner"* and then peddle them to tourists.

Mrs. Roosevelt aided her husband in organizing a society to feed destitute children and in setting up milk stations. He carried his program to the sugar companies, appealing to them to release plots of land to workers for truck gardening. Back at the Fortaleza, the governor pared expenses notably.

Roosevelt practiced his Spanish at every opportunity, occasionally with wry results. In one speech he attempted to describe his family and unwittingly stated he had given birth to four children. In a later discussion of the error, he was advised: "Mr. Governor, in the tropics everything is possible."

Between Roosevelt and Muñoz Marín, both sons of distinguished men, there was sympathy and mutual respect. They met on various occasions, mostly in Washington on Roosevelt's periodic trips to the States. The governor joined Muñoz in seeing no reason for "Americanizing" Puerto Rico. He visualized the island as a bridge between the United States and Latin America, and he advised the Puerto Ricans to preserve their culture but to learn English as preparation for their role. Observers have stated that Roosevelt also advised Muñoz to return to Puerto Rico and get into active politics in order to help his people more directly.

Muñoz has denied the suggestion, explaining that the impulse that brought him and his family back to San Juan in 1931 was a need to put his mother's affairs in order. Doña Amalia had been living with the family in New York. Muñoz Rivera's widow, having spent a lifetime in the shadow of the island's hero, seemed to take a more active part in the bustle of Luis and his small family. She became a storyteller for the Spanish-speaking children on New York's West Side, and in the family political discussions she lost no opportunity to espouse the convictions of her late husband. Amalia was a quick-witted and tart woman, lively and good-looking. As

long as *La Democracia* paid its rent on her home in San Juan, she
was content in New York. But payments fell badly behind, and the
family could not well afford to forego this income.

In late summer of 1931 Muñoz Marín sailed for Puerto Rico.
There he was hired by *La Democracia* for twenty-three dollars a
week, took possession of Doña Amalia's home, and sent for his family.

The home was an old house in the center of San Juan, not far
from the Fortaleza. Like most Spanish residences, it presented a flat
and forbidding face to the cobblestone street, its patio and garden
being in the back. There were enough rooms for some of *La Democracia's* facilities, as well as housing for the young people, their two
children, and one or two servants. The upper floor was kept for
Doña Amalia, and she guarded it like a bastion from the incursions
of Muñoz's political or literary friends. Standing at the top of the
stairs, she would greet visitors with a shout and the declaration, "The
social revolution stops at the second floor!"

For Muñoz the social revolution had far from begun.

Puerto Rican politics would have looked like a snake pit to any
sincere crusader in 1931. Its fiber had deteriorated steadily since the
departure of José de Diego and the deaths of Muñoz Rivera and
Celso Barbosa. Elections and jobs rather than causes had become
its lodestone. As early as 1924 Antonio Barceló, head of the Union
party, had attempted a combination with the Republicans. The effort was abortive, but it did split the Republicans into two hostile
wings. By 1928 the Socialists, founded by Santiago Iglesias, had allied with one of these wings, the backers of which were much
more concerned with higher profits for the sugar grower than wages
for the cutter. And the Unionists had finally combined with the
other Republican group in a new party called the Alianza. Now, in
1931, the Alianza had broken up its unholy marriage, and the Republicans within it had made off with the Alianza party name.

One could only conclude that principles had been sacrificed for
deals, that the objective of any party was to gain a majority vote and
most of the appointive jobs in the island government. It was true
that the Republicans, under any name, still proclaimed statehood as
their objective, that the Socialists still talked of social betterment,
and that a wing of the Unionists orated about self-government. All

parties joined in demanding immediately that Puerto Rico be allowed to elect her own governor, increasing the suspicion that job
distribution was the flaming ideal before them all. Through the years
of bellowing at deficient American governors, the leaders of Puerto
Rican political thought had lowered their standards to those of
municipal ward-heelers. Only two of these men had any emotional
appeal to the returned son of Muñoz Rivera: Santiago Iglesias,
whom he had once joined and left; Antonio Barceló, who had been
Muñoz Rivera's lieutenant.

Barceló was a professional politician whose greatest recommendation was his former loyalty to Muñoz Rivera. He was from the eastern town of Fajardo, one of the landing places of the Americans in
1898, and he never tired of repeating the story of his demand for independence on the occasion of the Americans' appearance. He was
an energetic individual, attaining his degree in law and maintaining
a clothing establishment first in Fajardo and later in San Juan. He
had enjoyed a political leader's power and a political leader's honors.
In 1928, with his Alianza in the majority, Barceló had been granted
an honorary Doctor-of-Laws degree from Columbia University.
Within weeks, at a ceremony in San Juan to celebrate the honor that
Columbia had conferred upon him, Barceló demonstrated his physical courage upon being stabbed before a gasping audience by an
individual whose ideas evidently differed from those of the great
university. Barceló recovered, but the attacker, one Justo Matos, was
shot on the scene. No one ever discovered whose bullet ended Sr.
Matos' career.

In 1931 Barceló was a leader with a following but no name for
his party, since his erstwhile associates had appropriated the Alianza
label. Accordingly, in December of that year he proposed at a party
meeting that the name of Muñoz Rivera's Liberal party, the one that
had so successfully associated itself with Sagasta's Liberals in Spain,
be revived for the reorganized group. The motion passed by accla-
mation. Muñoz Marín did not attend this meeting. He was busily
writing a series of articles for *La Democracia* stating the case for outright independence. He was also using his influence with Governor
Roosevelt to obtain a guarantee that all parties, old and new, would
be permitted to run freely in 1932.

Permission to put the new Liberal party on the ticket was granted
early in 1932, but not by Roosevelt. He had by then moved on to the

Philippines to perform in that difficult territory some of the services he had so well given to Puerto Rico. But his policies were continued by the new governor, James Beverley, who had been Roosevelt's attorney general on the island, succeeding him to the governorship on Roosevelt's enthusiastic recommendation.

Muñoz's first official appearance in the new career of Puerto Rican politician occurred on March 12, when Antonio Barceló proudly presented this newest political trophy to the party assembly. Now Barceló had the name of the father's party, Liberal, and in its grouping was the old hero's son, Muñoz Marín.

Muñoz had already created a stir by announcing that, should the Liberal party remove independence from its platform, he would vote for Albizu Campos, the militant leader of the Nationalist party. Now he brought to the new party's convention in March his own statement of the independence plank. He stated that independence was economically necessary, that without it the island would proceed to ruin. He pointed out that American tariffs were too high for the foods that Puerto Ricans needed to import and that no change could be expected because the island was an infinitesimal part of the United States. "The North American tariff," he said, "was set by the North American congress to protect the interests of the American people. And it will annihilate Puerto Rico obliquely, in passing, almost without thinking, with the brutal innocence of an elephant walking on a colony of ants."

The only remedy, he insisted, was independence, not the autonomy, self-government in a dominion status, that some of the Liberals espoused, as had his father during the Spanish regime. He qualified these autonomists as (1) those fearful that the goal of independence would prejudice the party before the colonial government, (2) those who feared its repercussions upon their positions as government employees, (3) the "monarchists" who did not realize the impracticality of being part of the American nation.

The weathered politicians who had been manipulating the island's interests while Muñoz was acquiring a broad education in New York may have raised eyebrows at the importunate enthusiasm with which the party's new acquisition promulgated his views. A few must have decided to rub down the bristly spots on the young man's hide. Others may have become nervous about his threat to their position in the party hierarchy. By the time one of the campaign assemblies was called in September, 1932, the whispering campaign of some sinister enemies had pierced the neophyte's still-thin skin. Nominated as one of the party's four choices to run for resident commissioner, Muñoz rose to thank his sponsors and to "disturb the peace of this assembly for a few moments." When Muñoz had finished speaking, there was no confusion in his listeners' minds as to the meaning of his words. His voice rising in fury, the young man declared:

"Throughout the island of Puerto Rico someone has promulgated an organized campaign of defamation against me personally. It has reached the extreme of claiming that I take morphine, and finally, as if that were not enough, of dispersing the rumor that Sr. Barceló and I have had a personal quarrel about this candidacy."

Muñoz disclaimed knowledge of the identity of his attackers but roared that they were known by his listeners. "Therefore, I now accuse these persons," he shouted, "of being ruffians, cowards, and blackguards; and I accuse them although I do not know them, but I know that you know them. It is possible and even probable that these calumniators are at this moment in the midst of this assembly. Look at them, because I don't know them. I would like to pause right now to allow, if he dares, the first ruffian to come to the rostrum. The issue I propose is serious, because calumny always leaves a residue; of calumny, something remains, the proverb says. I must also say that the relationship that unites me with my people is not limited to the next four years but will be projected to the next twenty years, in which I will live in Puerto Rico, working for my liberty. . . . It is necessary that I stay here, and here I will have to live as in a crystal bowl for all to see." Thereupon Muñoz withdrew his candidacy for the resident commissionership and gave his endorsement to Benigno Fernández García, of whom much would be heard later.

Muñoz never again was required or impelled to make a like statement in public. The envious now knew that he was in Puerto Rico to stay and that he would not easily accept the sneak attacks of immoral politicians. He has never since deviated from that demand for respect or the commitment to merit it.

Now, in 1932, as Luis Muñoz Marín put his shoulder to the rock of Sisyphus, he was already learning that "beasts of prey have taken shelter along its deep, dark crevices."

EIGHT

The Rise and Fall of
Luis Muñoz Marín

THE ELECTIONS OF 1932 brought Muñoz Marín to his first elective political post—senator at large for the Liberal party.

Headline writers of the Puerto Rican press emphasized the drama of his entrance into Puerto Rican politics. This was the son of Muñoz Rivera. This was the poet, the essayist, the reporter, the *bon vivant*, the moderator of conversations at midnight in New York and San Juan, the erstwhile socialist, the Puerto Rican brought up in the United States and now returned to his island to demand her independence from Uncle Sam. This was the headstrong young intellectual, married to the well-known American woman, and now come back to his island to take over the editorship of his father's former newspaper, *La Democracia*, and to take his place immediately in the councils of the island's largest single political party. This was the man who had publicly announced his sympathy for Albizu Campos, frenzied leader of the Nationalists. Muñoz was an exciting new personality in Puerto Rican politics.

Elsewhere in the world headline writers put other dramatic names in black type in 1932. It was the year Rafael Trujillo seized control of the Dominican Republic, never to relinquish his bloody dictatorship until his assassination in 1961. It was the year that Getulio Vargas, claiming fraud in the Brazilian elections, moved a division of troops up from Rio Grande do Sul to Rio de Janeiro to establish the *Novo Estado*—New State—in South America's gigantic republic. In Cuba students were in rebellion against the repressive Machado regime, and soon an army sergeant named Fulgencio Batista would take full powers over the convulsed island. In Germany a man named Adolf Hitler was shouldering his way into the Reichstag.

A landslide vote in the United States put the support and hopes of a great majority of Americans behind Franklin D. Roosevelt, whose jaunty courage was already dispelling much of the depression's gloom. Roosevelt's most quotable statement on the occasion of his inauguration was the declaration that "the only thing we have to fear is fear itself." Undoubtedly the epigram captured the imagination of Muñoz Marín, as it did so many of those who sought encouragement from the man who had been asked to lead the United States out of its wilderness. Muñoz later paraphrased Roosevelt's summation and later learned its limitations. Less poetic to the ears of his audience but more solidly descriptive was Roosevelt's admission: "I am in the midst of a stricken nation in the midst of a stricken world."

The year 1932 was a year of anguish, not only because of the economic failures that were bringing starvation to the doorsteps of so many homes, but for its wry observance of the death of one system of life and its unconscious welcome of another. Laissez-faire, a concept under attack since the early part of the twentieth century, when it had seemed so strong, was fast disappearing.

In 1932 the tide went out for economic individualists, and the idea that government should assume responsibility for the welfare of its people washed high upon the shore. It took different forms according to the stretch of beach on which it landed. They ranged from the authoritarian to the democratic, and the latter had its various interpretations. No one knows, including Muñoz Marín, whether he fully understood what was happening to the world in 1932. Perhaps no one else yet fully possesses that comprehension. Three tenets, however, became embedded in his heart and mind: that man's dignity depends upon his right to speak for himself, that man must not be alone, that man's liberty requires freedom from the enslavement of hunger. To these negatively expressed principles he added a single positive: one's best effort emerges from a desire, not to avoid injury, but to reach an objective. In the case of the Puerto Ricans, the objective that could firm their flagging muscles was—independence.

At this peak of social revolution, the politicians reasserted their power also in the exercise of their craft. The Liberal party designated Muñoz Marín as its representative in Washington. And Franklin D. Roosevelt appointed Robert H. Gore governor of Puerto

Rico. Discounting the possibility that the Liberal party may have visualized more peace of mind with the aggressive new star of its cast off the island, there were good reasons for involving Muñoz Marín with Washington. More than all other Puerto Ricans in public life he knew the American mind. More than most Americans in the United States he knew the intellectual content of Franklin Roosevelt's followers. And since he had contributed so significantly to the removal of Governor Reily in the twenties, he might be best qualified to kill the dragon that the American Presidency now unleashed upon the nation's Caribbean colony.

Robert Hayes Gore, politically obscure until his appointment, had been a newspaperman who turned to the insurance business to make his fortune. He had astutely foreseen Roosevelt's ascendancy many years before it became apparent to the American people, and after FDR's election to the Presidency Gore was in a position to recall this to James Farley, the new postmaster general. During the famous hundred days of Roosevelt's domination of Congress, Gore's appointment was approved without notice. Before leaving the United States Gore made a speech at the Chicago World's Fair espousing statehood for Puerto Rico, since this goal was part of the new Democratic party platform. Naturally enough, he was received in San Juan with more than ordinary curiosity.

The year 1933 had hardly dawned before the handicaps that Robert Gore brought to his task became apparent to the almost bloodthirsty Puerto Rican political stronghold. He represented the Democratic party, which could not be expected to harmonize with the Socialist-Republican coalition because of its Republican wing. He had expressed his party's declaration for statehood, an objective contradictory to the hopes of the Liberals. He had gained his appointment through James Farley, a politician at the height of his manipulative powers and the nadir of his humanitarian development. And two little-known foxes were ready to taste the blood of President Roosevelt's careless offering to a needy people. The first was Muñoz Marín. The second was his Washington correspondent for *La Democracia,* a lively, intelligent, and respected newspaperwoman named Ruby Black.

With all these tripwires in his path, Robert Gore proceeded to fall over each, one by one. First, Ruby Black was able to notify Muñoz's newspaper that Governor Gore would follow Mr. Farley's suggestion to hand the posts of commissioner of education and chief of immigration to two doughty lady supporters of the American Democratic party resident in Puerto Rico. They were Mrs. Jean Whittemore and Mrs. Henry Dooley, respectively. The former would replace Theodore Roosevelt's extraordinarily competent commissioner of education, Dr. José Padín. The latter was baldly an effort to pay a political debt. Already Muñoz had stated, ". . . over and above all of these things is the fact that our people are dying of hunger. . . . And in the face of this reality we are playing politics."

Gore pursued the effort to replace Dr. Padín with an American commissioner because he opposed the practice of teaching in Spanish, with English provided only as a second language course. He sought to establish a Democratic party on the island. He proposed a bill to reestablish cockfighting on the island, to attract tourists, he explained. His antics were so consistently ill-starred that Muñoz felt he could not long stay away from the island. He left Washington to the alert observation of Ruby Black.

A friend of Muna Lee, colleague in her public interests, a newswoman in the confidence of Eleanor Roosevelt, Ruby Black was one of the women who became part of the pattern of Muñoz's life during the years of the thirties. Her sources of information were so superior to those of all other correspondents interested in island affairs that she soon became a legend. Gossip had her a half sister of Muñoz, a fictitious person, a diabolical ruse.

The same wicked tongues that attempted to blacken Ruby had already started a story about Gore. It was said that he, born in Kentucky, was the answer to the old American debate about the greater idiocy of mules from that state or Missouri, birthplace of the unlamented Governor Reily.

As if to prove the theory, Gore preceded his appointments to cabinet posts by stating that he would require undated letters of resignation from his nominees. Ruby Black, of course, broke the story first. Antonio Barceló then withdrew all Liberal candidacies for the cabinet list. Gore denied the story of the letters of resignation, ascribing it to Antonio Barceló. Muñoz's sure sense of the dramatic moment impelled his move to the forefront of the crisis. Writing in English, he placed an editorial in the other leading island newspaper, *El Mundo*.

The statement was shockingly headed "Governor Gore, You Are

a Damn Liar." Placing all the facts in order, the editorial ended with the statement:

"Governor Gore, this is a damn lie. You who uttered it are a damn liar. . . ."

About the charge: "We make it deliberately so that you may sue us for libel and obtain a verdict if you have not lied. It is in your hands to demonstrate your veracity."

Sensing, probably with Ruby Black's help, that the White House was tiring of the Gore situation, Muñoz went to Washington in the fall of 1933. The tragic farce of Gore's short regime had already caused rifts in Roosevelt's official family. It was not difficult for Ruby Black to bring Muñoz Marín into the presence of another woman who would affect the turbulent early stages of his career. This was the President's wife, Eleanor Roosevelt. Seeing beyond the charm of the tall, dark-eyed Puerto Rican, Mrs. Roosevelt responded to the logic of his plea for government that could improve the desperate situation of Puerto Rico in that hungry depression-ridden year. Muñoz was taken to the President. Shortly, he cabled Barceló in San Juan a request to stop the attacks on Gore. The White House would not want to remove a man while he was under fire.

In December Robert Hayes Gore tendered his resignation. It was accepted on January 12, 1934.

On January 22, 1934, Muñoz Marín again returned to Puerto Rico. Hailed by a wildly enthusiastic populace, heralded on the front pages of the island newspapers, Muñoz was acclaimed as representative of the vigorous young generation that would replace the tired leaders of yesteryear.

If one's menu is meager, a slice of American governor may be tasty to the imagination. A beleaguered and hungry Puerto Rico was grateful to the gallant son of its old hero for at least serving its spirit with a taste of victory over an apparent oppressor. But there were ashes in the meal for the political party leaders. Old Antonio Barceló had been the most relentless in the pursuit of Robert Gore. And the governor's misdeeds had been so flagrant that, furtively, even Barceló's adversaries had helped to set the traps. They must have asked themselves why the neophyte Muñoz Marín was being credited with the kill. But they kept the question to themselves and cheered with the multitude for the brilliant, lusty, storied young leader who had aggressively gone to headquarters, in the Puerto Rican tradition, to alleviate a miserable situation.

Among the confidants of Muñoz Marín, there were second thoughts. He seemed to have thrown off much of the carefree querying of the young philosopher in search of a system. The nights of exploration over coffee and rum in smoky cafés were less frequent and often ended much before dawn. "Something has happened to Muñoz," said the lighter-hearted; "something is driving him, and now he wants to drive us." Then they too caught fire and kept his pace. They shrugged at his solution to *La Democracia's* economic difficulties.

"Expenses are higher than income," Muñoz announced to his staff. "Let's bring them even. We will simply split the income evenly among the patriots." The group responding to his gaze knew that he was cutting his own revenue to their level. All were patriots.

He wrote a friend in New York, "You must come back to Puerto Rico and work for *Democracia*. You will work like a mule, be paid like a slave, and be abused like a good patriot." The invitation was accepted.

The respondent was wise, for Muñoz had become an exciting companion for the lively-minded and the eager-spirited. Into the probing eyes of the poet and the seeker had come a light of purpose. He was still following a concept that he would one day renounce—the idea that Puerto Rico's only salvation rested in attainment of her independence. But now a more immediate objective—economic reconstruction for Puerto Rico—was triggering his questing energy toward immediate, dynamic action.

This new motivation had taken shape during his three months in Washington while pursuing the scalp of the hapless Mr. Gore. There, back with friends of the friends he had known so well in the decade of the twenties, those now charged with a responsibility to bring solutions to a nation whose complacency they had formerly decried, Muñoz was stirred by the planning philosophy of the New Deal. Since everything needed to be done, nothing was impossible. The idealists were at the wheel, but responsibility was making them pragmatic.

Teófilo Maldonado, reporter for *El Mundo*, has repeated Muñoz's account of how he at this time conceived the idea of a reconstruction plan for Puerto Rico. "The idea," Muñoz has said, "came into my mind during my first interview with President Roosevelt. I was talking to him about Governor Robert H. Gore. . . ."

During the discussion Muñoz pointed out that beyond Gore's damaging political action in Puerto Rico was the more important factor of the island's need for solutions to the problems that beset its labor, its agriculture, its commerce, its people. "The campaign against Gore became a campaign for an Economic Reconstruction Plan."

Muñoz's use of the word "reconstruction" was consciously in contrast to the new Emergency Relief Program already operating in Puerto Rico, with a fifteen-million-dollar budget. Santiago Iglesias, who as of 1932 was serving in Washington as resident commissioner for Puerto Rico representing the majority coalition, had urged this immediate action in Washington. When the plan's administrative chief, James Bourne, soon distributed most of the new machinery's jobs to island Liberals, Iglesias' Socialist-Republican coalition declared him a "public enemy," and the business of relieving human misery was mired in politics.

While President Roosevelt evidenced a lively interest in the idea of economic reconstruction for Puerto Rico, it was not exhibited in his appointment of General Blanton Winship to replace Robert Gore as the island's governor. This was the Janus-like conduct that so often bewildered his followers and infuriated his enemies.

Advisers had told the President that the island needed a "strong" governor, "a military man." Winship, a retired general from Macon, Georgia, had served with distinction in Cuba, the Philippines, and Europe during the First World War. He had been recognized by the Legion of Honor. His early university law training had later been put to use as an adviser to the military. He had no sense of economics and an air of being little interested in the workings of the desperately projected planning efforts stirring the atmosphere about him. In a time of peace and plenty, he might have satisfied Muñoz's definition of the ideal governor. In a period of stress his best contribution was to suggest that all visible areas be planted to flowers and that pageants be staged to attract the tourist to the tropical garden into which he would convert the island. When Americans could hardly keep up their payments on their automobiles, he would build a tourist industry in Puerto Rico. The socially attractive members of the island's landed gentry soon gathered about the genial governor, whom Muñoz would call "a nice old gentleman" in an editorial saying that "Blanton Winship came to Puerto Rico to live a life of perpetual sunshine, brilliant flowers, and fragrant air. His rich imagination dreamt of this in Washington, and he shut his eyes and extended his nostrils and smelled fine odors."

Winship was less easygoing in matters that recalled his military background. Almost immediately he set to work on the insular police force, adding personnel, equipping the units with tear gas and machine guns, providing new red cars for patrolmen, and establishing a modern summer training camp. A day would come when the political career of Luis Muñoz Marín would be caught in crossfire from the newly oiled machine guns of the governor's police force.

Meanwhile, in the view of the returning Muñoz as he looked at Puerto Rico in those early months of 1934, what needed oiling was not machine guns or even the machinery of the Puerto Rico Emergency Relief Administration. It was the thinking of the would-be helpers of the island that needed lubrication. With no plan for reconstruction, millions of dollars would be wasted in doles, food lines, emergency shelters that would sustain the bodies but weaken the resolve of an already supine people. While this holding action would prevail on the level of subsistence, it would accelerate a corrosion of the moral texture of the middle and upper classes. In that sector jobseekers were crowding out job-doers.

Muñoz was not an economist, but he was acquiring a strong feeling for the effects of economic influences on the will, the spirit, the morale of men. Consistent with his growing conviction that his people must be given not benefits but the means to earn them, he proposed at the opening of the 1934 legislative session that funds be found for public purchase of the United Puerto Rico Sugar Company lands for redistribution to small farmers. Support came from an unexpected source. Dr. Carlos Chardón, called in as an expert on sugar, not only testified in favor of Muñoz's proposal, but soon became a valued ally in Muñoz's developing struggle to bring full-scale planning to bear on the island's economic problems.

Chardón, chancellor of the University of Puerto Rico since 1931, was an internationally recognized scholar of the agricultural sciences, as well as a man of proven integrity and unusual administrative ability. He had never been involved in politics. A master of Cornell's Department of Agricultural Sciences in 1921, Chardón had reorganized university facilities for agricultural studies for the government of Colombia in 1926 and had been honored for services to the Venezuelan government in 1932. In Puerto Rico he was also known as the discoverer of the *Aphis maidis,* a pest reducing the yield of the canefields.

Muñoz, two years a senator, had now gained the stature of leadership. Physically he had matured. He was bulkier about the shoulders, developing toward the appearance that would later be described as "bearlike." He had grown a black moustache. There was more assurance in the probing, steady gaze. He had proven the value of his years in the United States. In Washington he had more influence than resident comissioner Santiago Iglesias.

Now Chardón, Muñoz, and Rafael Fernández García, head of the university's department of chemistry, who, with his brother, Benigno, had been an early colleague among the Liberals, joined in planning a long-term economic program for Puerto Rico. With the help of other qualified friends they worked intensively on preparations for talks with Washington authorities, talks that would eventually make the Puerto Rico Reconstruction Administration a reality.

Muñoz's Washington correspondent, Ruby Black, had sent word that important visitors were coming to the island. As if to guarantee her prediction, Miss Black came with the entourage of the most prominent caller, Mrs. Roosevelt. Good fortune, apparently not design, had Rexford Guy Tugwell on the same plane. Formerly a professor of economics at the University of Pennsylvania and at the University of Washington, Tugwell was one of the New Deal's original Brain Trust, first as assistant, then undersecretary of Agriculture. Mrs. Roosevelt's inspection of conditions in Puerto Rico interlocked with Tugwell's conferences with the proponents of the new reconstruction plan. His impression of the Puerto Rican group was summarized in the statement: "The best thing I have found here is that you have no fear of ideas and are not afraid to try something new."

It was agreed during these meetings that Dr. Chardón should head a commission to Washington to propose what would become known as the Chardón Plan. The program was essentially based on land redistribution according to the neglected five-hundred-acre limitation on ownership of sugar lands that had been written into the Foraker Act in 1901. There were many other provisions for building the island economy, prominent among them being a refurbishing of its public utilities. Muñoz Marín accompanied the commission as an observer, and Rexford Tugwell became a one-man steering committee for the commission's negotiations. Eleanor Roosevelt also was committed to informal sponsorship of the plan.

Ranging themselves against the Chardón Plan were the landowners on the island and in the United States; owners of the public utilities; administrative officers of the Puerto Rico Emergency Relief Administration, who foresaw a new program replacing their functions; the political cronies of this group; and most of the Republicans in Congress, with a notable exception. This was Everett Dirksen, who proved to be a valuable supporter of the new plan when it came to Congress as the proposed Puerto Rico Reconstruction Administration.

During the course of tangled negotiations and a great deal of vicious political infighting, the President moved jurisdiction over the island from the War Department to the Department of the Interior, and appointed Ernest Gruening director of the newly formed Division of Territories and Island Possessions. Gruening was somewhat of an expert on Latin-American affairs. He had been president of the Spanish-language *La Prensa* in New York in 1920, had spent considerable time in Mexico, and had served as an adviser to the United States delegation at the Inter-American Conference in Montevideo. During the early twenties, he had been managing editor of *The Nation,* and had been publicity director for the La Follette Presidential campaign in 1924. In those years Ernest Gruening was often in the company of Muñoz Marín and Muna Lee. His appointment now was not a casual one.

As Rexford Tugwell was later to observe, Muñoz Marín, as a Puerto Rican legislator, was not entirely comfortable in the spittoon-decorated offices of Congress, but he was extraordinarily influential in the taproom of a Washington hotel. He would take an inconspicuous table at the back of the room. Soon congressmen, diplomats, and White House attachés would join him. And something that Muñoz wanted to be known would be learned by the group. Occasionally something Muñoz hoped would be done was initiated at these informal gatherings.

Gruening's appointment forwarded the PRRA project but did not put its enemies to rest. The jungle through which the plan was being guided was thick with complexity and infested with obstructors. While funds for emergency and relief were being withheld, those for reconstruction were caught in the web of political impediments. The year 1934 was a grueling battle of conflicting interests struggling over the weakening bodies of a famished people. Desperately Muñoz sought to break through the squeeze and emerge into the open with his plan. In December he brought an eloquent appeal to the President, asking, if not for action now, at least for hope for his people.

The response was the most dramatic possible. On the night of December 22, 1934, a radio loudspeaker was in place in every town square in Puerto Rico. Throngs strolling slowly through the plazas stopped to listen as the first announcement heralded the ceremony at Hyde Park. Impressed, they heard the President of the United States present Luis Muñoz Marín to read his message to Puerto Rico. Then came the words in Spanish. It was Muñoz's low, pleasing voice reading the President's message to Puerto Rico:

> I can and do assure you and your people of my complete goodwill and firm determination that permanent reconstruction shall be initiated at the very earliest possible moment on the basis of the Chardón Plan, the principles of which have received my approval.

Muñoz's prompt return to Puerto Rico was the second occasion for public acclaim since the announcement of Governor Gore's resignation exactly twelve months earlier. As he stepped off the boat into the soft air of San Juan, it was clearly apparent that the son of Luis Muñoz Rivera was becoming a hero in his own right. To the now embroidered legend of his career as a writer for American publications was added the triumphs of his negotiations with American heads of state. And admirers were exaggeratedly whispering to each other of his cleverness in arranging the appointments of friends to positions vital to the program for aid to the island.

None of this applause reduced his enemies in numbers or intent. They had consistently fired salvos straight to the White House to remind the administration that Muñoz was a strong adherent of independence for Puerto Rico, not to be trusted with political responsibility. Muñoz found it necessary to answer their charges so that he could continue the battle for Puerto Rico's economic salvation.

"I want my people to want independence," he declared. "Once they do that, they will set powerful forces in motion and may bring things to the point where independence is unnecessary or even bad." He was reiterating a philosophy that he has never abandoned in principle but has frequently altered in application: a great drama requires a great objective.

The current objective was to put PRRA into motion. Seven months passed before President Roosevelt's executive order could formalize the program. Gruening was named administrator in August, 1935, and Dr. Chardón regional administrator for Puerto Rico. The opposing coalition called a public mass meeting to protest the alleged political appointments to the administrative body. Muñoz Marín immediately broadcast a spirited defense throughout the island, becoming thereby the plan's popular advocate.

PRRA went into action with a budget of $40 million from Washington and an estimated additional $7.5 million from sugar taxes. It also started with a full complement of political rivals jockeying for control. A more astute and less idealistic politician than Muñoz would not have allowed himself to be held responsible for such an unwieldy operation, especially without any means of control other than personal influence.

PRRA lumbered under the weight of political quarrels in Washington and in Puerto Rico. Gruening, finding that his old friend Muñoz, the poet of yore, was not as malleable as he had anticipated, was cooling toward his Puerto Rican colleague. Muñoz was discovering that Gruening's essential conservatism was overtaking the free-thinking tendencies of his younger years. Others moved between the two men to seek a share of control of PRRA's mammoth budget. And the sugar interests fought back stubbornly against the onslaught of the "socialists."

Then, two months after President Roosevelt signed the August, 1935, order to establish the Puerto Rico Reconstruction Administration, the fanatic Nationalists again broke into the headlines. Albizu Campos, Nationalist leader, had been trying to enlist the support of the students at the University of Puerto Rico. Finding them unenthusiastic about his aims, Campos made a public statement impugning the virility of the student group. The response, on October 24, was a student demonstration on the campus in Rio Piedras, a town near San Juan.

Armed Nationalists arrived to break up the meeting, and Governor Winship's police appeared to dispel the Nationalists. In the course of the riot, one policeman and four Nationalists were killed, and forty participants and bystanders were wounded.

Albizu Campos called a Nationalist party meeting in December, 1935, to declare that his party would no longer enter "colonial elections," that the government of the United States must abandon the island immediately, that all Nationalists must enter military service within the party, and that an international campaign would be launched immediately to raise funds for the Nationalist cause.

It was now February 23, 1936. Muñoz Marín was in Washington attempting to iron out PRRA problems.

In San Juan Colonel E. Francis Riggs, police chief, an old friend of United States Senator Millard Tydings and appointed to his present position through the senator's influence, was keeping a sharp eye on potential sources of island disorders. Although efficient as a police administrator, Riggs was popular in Puerto Rico for his native courtesy and affable manners.

On this particular morning Colonel Riggs, prayer book in hand, waved to some friends as he left the cathedral in San Juan. He took only a few strides before two men who had been standing near the cathedral door moved swiftly toward him. As he turned to greet them, Hiram Rosado and Elías Beauchamp, Nationalist gunmen, shot repeatedly at Riggs until he slumped dead in the street. Police closed in quickly. The men were taken to headquarters. Riggs's body was removed from the scene.

Within hours the story was known throughout San Juan. The police chief had been murdered by two Nationalists, and the culprits, in a skirmish in the police station, had been killed by their captors. On the island the first burst of shame for the brutal murder was followed by indignation over the shooting of the killers by the insular police. Nationalists fed the clamor with a new outburst of demonstrations. The seething atmosphere was kept boiling by Governor Winship's order for raids and investigations directed against the Nationalist organization and the eventual arrest of Albizu Campos and seven Nationalist leaders.

In Washington and elsewhere in the United States the reaction was one of unmitigated outrage. Muñoz Marín, long denounced as a proponent of Puerto Rican independence, shared the administration's anger and embarrassment, but he also joined in the island's repugnance at the police killing of the Nationalists. In recent months Muñoz had been unsympathetic to many of Ernest Gruening's political moves to solidify his control over PRRA. Now he was called upon by Gruening to dispatch a statement to the Puerto Rican press denouncing the murder of Colonel Riggs. As he faced his former friend, Muñoz realized that the web of his relationships in Washington and in Puerto Rico was vulnerable to the violent pressure of Riggs's murder. Muñoz's reply was decisive. He would send such a statement only if Gruening would likewise condemn the police brutality that had followed the murder. The breach between Muñoz and Gruening was now virtually irrevocable, even though Muñoz attempted to alleviate the situation by sending a letter to the *Washington Post* expressing his sorrow over the tragedy of Riggs.

In the wake of these events Senator Millard Tydings asked the Department of the Interior to draft a bill offering Puerto Rico a plebiscite for or against independence. Secretary Ickes, in consultation with President Roosevelt, stated that "if Puerto Rico wants its independence, it ought to be granted it, but if it should vote against independence, then such agitation as has been going on in Puerto Rico recently will be put to an end for probably twenty years." Gruening and Ickes wrote the bill for Tydings to introduce to Congress in April.

Announcement of the bill had anything but a quieting effect. Every shade of political opinion in Puerto Rico became immediately white or black. Every politician took a firm position. Parties broke into violently hostile groups. Students throughout the island staged strikes for the bill. The governor's office called out police reserves to quell disorders. The conservative Republican leader, Martínez Nadal, reversed his lifelong position for statehood, loudly demanding that Puerto Rico accept the Tydings challenge. The Liberal party split into the Independence wing, which had always followed Muñoz Marín and now gave wavering support to Antonio Barceló's clamor to accept Tydings' offer, and the conservative group that interpreted the bill as a reprisal that might condemn the island to years of inde-

pendent starvation. Dr. Chardón accepted a request of the conservatives to write an analysis in depth of the bill and its possible damaging consequences.

The proposal of the Tydings bill was an exercise in human motivation meriting a voluminous study of its own. At the moment,
Senator Tydings might have been impelled, because of his friendship with Riggs, to represent a wave of American resentment and
disgust caused by the Riggs murder. That he should repeat his sponsorship of independence proposals up to the year 1945, while maintaining a sympathetic relationship with American sugar interests in
competition with Puerto Rican sugar, has since cast some doubt
upon his sincerity. Secretary Ickes, as adviser to President Roosevelt,
and the President himself seemed to have shared an opinion that the
United States had dealt fairly with the Puerto Ricans and that the
time had come for them to answer in kind, or risk the consequences.
Dr. Gruening, while appearing to hold the same view, displayed
such a vengeful spirit in the course of the following year that he was
removed from his post as chief of the Puerto Rican Reconstruction
Administration.

In the midst of this welter of contradictory forces, Muñoz faced
an island whose people considered him a champion of their desires
for independence. But the Tydings bill, written without his consultation, undercut his leadership in the independence issue. If Muñoz
now sponsored the bill and the elections of 1936 should return a
majority to the Liberals, this would be a pre-plebiscite forecast of
the island's future. If he opposed it and the Liberals under Barceló
held steady for the bill, the party, split between his adherents and
those of Barceló, would lose the election; the vote for the Republi-
can-Socialist coalition could be interpreted as a popular decision
against the prospect of independence. The brilliant young leader had
obviously lost his touch in Washington and was in danger of losing
his leadership in a party whose aging chief, Antonio Barceló, was
jealous of Muñoz's recent rapid gains. As he weighed these premises,
the Nationalists annnounced their readiness boldly to accept the
Tydings challenge. They would lead the island through its greatest
expression of hatred for the Yankee to its glorious independence as
an inimical republic in the Caribbean Sea.

Muñoz sifted through the convictions that he had so bravely expressed in his articles of the twenties and his statements as a Liberal

party senator. The long nights of talk with Nemesio Canales and Luis Lloréns Torres and other friends in La Mallorquina; the midnight debates with Sara Teasdale, Horace Gregory, and Earl Parker Hanson in New York; the trenchant iconoclasm of H. L. Mencken; the humaneness of Edwin Markham; the last eager conversations with his father in the tiny apartment in Washington; the observation of Theodore Roosevelt's honest efforts; and his own awareness of the desperate plight of the Puerto Rican people were all brought into balance.

Muñoz declared against the Tydings bill. He stated that it presented Puerto Rico with a choice between independent famine or abject acceptance of a colonial regime. But Muñoz did not abdicate his sponsorship of independence. He qualified his position with a demand that independence be joined to an opportunity for his people's economic salvation. A plebiscite for independence, he stated, should be conditioned upon guarantees of preference for United States manufacturers selling to Puerto Rico, assurances of quotas for the sale of Puerto Rican sugar in the United States, an American loan sufficient to achieve the objectives of the economic efforts initiated by the New Deal. Then Muñoz returned to his island, this time not in triumph, but quietly and with some reluctance.

As he anticipated, the Liberal party was divided between the "conservatives" favoring Muñoz's position and the "radicals" following Barceló, whose enthusiasm for an election victory had even led him to negotiations with the Nationalists for immediate unconditional independence. Muñoz was convinced that the Liberal party, split by divergent opinions, would lose the 1936 elections. Believing that this would be interpreted as a popular vote against independence and for knuckling under a colonial regime, he insisted that the party should withdraw entirely from the coming electoral contest, and he withdrew his own candidacy for any post.

Barceló vigorously opposed Muñoz Marín and wagered his control of the Liberal party by taking the issue to an intraparty vote. Muñoz, losing by a narrow margin, agreed to support the party election campaign, but the rift between the old Liberal leader and the young challenger brought into play new forces that were leading to unforeseen ends—unforeseen, that is, by all but perhaps Luis Muñoz Marín. He began organizing the conservative independence wing of the Liberals into a group called the Acción Social Independentista, with a hurriedly established network of political representatives throughout the island. This group continued officially to support the Liberal party.

The murder of Riggs, the refusal of Muñoz to condemn it without censure of the police killing of the assassins, the break between Gruening and Muñoz, the division within the Liberal party—all had worked to reduce the party's influence in Washington. Gruening was reacting by replacing Liberals with coalitionists in the PRRA organization. He was also calling attention to the educational policies that made Spanish the primary language in Puerto Rico's schools. This charge won the support of Secretary of the Interior Ickes and of Eleanor Roosevelt, causing the resignation from PRRA, and from the chancellorship of the University, of Dr. Carlos Chardón, one of the island's finest public servants. Only the reform of the election law, requiring new registrations and stricter controls at voting places as well as better supervision of the count, acted to favor the Liberals.

It was no surprise that the Liberals lost the election, only that they did well enough to move their share of the vote from their former forty-six percent up to forty-eight percent. Barceló and his followers were convinced, possibly correctly, that Muñoz's attitude could be charged with the defeat. In December, 1936, after the election, Barceló made his resentment more obvious by declaring that *La Democracia* was no longer a party organ and that he would have no more to do with it.

In April, 1937, Muñoz made his ill-starred move to capture the party machinery. Returning from another stay in Washington, he proposed a Liberal convention for the purpose of healing party wounds. Muñoz was convinced that the Tydings bill had lost its momentum in Washington's slow procedures and that he could now again espouse independence firmly linked to economic safeguards. To this end he brought his Acción Social group together in a declaration that the Liberal party still represented the policies of Luis Muñoz Rivera. The first stage of his father's program, he declared, was the achievement of autonomy, which had been done through the Jones Act; the second stage was the proof that Puerto Rico was capable of managing her own political affairs, which had been amply demonstrated; the third stage would be the effort to achieve independence. Analysts could only excuse the insincerity or incompetence of Muñoz's definition of the first two stages on the basis of an impetuous enthusiasm for the third. More likely, Muñoz's determination to seize the Liberal party machinery was tempting him toward the sins that he deplored in other politicians.

If so, Barceló's sharp rebuttal at the party convention called in May set Muñoz back on the track of responsible political action. The convention took place on a party leader's farm, called Naranjal. Here, under Barceló's leadership, the majority of the Liberals supported a resolution expelling splinter groups from the party. Here, in the view of all observers, the political career of Luis Muñoz Marín seemed to be coming to a close.

The tempestuous young man who had espoused socialism in its Fabian and later its Puerto Rican form, who had moved to the Liberal party and scored its two great triumphs in ousting Governor Gore and in bringing in PRRA, who had endorsed independence but fought the form in which it was proposed by Tydings, who had broken all the rules of politics by abstaining from a candidacy that would help bring victory to his party, who had formed his own party within the party, who had attempted to wrest the party leadership from its chief, who had finally resorted to claims based on an ill-defined reference to his father's program—this new light in Puerto Rican politics was dimmed like a guttering candle at Naranjal. Muñoz, in the view of all but his closest adherents, was out, finished. His posture on the island was the absurd one of a rebel who has lost. His standing in Washington, accordingly, was a forecast of oblivion.

As if to underline his failure, Gruening's interference with PRRA, the first organized American effort to aid the island's economy, was debilitating the program so that it had lost the support of Congress and the faith of Puerto Rico. Its declining budget and the petty plundering of its new administrators already foreshadowed its early and final failure. The Socialist-Republican coalition, now in control, was urging PRRA toward the cliff. At the bottom, as it went over, the ruined plan might find the rock of Sisyphus, lost from the hands of Muñoz Marín, resting again in the Plutonic depths where Luis' father, Muñoz Rivera, had first discovered his destiny.

Muñoz Marín and his father have often been quoted on the subject of destiny, Muñoz Marín particularly on the destiny of being a

Puerto Rican. Muñoz is not religious in the sense of a close affiliation with a church, but he has an almost pantheistic belief in the permeating presence of God and a nearly superstitious feeling about the accidental effects of outside occurrences on the lives of individuals.

When the currents of 1936 and 1937 were carrying Muñoz off to sea, they swept across his course two other Puerto Ricans whose association with Muñoz thereafter might have contributed to his respect for the forces of destiny. Significantly, both came from Puerto Rico's poorer class.

Ernesto Ramos Antonini was the first, chronologically, of the two new personalities in Muñoz's life. He appeared on the scene some weeks before Muñoz's defeat at the party convention in May, 1937. Born in the same year as Muñoz, Ramos Antonini was the son of the Puerto Rican composer and pianist Federico Ramos Escalera and of Rosa Antonini. The blood strain flowing to the boy was predominantly Negro. Young Ramos worked his way through college and law school by playing the piano at a movie house in the university town of Rio Piedras. A year after his graduation in 1922, he entered politics with the Unionist party, then under Antonio Barceló's leadership. In court, concentrating on labor and criminal cases, he developed a talent for public speaking that eventually made him one of the island's brilliant orators. Away from the law library and the speaker's stand, Ramos Antonini was the slight, dapper center of gatherings that delighted in his urbane flow of talk and his supply of gay music at the piano. But the core of his devotion after his schoolteacher wife, Josefina, was the defense of the poor island worker and the wretch whose misery had led him to crime.

On Palm Sunday, March 21, 1937, in the town square of Ponce, the threads of violence were weaving a drama that would have a signal effect on the career of Ramos Antonini. The Nationalist party, incensed at the seven-year prison terms to which Albizu Campos and seven other Nationalists had been sentenced after the Riggs murder, planned another in a series of demonstrations on this day of peace. Other parades and meetings had been stopped by the police under orders of Governor Winship. The American Civil Liberties Union was already concerned about the governor's totalitarian reaction.

In this case, however, the mayor of Ponce had acceded to the Nationalist request for permission to walk peacefully in protest through the streets of Ponce. He also sent the governor's office a routine report of the expected procession. Winship ordered the insular chief of police to Ponce to survey security measures, then sent him back on the morning of Palm Sunday to cancel the mayor's permit. In a hurried meeting that lasted up to the hour scheduled for the parade, the Nationalist leaders, the mayor, and the chief of police failed to reach an agreement. The Nationalists insisted that police rejection of the mayor's permit had arrived too late. Their Cadets of the Republic and Daughters of the Republic were already in from the countryside and assembling for the event. The mayor sympathized with them but was disauthorized by the chief of police, and the chief had no recourse but force, which he wished to avoid.

The parade began peacefully enough in the hot Sunday sun, with the town's worshipers stopping on their way home from church to watch the silent youngsters line down the main street. The holiday atmosphere was accented by the palm leaves carried by bystanders wearing their Sunday best. With the church's message of peace still within them, the townsfolk might have found this an occasion for some gaiety had they not observed the grim contingent of 150 insular police ringing the square, their automatic carbines gleaming in the hot Caribbean sunshine.

As the youngsters approached the square, everyone could see how cleanly starched the girls' white dresses were and how neat the boys looked in their white shirts, black trousers, and small caps. Then the spectators saw a police officer, Captain Soldevila, step into the street and order the procession to halt. The police force sharpened its alert. The youngsters looked to their leader for instructions. The crowd watched tensely. A shot rang out. The crowd and the paraders broke ranks. More shots. Panic. Screams, curses, and the repeated sound of firing filled the square. When quiet returned to the city of Ponce, there was blood on its streets, tragedy in the families of nineteen dead civilians and policemen, sorrow in the homes of over a hundred wounded citizens.

This was the "Ponce Massacre," a disgrace whose repercussions reached into the White House and finally wrote the termination of Governor Winship's inept regime. Investigators and survey commissions were never able to place blame for the initial shooting. Nationalist leaders were brought to trial. The attorney for the defense was

Ramos Antonini. The law was on the side of the defendants, who were acquitted. The hearts of Puerto Ricans, and many Americans, of all political creeds were with the young lawyer whose brilliant conduct of the trial vaulted him into the forefront of Puerto Rican public life.

The cause of justice, the defense of the weak, and a genius for debate were the tools that Ramos Antonini brought to Muñoz Marín in his mortifying confrontation with Antonio Barceló. Ramos Antonini, veteran colleague of Barceló, attempted to hold the party together on Muñoz's terms. When Muñoz's Acción Social Independentista was voted out of the party, Ramos went with it. For the rest of his life his great talents served the objectives of Muñoz Marín, strengthening the bridge between Muñoz and the people of Puerto Rico.

The Ponce Massacre also brought, though indirectly, the second of Muñoz Marín's important associations that originated in 1937. Notable among the reports on the massacre was one drawn up by lawyer Arthur Garfield Hays for the American Civil Liberties Union. Hays's objective analysis led to a Washington request for further studies of island conditions. Among the issues considered by the Hays Committee was the use of the English and Spanish languages in the schools, and teachers were invited to state their views. Meanwhile the new commissioner of education, Dr. José Gallardo, was interpreting Washington's wish to increase the teaching of English as a mandate to remove teachers with a contrary viewpoint or those known to support the cause of independence. Accordingly, over Hays's protest, those teachers who expressed these views to the Hays Committee were fired from their posts by the Department of Education.

Among those so briskly treated was one Señora Inés María Mendoza de Palacios, teacher of Spanish in the Central High School of Santurce. A strong believer in independence, she also supported the predominant use of Spanish in the island schools. Nor was she one to accept dismissal without a struggle. Her protest to the Hays Committee received American Civil Liberties support, reaching Eleanor Roosevelt and the President.

Perhaps not even Muñoz Marín could say whether he became interested in the case because of Inés Mendoza or whether the situation brought her first to his notice. The fact is that in 1937 Inés

María Mendoza came into Muñoz Marín's life, and she is still there. Inés was a vibrantly beautiful young woman. People first noticed her abundant jet-black hair, then the passionate dark eyes and ivory skin, finally the petite body with its quick movements, hands gesturing as she talked, her posturing tense as she listened. Inés had been brought up on a cattle farm in the interior. She had adored her father until his death, when she was eight years old. She has said that the lesson of her father helped her to understand Muñoz. "I could not have known who Muñoz was if I had not known my father. My father was illiterate. He bought many books and my mother read them to him. . . . He valued human beings above all else . . . the people were the most important thing. He had a great deal of courage and he was very humble. I only lived with him for eight years, and yet he taught me the pattern of everything good."

After her father's death, her mother lost the family's small plot of land to an expanding sugar economy. Inés never forgot. She became a Nationalist, an ardent fighter for Puerto Rico's independence, a devoted protector of the Spanish cultural heritage of the island. The flint of her passion for her people sparked against the hard-grained urge of Muñoz to free them from hunger before liberating Puerto Rico from her political masters. If Muñoz moderated the flaming Inés, she illuminated hope for him at a time when there was no place for Muñoz to go—but to the people.

NINE

The Electorate

In one of the speeches of his middle years, Luis Muñoz Marín said, "We learn by planting things in the mind that later bear fruit in understanding." For public leaders who store impressions that later develop into policies, the moment of fruition is often unpredictable. Muñoz, leading the independence group of the Liberal party, when faced with a flat offer of independence, drew on his understanding of things formerly planted in his mind and rejected the offer. Now, in the intense period of reflection that his first great failure forced upon him, Muñoz could plant in his mind the things that would enable him truly to understand his people.

Years later he described some of them. One was the idea of his country that the Puerto Rican profoundly cherishes. He described it in a speech in 1951 honoring the birth date of his father:

> To the Puerto Rican, *patria* is the colors of the landscape, the change of seasons, the smell of the earth wet with fresh rain, the voice of the streams, the crash of the ocean against the shore, the fruits, the songs, the habits of work and of leisure, the typical dishes for special occasions, and the meager ones for every day, the flowers, the valleys, and the pathways. But even more than these things, *patria* is the people: their way of life, spirit, folkways, customs, their ways of getting along with each other. . . .
>
> Love of the country must mean love of all the country—both the *patria* and the people. But some of us confused love of the homeland with the narrow and bitter concept of the national

state. We felt that love of Puerto Rico had as a necessary corollary the desire for separate independence. We had not yet comprehended that no law, divine or human, commands that countries must be suspicious, vain, and hostile, that they must live separate from other countries whose peoples are a part of the broad equality that the Lord created on the earth. Because of the rigidity of our thinking, we could not disentangle the concept of love for our country from the fixed idea of separate independence. . . .

The difficult process of clarifying these ideas began when the Tydings bill was introduced in Congress in 1936. . . .

The process of clarification now led Muñoz Marín to his people. It took him the length and breadth of their island, into their most remote hamlets, along the lost roads that threaded through the hills, the highways that flanked the shores, and back to the cities teeming with a kaleidoscopic populace.

He again observed an island some one hundred miles long and thirty-five miles wide, about half the size of the state of Massachusetts. For centuries ocean breezes had held its mean temperatures the year around between 73.4 and 78.9 degrees. Columbus had replied to Queen Isabella's request for a description of the island by crumpling a piece of paper and throwing it on a table. "It is like that," he said. Puerto Rico's 3,345 square miles, including three other tiny offshore islands, contain twelve mountains over 3,000 feet high. The highest is 4,400 feet high and is called Ala de la Piedra (Wing of the Rock). The hills whose steep slopes have deprived Puerto Ricans of thousands of acres of otherwise tillable land have also sheltered them from the onslaughts of the eighty-five hurricanes that have swept across the island since 1500. The storms were recorded under the names of saints until 1955, when "Connie" was acknowledged as the successor to "San Mateo," which had lightly flicked the island in 1949.

There are no deserts in Puerto Rico, nor extended jungles, nor far distant mountaintops where a man can lose himself. Yet of the 1,869,255 Puerto Ricans recorded in the 1940 census, the only group separately known by a generic term was labeled by a word signifying, roughly, "one escaped from civilization." This was the *jíbaro*, originally the man of the hills, then the man of the countryside, eventually to become the man of all work. By the time Muñoz Marín began his personal study of the *jíbaro*, the term was an anachronism, for Puerto Rico, with over five hundred persons per square mile on the island, was one of the most densely populated areas on the globe. But the legend of the *jíbaro* persists, and the background of his nickname is rooted in Puerto Rican history.

The Indians who hid in the hills of Puerto Rico to avoid being pressed into service by the first Spanish seekers of gold are said to have led the "first flight of the *jíbaro*." A hundred years later they were joined by the runaway Negro slaves who escaped from the sugarcane fields in the "second flight of the *jíbaro*." Drifting into the countryside and slowly climbing the slopes of the interior of the island were also the Spaniards who had found no comfort in the company of their fellowmen in Spain or in Puerto Rico. Theirs was the "third flight of the *jíbaro*."

The trinity of the *jíbaro* recurs in most Puerto Rican discussions of the island's culture. One of Puerto Rico's writers, Salvador Brau, applied it to his observations of Puerto Rican character: "From the Indian came our indolence, taciturnity, indifference, and the sentiment of hospitality; the African brought his endurance, his vigorous sensuality, superstition, and fatalism; the Spaniard injected his gentlemanly gravity, his characteristic aloofness, his festive pleasures, his austere devotion, constancy in adversity, and the love of the *patria* and independence." *

In the music of the people (and nearly every Puerto Rican is a dancer and musician until he is laid away in some crowded graveyard) the Indian is said to have contributed the *carracho* and the maracas; the African the drum, the bongo, and the *bomba*; the Spaniard the guitar, which the Puerto Rican has altered into an instrument called the *tiple*.

In stories for those greatest of realists, the children, the legend of the *jíbaro* has been perpetuated in tales that divide his character into three personalities known as Juan Bobo, Juan Animala, and Juan Cuchilla. All are poor young men facing the problem of survival in a land of scarcity.

* Salvador Brau. *"Las Clases Jornaleras de Puerto Rico," Disquisiciones Sociologicas.* University of Puerto Rico. Instituto de Literatura, 1956.

Juan Bobo (Silly John) is not a stupid man. He is merely ingenuous and unlucky and, of course, comic. Juan Bobo is also the children's favorite of the three Juans. His misadventures are caused by his distrust, which often induces him to reject opportunities for gain, paradoxically linked to a candor and good faith that make him the butt of clever manipulators of men. His only desire is to solve his problems humbly and peacefully. His failures are pathetic, sometimes tear-provoking, but never bitter or tragic. He is the hero-son of Puerto Rico, beloved by her children, fondly recalled by their parents. He is related to our Simple Simon of Mother Goose days, to World War II's Sad Sack, to the Manoel of many Brazilian anecdotes, to the lovable, open-hearted, but suspicious countryman of many lands.

His antithesis is Juan Animala, a strange name for a Robin Hood sort of figure who outwits the governor, the businessmen, the politicians. He is a popular Fearless John who weaves the most intricate of plots to deceive his betters and emerges successful and unharmed from the most threatening of situations, mostly of his own creation. He is the *pícaro* of Spanish legend, the adventurer of many lands, the Thin Man or James Bond of detective literature. He can be dangerous and perfidious for strangers, but is always affectionate and loyal to his own people.

The third of the three Juans is perhaps the most interesting as a legendary representation of the individual in conflict with society. He is Juan Cuchilla, John the Knife. He comes into the world as a being of natural goodness, but the conditions he encounters transpose his innate decency into laziness, deceitfulness, and malice. He is thrown in with thieves and lives their life. Mired in an atmosphere of crime, he commits petty misdemeanors but never harms anyone seriously. He is not violent or cruel, merely another "man gone wrong." John the Knife is a less romantic version of Mack the Knife of *The Threepenny Opera*, a man molded into perverseness and driven to crime by the misery that surrounds him from birth.

As if the children and their nurses and grandparents had not done well enough in defining the nature of the *jíbaro*, stern-browed observers of the sociological scene have felt the need to make their own pronouncements. Their inconsistencies have reflected more of themselves than of the theme. The *jíbaro* is shrewd and calculating; the *jíbaro* is stupid and naïve. The *jíbaro* is kind and hospitable; the *jíbaro* is a moral vagrant; the *jíbaro* is a sturdy and steady worker; the *jíbaro* only cares for cockfights, dice, song, and rum.

Novelists, poets, and essayists have written of the *jíbaro*. Orators have spoken of him. One critic of Puerto Rican literature said, "The persistence of the *jíbaro* theme in Puerto Rican literature is one of the strongest evidences of the uneasiness embedded in the thought of our men."

Luis Muñoz Rivera, writing in the cool tranquillity of his mahogany-paneled study, had recorded his observation on the *jíbaro*: "He gazes at the bureaucrats, those who meddle with their corrupt practices, looming above him. He believes that laws are something mysterious, constructed not to protect him but with oppression as their purpose. He sees the mayor of his town as a sort of demigod, the priest a human being verging on the divine . . . by instinct he loves liberty just as growing things love the sun; he has no precise ideas of his existence because he has never gone beyond the boundaries of his mountain and his river."

Finally, Luis Lloréns Torres, lawyer and poet who had often discussed the *jíbaro* and many other subjects with Nemesio Canales and Muñoz Marín over La Mallorquina's best rum, put the *jíbaro* into verse and into the context of the late 1930's.

> A *jíbaro* came to San Juan
> And a bunch of Yankee-lovers
> Came upon him in the park
> Hoping to win him over.
> They told him about Uncle Sam,
> About Wilson and E. Roote,
> About liberty, and the vote,
> About the dollar, and about habeas corpus,
> And the *jíbaro* answered: Mmmmm.

In 1937 the *jíbaro* was still saying "Mmmmm" about the Puerto Rican Emergency Relief Administration and the Puerto Rican Reconstruction Administration and the Liberals and the Nationalists; and only the poets thought his diffidence worth a comment.

Except to a poet, what did it matter that the *jíbaro* should say "Mmmmm" about the words of politicians and employers who had defrauded him habitually? What did it matter in the rest of Latin America? Who but the makers of legend and verse and music were concerned with Mexico's *campesino*, Argentina's gaucho, Brazil's *caboclo*, Chile's *roto*, Venezuela's *llanero*, or Peru's *Indio*?

The poet in Muñoz Marín counted the *jíbaro's* miseries; the pragmatist in his nature scored his numbers and saw the threat of their increase.

The birth rate of Puerto Rico, 39.2 per thousand, was among the highest in the world. American health aid was reducing the mortality per thousand, and the population rise was surpassed by very few nations on the globe. What could be done to take care of the new babies? The PRRA was dying, and charity was a solution without dignity. Of the agricultural countries above the level of bare subsistence, none matched the density of Puerto Rico's 546 persons per square mile. And of the beauteous lands of the mountainous tropical island, only twenty-five percent of the acreage could be called productive. Yet, since there was little industrial development to provide goods or work, Puerto Rico was consigning over forty-five percent of its labor force to agriculture. To compound the problem, less than a third of the island's population was in the labor force—against forty percent for the United States—because some forty percent of the people of Puerto Rico were fourteen years of age or under. The future could be read in the ten percent of unemployed, the five percent on emergency relief work, and the more than ten thousand persons per year being added to the work force. It was little wonder that Puerto Rico's writers had romanticized the *jíbaro*. In their hearts, it was his stoicism they were extolling.

Muñoz Marín, in his probing, searched for the factor that kept the song in the heart of the *jíbaro* who received from nature so little more than the sweetness of the hillside air, the odor of flowering trees, the sound of bacteria-infested streams, and the love of women who continually presented him more children to keep alive. All the forms of the church were there, but the *jíbaro* rejected its content. Spain's priests had never really reached the people outside the cities, and the American churchmen mystified the Puerto Rican with their urgency and their litanies in a strange tongue. Some spiritualism combined with a natural superstition to attract a few groups. Some women took their sorrows to the quiet shadows of a nearby chapel. But many never were able to bring their mates to its sacrament.

Nearly half the marriages were consensual, but not promiscuous. They endured as unions, but money was needed for food rather than ceremonies. Only baptisms were taken seriously, in part because they were given more freely by the church. Discreetly, priests avoided questions about the legitimacy of the child.

From the baptism emerged a relationship that helped each *jíbaro* aid another through his tortuous life. It was called *compadrazgo,* a word derived from *compadre,* or godfather. In a land with a life expectancy of forty-six years, the responsibilities of a godfather were not lightly conferred, nor disdainfully accepted. From this promise of faith mutually and voluntarily expressed, it was a natural step to similar avowals unattended by the circumstances of baptism. In the spirit of the American Indian "blood brother" or the American "buddy" concept of the First World War, *compadrazgo* became a voluntary brotherhood of individuals in need of help to buoy the scant resources of their own families.

The practical uses of the bond among this peaceful people were not defense or attack; they were simply prosaic, day-to-day assistance. The one who was a carpenter would spend his Sunday helping his *compadre* fix the roof of his hut, and the latter, who was a fisherman, would return the favor with any excess from his catch. The same relationship might exist between women, with exchanges of child care and housecleaning. Little as it may have meant to the political or economic structure of Puerto Rico, the *compadre* system threaded through the social atmosphere of the island a sense of loyalty and of reciprocity. This Muñoz Marín came to understand profoundly.

He also came to believe that just as the trust and confidence on which *compadrazgo* was based could account for the honest, loyal, and ingenuous traits credited to the *jíbaro,* so the suspicion, taciturnity, and malingering ascribed to him may have resulted, in part, from his disenchantment with outsiders. Puerto Rican leadership under the Spanish or the American flag had made up a thin crust on the surface of the island's society. Only in the almost golden days of Muñoz Rivera's preeminence had political leaders attempted to speak for and act for all the people of Puerto Rico. Muñoz Rivera had won their adulation by his valor and his essential decency. Celso Barbosa, colored himself, had attracted the loyalty of the Negro strain, who visualized in him an island projection of the American Emancipator. José de Diego had lit a spark of rebellion with his poetic vision of independence for all. And Santiago Iglesias, the boisterous street fighter, had organized the ranks of laborers already joined in industry, artisanship, and the great landholdings. Then the deaths of Muñoz Rivera and Celso Barbosa, the flight of José de Diego, and the aging of Santiago Iglesias had left the island in the hands of politicians who sought not to help but to manipulate Puerto Rico's workman and *jíbaro*.

The middle class, a small group, consisted of the successful farmers who had bought their way into urban trade, of the heirs who had lost their land and descended to commercial circles, and of the group of importers and exporters who had prospered on an island dependent on their services. To it was joined members of the professions. Here was the independent and competent group whose support was sought by all political parties. But financial support for political organizations came from the large landowners and the select leaders in trade.

This group gave itself the label of aristocracy, taking the anachronism from Spain. By 1937 it had divided into two branches: one with strong commercial ties to the United States, the other turned toward Spain. The former belonged to the same clubs as the Americans, except those that prohibited Puerto Rican membership. The latter were members of the Spanish Club, and when Primo de Rivera founded the Falange in Spain, many became its overseas adepts. They cheered as General Franco carried the Falange banner over the bloody battlefields of the Spanish Civil War. In their homes the old customs were ardently preserved: the double standard, chaperonage of daughters until marriage, the lavish show of Carnival, the sense of race, the drawing of class lines, pride in the manners of Spain.

The funds of the "aristocracy" and the successful merchants helped the politicians to buy the votes of the disappointed and skeptical *jíbaro*. Unless he gave his pledge for money, up to two dollars a vote, the *jíbaro* would be kept from the polls by the plying of rum at an election-day fiesta on the hacienda. It mattered little to this voter, since for some twenty years he had been promised everything before election day and given nothing after the returns were counted. Even the election-reform statute of 1936 made little difference. This had provided that voters would be brought to buildings in groups of 150 before one o'clock in the afternoon. Then the buildings would be closed and the vote would begin. Duplicate voting was eliminated, but not the sale of votes.

Muñoz could now clearly see a rejected mass, multiplying its problems by its own proliferation in a rising swamp of misery that was creeping over the island. Yet in this group he perceived the courage that struggle had wrought, the resourcefulness that, with tools, might drain the slough. On higher land, his view could take in the limitations of a stagnating system. The influx of federal-aid funds had started a few industries and some activity in public works; but their benefits were superficial and would be temporary. Sugar exports had reached a plateau. The island was deprived of most of their benefits. Nearly half of Puerto Rico's sugar exports were produced by four American-owned companies whose stock was owned in the United States. Most other land was in tobacco and coffee. As Muñoz had said: "We produce the after-dinner pleasures, without the meal." The meal had to be imported from the United States at American prices that an impoverished people could ill afford.

As Muñoz reviewed the conditions of his overpopulated island, he might have been struck by some of its similarities to and some of its differences from other underdeveloped countries in South America. Puerto Rico shared with them a long history of poverty and stagnation. It was, like the others, an agricultural country. But unlike the nations on the continent, Puerto Rico did not have vast stretches of uncultivated land that could be broken up and developed. Her soil, though closely held, was producing at close to capacity. True, like her Hispanic cousins, Puerto Rico was largely populated by landless laborers. Unlike them, the island had no other resources on which to employ her people, no oil, no mines, no great forests, no great plains feeding livestock, no fisheries, no untrapped torrents for conversion to hydroelectric power. Like the others, Puerto Rico had a small, strongly entrenched class in which most wealth was concentrated. Unlike them, she did not have an army standing by to protect the dominant group and to overthrow whatever progressive government might endanger the holdings of the wealthy.

If anyone had told Muñoz Marín of Puerto Rico's great difference, her link to the United States, he might well have shrugged and pointed to the statistical picture of poverty, disease, hunger, and unemployment that had ravaged the land throughout the forty years of the American occupation. And Muñoz could have indicated another overwhelming similarity joining Puerto Rico with the poorer of her neighbors: a mass of men sunk in poverty, without hope, without confidence, but nursing in the embers of survival a spark that could be fanned into the flame of accomplishment.

Now the tall and brooding Puerto Rican knew what had to be done.

TEN

Jalda Arriba!

O<small>N</small> J<small>ULY</small> 22, 1938, Puerto Rico awoke to the news that a new political party had entered the listings. The Popular Democratic party announced its registration in the voting districts of Luquillo and Barranquitas. Its leader was Luis Muñoz Marín.

The news was received with an indifference reflecting the serenity of the sites where the party was inscribed. Luquillo was a sleepy village near one of Puerto Rico's idyllic, remote beaches. Barranquitas was best known as the quiet hill town in which Luis Muñoz Rivera was born.

The coalition majority, still combining the Socialist and Republican parties, was amused and even pleased. The new party had drawn off much of the best Liberal talent. Although its announced followers were known to favor independence for Puerto Rico, the party's leader had placed himself against the offer of independence contained in the Tydings bill. And this man, Luis Muñoz Marín, the son of the island's great patriot, had publicly demonstrated his political incapacity by losing his prestige as a dominant member of the Liberals. Now he had set up a new group without public endorsement, without funds or hope of financial support, without a program to win the adherence of any substantial sector of the electorate. Most encouraging, he had weakened the Liberals, the only strong opposition to the coalitionists.

The Liberals were equally scornful but less amused. Muñoz's final departure from the Liberal ranks was followed by the old party's most fervent believers in social reform and in independence.

Their names were destined to become part of Puerto Rico's political history.

Ernesto Ramos Antonini led the list. He was already known for his defense of the Nationalists accused in the case of the Ponce Massacre. Jesús Piñero, head of the Sugar Tenant Farmers' Association, was known and loved throughout the countryside for his simple honesty and personal charm. Samuel Quiñones, a brilliant young lawyer, Dr. Fernós-Isern, Antonio Berríos Berdecía, and Emilio Colón all came from the alert and eager professional side of the middle class. They were joined by Elmer Ellsworth, a moneyed American idealist who considered himself something of an agricultural expert, and Josefina and Felisa Rincón, fiery sisters prominent in the garment workers union. There were others: Jaime Benítez, brilliant young university professor who had been suspended for his stand on the issue of language teaching in the schools; and Inés Mendoza, the young teacher whose dismissal had brought her into Muñoz Marín's orbit.

There was also an ex-Nationalist university professor named Antonio Colorado, with an amateur's flair for drawing. In the secrecy of his study he sketched the symbol that would identify the new party: a profile of a *jíbaro* wearing the typical countryman's straw hat. On an island where the illiteracy rate was still high, party lists on the ballots were headed by symbols, and Muñoz sought one that would be easily recognized by his potential followers.

When Colorado brought the drawing to the party meeting, Muñoz scrutinized it carefully. The group drew about their new chief and peered at the drawing with nods of approval. Muñoz pushed away the usual half-empty coffee cup and put out the constant cigarette. Dressed in a sport shirt, as always, he leaned his bare arms on the wooden table and printed under the drawing the words: *Pan— Tierra—Libertád* (Bread—Land—Liberty). Holding it up, he announced it as the party's first poster. Then he lit another cigarette. Someone brought another coffee. Muñoz's colleagues went back to their chairs, scraping them along the floor of the loft that was their meeting place. Then Muñoz spoke, explaining as he had before, the difference between freedom and independence.

Man, he said, could not find freedom in political independence alone. He must first be liberated from the binding grip of hunger. He must be relieved of the ubiquity of filth, and escape from the ex-

posure of seminakedness. He must have a shelter safe from rain or
the burning heat. His freedom requires a fair chance to live without
sickness wringing his intestines, boiling his blood, or throbbing in
his head. He needs an opportunity to earn a living and to work
without the nagging fear that disease and malnutrition may be
debilitating his children. Liberty, if a man is industrious enough, includes a parcel of land on which he may raise some food for his
family and, luckily, a bit more to sell. Freedom is being a man, not
a beast of burden. When this liberty is won, and only then, can
political bonds be challenged as obstacles to liberty. Then independence might mean liberty too.

As Muñoz talked, his small audience was intent, some quickly
understanding the first words of his softly spoken message, others
responding to the rising inflection in his final phrases. There were
those who still believed the crusade would be only a stepping-stone
to a final thrust for independence. These followers had to be convinced before Muñoz could ask them to go to the people. He was
tireless, lucid and, finally, persuasive. The first public pronounce-
ment from the Popular Democratic party was: "Status is not an
issue." Statehood, independence, or any other system of political
status would not be the subject of the Popular party's argument. A
decent life for the people of Puerto Rico would be its goal.

But Santiago Iglesias had made the same declaration when he
formed the Socialist party fourteen years ago. He had also made the
same plea that the Popular party was about to propose to the people:
"Don't sell your vote." He had known then that his funds could
not match those of the wealthier opposition and that the skeptical
jíbaro thought the dollar or two for his vote was worth more than
the politicians' promises. And Santiago Iglesias had not been heard.
How could Muñoz Marín, without even the support of the labor
unions who had backed Iglesias, expect to reach the Puerto Rican
masses who had just recently observed his failure with the Liberal
party? It would not be through the press, for the island's leading
newspapers were on the side of his opposition. *La Democracia* was
defunct. Only a few dusty presses remained to print the party's post-
ers and some handbills. Not through the radio, because the Populares
could not pay for time on the air. Not through the party organization,
because it was newer, smaller, and poorer than its opposition. Not by
means of those night-long meetings in the creaky, cramped quarters of

the zealots who gathered about Muñoz Marín ready to talk interminably about the project before them.

These followers were seeing what seemed to be a changed Muñoz Marín. In truth the man had not altered; he had marshaled his formerly dispersed energies for a single purpose. Although he was still ready to talk until dawn, now the conversation must revolve about the strategy of victory in the 1940 election. There was no time for philosophical or poetic exploration. Although he still enjoyed his rum and his food and wine, he was ready to go on rations to accumulate dollars for campaigning. The humor that he preserved, and the love of parables and stories, became gunshot against the adversary and support for the Populares argument. The surging energy that had never measured time for rest demanded that all who joined him put aside their private lives and sacrifice all reserve of their own resources.

He had decided that he and his supporters must go directly to the people, that they must speak clearly and honestly to every man and woman in Puerto Rico if possible. They must listen, too, to learn what was really in the heart of the people before the Popular party's program would be announced. They must leave San Juan, disperse throughout the island, appoint local leaders where they could. They must first make two points clear: one, that the island's political status must not be an issue in the election, for status could not solve the problem of the people; second, that the people must not sell their votes, for by doing so they abdicated their right to participate in their government. Once this was understood, Muñoz reasoned, the people could freely decide to support or reject the program that the Popular party would offer. With this plan established in the party councils, Muñoz sought the first means for his campaign.

He needed a car and a driver "who could make an automobile move without gasoline, who could live without food, and who would work for pennies a day." He found two brothers, Erasmus and Virgilio, who believed in Muñoz and were charmed by him. There was also a friend named Raul Gándara, even taller and brawnier than Muñoz. The car lacked the youth and energy of its drivers, but it moved into the countryside bearing its evangelist in his sport shirt, leaving behind the scatter of cigarette butts that traced Muñoz's path over the island.

Whenever Muñoz encountered two or more men by the side of the road, he stopped the car and engaged the countrymen in conversation. He talked with them as he had talked with people in his New York apartment and as he has conversed ever since. He spoke well, clearly, with imagery, and with sincerity; and he listened with deep attention, his large eyes fixed on the other speaker as he weighed the man's thoughts. Listening, questioning, he soon learned that the *jíbaro* cared much less for the island's status than for his own chances of survival. Although the Populares' declaration that status was not an issue may have caused a mixture of consternation, perplexity, and amusement in political circles, the man of the soil found it logical enough.

These roadside discussions also convinced Muñoz that the purchase of votes was far more menacing to his campaign than the question of Puerto Rico's political status. The long disappointed and defrauded *jíbaro* could easily believe that political status meant little to him. He might succumb to the charm and logic of Muñoz while conversing with him and so agree that selling a vote was like selling a birthright. But recalling the futile past, would the *jíbaro* on election day be ready to reject two dollars and gamble on a man expelled by the Liberals, who were still in the race? Muñoz's argument became a litany, a fugue, and a rondo.

"I know two dollars will buy a lot of beans and rice for your family. But if you don't sell your vote, you can use it to get justice for your family. So remember: Justice or two dollars. But you can't have both.

"Parties that win elections by buying votes do not need to comply with their promises to the people. They are obliged to take orders from those who provided the money to buy the votes.

"If you sell your vote, you sell your rights in your government. You sell the future of your children."

Then the *jíbaros*, first intrigued by the famous man who sat beside them at a roadside bar and talked in an idiom they could understand, then charmed by his stories, his ready smile, his obviously deep desire to convince them, would ask for the alternative. And if they did not sell their votes—what? "Lend me your vote," answered Muñoz, "if you are satisfied with the program my party offers you. And if we do not comply, vote us out of office in the following election."

But Muñoz could not long delay at least some informal indications of the party's program: land, minimum wages, shorter working days, health measures, elimination of the salt tax, control of prices on basic foods, public health measures, extension of education, much more to be listed when the program would be announced. Word of these promises came back to the opposition, causing alarm to mix with the derision with which Muñoz's campaign was being observed. This obvious socialist must not be allowed to run wild without comment. Newspapers began to carry the sarcastic attacks of Coalition and Liberal party leaders. The Popular party meetings were called "the boys' club." Muñoz was accused of being a Communist and finally obtained a letter from the parish priest of Humacao absolving him of the charge. He was called an anti-American and eventually produced a letter from American federal judge Cecil Snyder absolving him of this charge. The owner of a large sugar holding on the southern shore barred Muñoz from the property, but he slogged over the beach in the night to find the workers waiting there to hear him.

When Antonio Barceló died in October, 1938, Puerto Ricans were still more interested in the fortunes of the Liberal party and its opposition, the coalitionists, than in the desperate efforts of Muñoz Marín. The leadership of the Liberals fell to José Ramírez Santibáñez, whose almost immediate search for new alliances followed the lowest standards of Puerto Rican political action. Muñoz must have wondered, momentarily, what would have happened had he stayed with the Liberal party. Would he have succeeded to its leadership?

There was no time for reflection. Petitions to inscribe the Popular party in the 786 voting districts were lagging. The *jíbaro* was not yet massed behind the straining new party chief. New measures were taken.

Jesús Piñero was asked to return from Washington, where he was representing the Sugar Tenant Farmers' Association, to go out and talk in the countryside. Piñero was a wise choice. His mild manners, easy smile, and relaxed plump figure were a disarming background for his crusading message.

The party obtained a recorder so that copies of Muñoz's speeches could be distributed for replaying, since the radio stations were still closed to the restricted Popular budget. And in the tradition of

Puerto Rican politics, the party rolled its own newspaper out of the rusty presses that had produced *La Democracia*. This was called *El Batey*, taken from an Indian name for the clearing beside a country hut where the family and friends gather for talk in the evening and on Sundays. Muñoz wrote the entire first issues himself. Other party members attempted to finance the publication through the sale of advertising.

Meanwhile José Ramírez Santibáñez engineered a turnabout for the Liberal party resulting in a statement to favor statehood. The remaining independence-minded group who had not followed Muñoz out of the party defected now and strengthened the ranks of the Populares. Here was encouragement to Muñoz's heart, and, more important, money to help with the Popular party campaign's mounting needs. Good news also came from the field, with reports of Piñero's travels. Jesús had adroitly packed first-aid medicines in his car, and he had located a trailer, an antique movie projector, and some old films. He ministered to the sick who could be aided by aspirin and iodine while entertaining others who could not ordinarily afford cinema entertainment. He had troubles, but he was getting petitions signed. His technique for attracting a movie audience was to fire a few rockets into the dark stillness of the countryside. After the show Piñero would deliver the message. One night he lost the opportunity to do this when the rockets went off before going up, and the gathering crowd spent the night putting out the fire started in a canefield.

Now Muñoz was driving himself beyond credited endurance. His meetings were scheduled for evenings and Sundays, when people were not working. His car was rumbling over the starlit countryside. The gatherings awaiting him were becoming larger, more enthusiastic. They were talking about him, stimulated by the prospect of hearing his stories. He was gaining a new name, one that has never left him. He was El Vate, the Bard. He was going without meals or sleep, sustaining himself on cigarettes, shots of rum, and fervor. But stories of his adventures preceded him and attracted crowds.

One night some hundred followers gathered to hear him in the *barrio* Guayabota de Yabucoa. There was nowhere else to go that night, and the only sleeping accommodations were four cots in a shack. Neighbors found six more cots. *Jíbaro* strategy devised a solution. One *jíbaro* brought a guitar and a dance was started in the clearing. With two in a cot, twenty of the party could sleep while the others sang; and after two hours they would give their beds to the next twenty participants. The dancing and singing continued all night, while exhausted members of the party each slept at least two hours before rejoining the dance. At dawn Muñoz, laughing and shaking hands with all the crowd, pushed into the car. As the *jíbaros* watched it rattle down the road, they saw Muñoz's head fall back on the seat, his eyes closed in sleep. As the car disappeared around a bend, the *jíbaros* joined to shout the Popular party's new fighting slogan: *Jalda arriba!* (Up the hill). New onlookers were cheering for a new Sisyphus as he urged the rock up the mountain-side.

El Batey, meanwhile, was becoming successful, eventually reaching more readers than all the other island newspapers combined. Members of opposition parties found themselves compelled to use it as an advertising medium. It was no longer a financial burden. Muñoz's campaign was throwing the opposition off balance. The reaction was a series of political maneuvers that produced another new party.

In Jackson Heights, New York, Ramírez Santibáñez met with Prudencio Rivera Martínez, leader of a dissident Socialist faction, and Miguel Angel García Méndez, representing defectors from the Republican group. These three decided to form the Tripartite party, in the belief that they were duplicating Muñoz Rivera's feat in establishing the Unionist party in 1904. Since they attracted only splinter groups from the three parties they purported to represent, they only succeeded in destroying the Liberal organization and weakening the coalition. There was jubiliation in the ranks of the Populares. A stronger ring of confidence entered the tones of Muñoz Marín's speeches. El Vate went on the road again.

Drama often attended his travels. In one town, late at night, his car ran out of gas and the sole service-station owner, a Republican, refused to sell him any fuel. Muñoz with some difficulty restrained his driver from burning down the man's home, while he sought the police chief to order the sale of a few gallons of gasoline. But it was a different story on another night, in the town of Guánica, where the Americans had landed in 1898. Muñoz was late for a rally in

the next town, Lajas, and again his driver roused the only service-
station owner, again a rigid Republican, to beg the purchase of a few
gallons.

"I will vote against him a hundred times if I can," said the
gas-station proprietor, "but he is our greatest patriot—let's fill his
tank." When the car rattled into Lajas at one-thirty in the morning,
Muñoz found the town square full of waiting townspeople.

Still another time, while he was speaking to a crowd in Sábana
Grande, his driver, Raul Gándara, moved quietly through the crowd
begging money for gasoline to go on to the next town. He collected
ten dollars, enough to take Muñoz across the island. But as Muñoz
was warming to his speech, the cry of "Fire!" was heard, and an old
woman in the crowd screamed.

Muñoz stopped abruptly and stared about. People were already
running from the outskirts of the crowd. As the speaker's eyes followed them, he saw the fire demolishing a shack a few blocks from
the square. It burned quickly. In minutes a home had been destroyed
and the crowd had gathered around a weeping old woman.

Raul Gándara had reached Muñoz and handed him the ten dollars.
The campaigner's voice rose again, and the crowd straggled back to
his makeshift platform. Holding the ten dollars high over his head,
Muñoz offered it as the start of a collection to buy boards and nails
to rebuild the old woman's home. The crowd willingly added its
pennies and nickels to the fund, and neighbors offered to do the
carpentry, and before the meeting ended the destitute woman was
promised a new house.

What happened another night was probably one of the most
moving experiences in Muñoz Marín's lifetime. The growing impetus
of his campaign was arousing sharper resistance, especially as landowners interpreted his appeal to their workers as incitement to a sort
of class warfare. Increasingly this opposition tried to obstruct the
night meetings and Sunday rallies that attracted the *jíbaros*. Threats
of dismissal became common. When Muñoz was known to be ap-
proaching a certain area, employers tried to bar their workers from
leaving the haciendas. But now Muñoz was in possession of a loudspeaker to carry his voice into the canefields.

It was a clear night, lit by Puerto Rico's tropical profusion of
stars, when Muñoz and his helper made the ascent in a road to a

clearing where he was scheduled to speak. They climbed out of the car and set up the loudspeaker. Muñoz drew his last puff on a cigarette and crushed out the stub in the dirt. Then he looked about. To hear his talk, there were only two or three *jíbaros* standing by the road, and innumerable fireflies chasing each other in the bushes by the roadside. He needed no loudspeaker for them.

But where were the people whose shacks were huddled in these hills? Where were the people who lived behind the mango trees whose great branches loomed in the star-studded sky?

One of the *jíbaros* pointed to the microphone and amplifier and smiled. "Go ahead," he said, "talk. Talk loud."

Nearly alone on a hillside overlooking a softly sloping valley, Muñoz stood on the running board of the car and began his speech, feeling a bit foolish as well as chagrined. He had spoken only a few minutes when he perceived tiny lights burning in the blanket of darkness before him. Then he noticed more coming on, and more, until they seemed as numerous as the fireflies. Questioningly, he looked aside at the grinning *jíbaro*.

"They light their candles," he explained, "to let you know they can hear you. Go on. Talk to them."

Muñoz talked to them that night and continued talking other nights. As his campaign gathered speed and power, more changes occurred in the opposition's camp. Most important, and most saddening, was the death on December 5, 1939, of Santiago Iglesias.

Iglesias, resident commissioner in Washington since 1932 and dean of Puerto Rican politics, died of malaria, a disease he contracted while attending a labor conference in Mexico City. United States congressmen made the trip to Puerto Rico to attend his funeral. The American flag flew at half mast in Washington. Some years later, on the eighth anniversary of Iglesias' death, Muñoz Marín acknowledged the old warrior's endowment to Puerto Rico.

The history of our people during the last half century cannot be written without the name of Santiago Iglesias appearing prominently in the pages of the story. Iglesias taught the workers . . . their rights in the scheme of social justice. He showed them that there is strength in union and he won many great gains of true worth for the laborer.

Successor to the leadership of the Socialist sector of the coalition was Iglesias' son-in-law, Bolívar Pagán, a brilliant lawyer whose career had included a judgeship in the town of Fajardo and a term as mayor of San Juan.

On the night of July 21, 1940, one of the largest crowds in San Juan's history converged on the Parque Sixto Escobar, the Polo Grounds of San Juan, named after Puerto Rico's first world-champion boxer. The crowd filled the field where baseball games were usually played; crowded the stands, boxes, and aisles; and overflowed into the streets outside, and into the adjacent public park. The mob was a joining of the *jíbaros* who had been streaming into San Juan all during the day and the Sanjuaneros who had now begun to wonder whether the son of Muñoz Rivera was going to change the history of their island. It was an orderly crowd whose enthusiasm was tempered by a great sense of expectancy. It was rumored that tonight the Popular party would announce its full platform for the 1940 election. Despite the disclaimers of interest in independence that had been made in the countryside, everyone knew that the party leaders had been strongly for independence. No one believed this inflammable issue could be avoided.

The meeting began awkwardly. Muñoz Marín, lost in the mob, was delayed trying to find his way to the platform where the party leaders were waiting for him. It was a tired, bedraggled Don Luis in a mussed sport shirt who finally stood before the sweating throng. On this occasion of the official constituting of the Popular Democratic party, Muñoz Marín was as nervous as a high school valedictorian. A master of polemic in a taproom, on a roadside, or in a town square, the exhausted party leader did not feel up to opening the meeting and turned the gavel over to María Libertád Gómez, the party's vice-president. She then became the first woman to preside over a political assembly in Puerto Rico.

Then Muñoz Marín assumed the role all had come to see him play. He stated that "this meeting of the Popular Democratic party is the first truly democratic act of our public life. For the first time, there will be direct representation from the forgotten countryside of Puerto Rico. . . ."

Quietly he began to read the statement of party policy. The issue of independence was dealt with immediately. Declaring that Puerto

Rico could best fulfill her destiny and best contribute to that of the Americas as an independent state, the proclamation continued:

> . . . no political solution regarding the final status of Puerto Rico should be undertaken without submission to prior consultation with the people of Puerto Rico in a vote especially designated for the situation.

In declaring that the political status is not in controversy in these elections, the Popular Democratic party wants to say that it has a solemn obligation to the people not to interpret the votes cast in favor of the Popular Democratic party as votes in favor of any particular political status.

After the ovation that this statement caused, the party leadership presented its program for approval. Its principal items were:

1. Support for the law limiting corporate land ownership to five hundred acres.
2. Readjustment of taxes.
3. Protection of agriculture and farm rights.
4. Marketplaces for produce and fruit.
5. Agricultural cooperatives.
6. Aid for redemption of foreclosures.
7. Moratorium on uncollectable taxes.
8. A higher sugar quota in the United States market.
9. Designation of sugar as a public industry.
10. Creation of a People's Bank.
11. Minimum wages.
12. Homes for sharecroppers.
13. A Food Commission to reduce the cost of living.
14. Promotion of new industries.
15. Social security against unemployment, disability, old age, maternity, and sickness.
16. Slum clearance.
17. Expedition of personal loans for workers and the middle class.
18. Legislation to encourage organized labor.
19. Legislation against absentee ownership and the coastal shipping regulations.
20. Support of civil liberties.

21. A program for water supply and water power.
22. A commission of all parties to investigate the performance of the majority party in power.
23. A fifty-percent reduction in costs of operating the Capitolio, the Senate and House of Representatives.
24. Elimination of nepotism in government.

The jubilant roars of the Parque Sixto Escobar crowd penetrated the night air to nearby Santurce and across the lagoon to Calle Ponce de León. Faintly they could be heard in old San Juan. The party council was ecstatic about the meeting as a demonstration of popular support.

Muñoz Marín was still troubled. How could a new party prove indisputably that it would fulfill its preelection promises? Its candidates could avow their sincerity, and it might be so genuine that their arguments might be persuasive. But on election day, how would a hungry *jíbaro* maintain such a profound belief in this newly grouped organization as to withstand the offer of two bright hard dollars for his vote for the opposition? He had been duped by promises before. Much as he might admire Muñoz Marín, he might recall that the new leader had been unable to do much for him as a Liberal. And two dollars could feed his family now for a couple of days.

This nagging worry never left Muñoz. It was discernible in his speeches right up to the election. But seeing the problem, he decided to tackle it. On September 15, 1940, Muñoz led a Popular Democratic party rally at a street corner of Santurce known as Parada 22, (Bus Stop 22). There, before a crowd of some fifteen thousand people, half of them hidden in the shadows cast by torchlight, the party leaders again read their program publicly. Then each of the candidates for the island's legislature was presented individually and each man publicly swore to vote, if elected, for every plank in the party platform.

This unique performance, added to the many innovations in Muñoz's campaign, plus the party's adroit handling of the independence issue, attracted attention throughout the island and even in Washington among circles that had given Muñoz up for destroyed in 1937. The Department of the Interior was no exception. Taking its cue from Secretary Harold Ickes, department officers remained cool to Muñoz's effort, tending to favor the new Tripartite party, headed by Miguel Angel García Méndez.

Elsewhere in the United States, however, only a few of Muñoz's old friends were conscious of the Puerto Rican campaign. Franklin Roosevelt was breaking with tradition in his candidacy for a third term as President of the United States, and most of the nation saw the threat of war looming over all other issues. Perhaps it was unfortunate that the rest of the world was so occupied with other affairs, because it lost notice of an almost Shakespearean play on the minds and hearts of men by a poet whose politics were already cast in structures of the future.

As the November election approached, Muñoz worked on his final speeches. He had personally covered over 500 of the 786 electoral districts. Finally, the island's radio network would be open to him for two preelection speeches. The first of these was broadcast on November 3, two nights before the election, probably reaching the largest single radio audience the island had ever known. Those who had heard and met Muñoz, those who had heard of him, those who loved him, and those who prayed for his defeat tensely listened to his words. Muñoz's radio delivery was less impassioned than his personal appearances. The soft voice retained its almost diffident intimacy, but the content of his talk put the entire radio audience on notice. His theme was *"Ahora les toca a ustedes!"* (Now it is up to you).

I appear before you to close this campaign, which has been carried on not merely to bring triumph to the Popular Democratic party. This has also been a campaign to mold a real public out of what others would like to make an electoral herd of sheep. This has been a campaign to urge you who hear me across the countryside and towns of Puerto Rico to act as a people, to begin to save yourselves instead of continuing to act like mere politicians, Republican, Socialist, "Alliancist," Coalitionist, or any other party name. . . .

Weeks, months, years, I have been at this work so that you might learn that . . . the only way to end the misery, the insecurity, the injustice that you have suffered under every party and its hangers-on is in your hands. . . . This part of my work is finished. Now it is up to you!

Listeners were amazed. No man before had talked to them like this. None had thrown upon them responsibility for their own destiny. Only a few realized that Muñoz was this night planting in the spirit of the people the confidence and the power that would cause Puerto Rico to lift itself to an undreamed height of dignity and well-being.

Muñoz did not confine his appeal to the underprivileged. His speech contained a plea and a warning that might have sounded like a prophecy elsewhere in the world, had there been listeners beyond the island.

I speak to the working class, I speak to the agricultural class, I speak to the middle class. And to the powerful ones in this land I speak, because only with justice done with order and in time will chaos be avoided, chaos within a few years, wrought by a people carried to the final limits of misery and desperation!

As he developed his theme, Muñoz paid particular attention to the middle class, knowing that it contained the competent, the professional, and the scholarly, whom he would need to organize and administer the program he had promised to all the people. In offering the Popular Democratic party as the vehicle through which the people could assume their rightful place in their government, he contrasted its policies to the vote-purchasing practices of its opposition:

The Popular Democratic party makes it clear that it does not buy men, it does not buy votes, and he who, calling himself a Popular, is thinking of selling his vote to the Popular Democratic party—and I say this clearly and finally, forty-eight hours before the election—should immediately withdraw from the Popular Democratic party, because this is not a party of animals for sale; this is a party of burdened men and women who know how to defend, as creatures of God, the justice that God wishes they should have in their passage through this life.

Finally Muñoz tackled the problem that had been worrying him so constantly: how an untried party could persuade voters that it would keep its promises.

During this campaign I have told you that . . . no one could be a candidate of the Popular Democratic party for the House or the Senate—where laws are approved—if he did not swear before the people to vote for our proposed laws of social justice. . . . The Popular Democratic party complied with this promise. . . .

I have kept faith with you. Now you keep faith with your own futures.

The next day Puerto Rico's coffee shops profited from Muñoz's speech. His followers were lashed to feverish enthusiasm. His opponents, still disdaining his prospects, were concerned with the militancy of his campaign.

Muñoz Marín again took to the air the night before the election to persuade an eager but frightened electorate that it need only believe in itself, and to remind the people of provisions taken to assure security for the individual voter. He referred to the guarantees promised by the governor who had replaced the trouble-marked Winship. Admiral William D. Leahy was now responsible for orderly government in Puerto Rico, although his tenure would be short. Within a month, he would be asked to serve as ambassador in Vichy, representing the United States in unoccupied France. Now he was one of the few American governors who had gained the respect of the Puerto Ricans.

Throughout the talk, Muñoz drove in the point that democratic action honestly and honorably taken lends greatness to the individual, and he should not allow himself to be corrupted or diverted from its practice.

For all its content of emotion and touches of demagoguery, the speech was a continuation of Muñoz's long lesson in democracy. Those who had credited Muñoz Marín with great foresight might point to this night when he attempted to form a body politic that would cast its votes objectively in judging government action. He knew how he planned to perform, given the opportunity. Now was the time to assure support against political resistance. ". . . And I, who am the chief of the Popular Democratic party, tell you that no one is obliged to be a Popular for all his life. It is the Popular Democratic party that has the obligation to comply with its word first and to bring you justice. But if the Popular Democratic party does the same as the others, does not fulfill its commitment to bring you justice, you, in the future, should repudiate the Popular Democratic party also. . . ."

Finally, Muñoz brought his last preelection message to bear upon the great obstacle before him. Man to man, he felt victorious. Facing the customs that had so long beset the mass of Puerto Ricans, he launched a last, almost despairing plea:

> Let no one stop you from voting! If it rains, remember that the hunger of your entire future is worse than one day's rain. If the rivers rise, remember that the injustice of a lifetime is a current worse than the waters of the rivers of Puerto Rico for a day. If you have no clean change of clothing to wear to the booth, come in your work clothes—there is your future! With your votes you are working for your future. It is not a holiday; it is the most serious day of work since you were born. Better to come in clothing dirty from work than . . . with your soul filthy for having sold your own right to justice, your future and the future of your children—to those who profit in millions by your misery. . . .
>
> Come to vote, as you will. Come seriously. Come without foolishness. You don't win justice with fooling. Come without having one shot of rum or any other intoxicating drink. Come without provoking anyone or allowing yourself to be drawn into provocation. . . .
>
> And above all other things, have faith in yourselves. Believe in yourselves. . . . Have faith in your own honor. . . . Be the men and women that God wanted you to be. . . .

Election Day was peaceful. As provided by reforms legislated in 1936, citizens gathered in designated buildings before two o'clock, voted secretly, departed, and could not again enter a voting area. Each voter was scrutinized by representatives of the contending parties. Police protection assured the carrying out of orderly procedures. Heading each ticket were the candidates for resident commissioner. For the Populares there was Antonio Fernós-Isern; for the coalition, Bolívar Pagán; for the Tripartite party, Miguel Angel García Méndez. With their leader, Albizu Campos, jailed in Atlanta, the Nationalists abstained from entering candidates. Muñoz

Marín, having led the Popular campaign, was a candidate to be senator at large.

As if the radio had become part of their blood, the people of Puerto Rico were again nestled to their speakers that night. Now Muñoz Marín, sitting at home with an old friend and colleague in politics, Jorge Font Saldaña, was part of the anxiously listening public. Earl Parker Hanson, friend, co-worker, recorder of many of the years of Muñoz's maturity, took note of the scene at the Muñoz Marín home. In appearance it was like any other night with friends, men lounging in sport shirts, women keeping the coffee hot, the radio playing—except that tonight the radio was the only voice to which all listened.

Of course there were the interminable descriptions: the weather throughout the island, the scenes of peaceful voting, the reports of a few minor squabbles, the estimates as to the number of voters, the reading of the names of candidates from all districts, the commercials, the brittle dialogue between announcers waiting for the real news. Then came word of the first returns from Bayamón, a town not far from San Juan. A strongly Republican district, it reported a modest registration of coalition (Republican and Socialist) votes and a strong showing by the Populares.

Muñoz, who had been sitting as though prepared to spring at the radio, shouted, "They are doing it! They are doing it! They have refused to sell their votes!"

All conversation stopped as new returns were announced from the mountain districts. The Popular Democratic party was leading in the countryside. Muñoz's shoulders began to shake, tears appeared in his weary eyes, and his voice broke as he turned toward Font Saldaña. "They are doing it, Jorge," he repeated. "Those wonderful people. They are starving and they haven't let me down. They haven't sold their votes!"

As more news crackled over the radio, the atmosphere in the hot room became ebullient. Muñoz's arms were waving. Others were shouting. They must celebrate. This was the hour, this was the goal, this was the mad end of the prayer and the beginning of many more. Muñoz looked about, grinning foolishly. He had no money, no champagne. Prepared to meet all other challenges, he had forgotten any arrangements to greet victory. He turned to Font Saldaña.

"Listen, Jorge. Do you have any whiskey at home?"

The guest rushed to the phone. Miraculously, he got through the usual obstacles of the Puerto Rican telephone company. His cook answered. Panting, he shouted, "Tell my wife—tell Doña Carmen to come here and bring the half-bottle of whiskey that's in the pantry!"

The cook, hearing not only the master's voice but the shouting in the background, reached her own conclusions and ran to the window. "We've won!" she announced. "Listen, all of you out there in the street. We've won! The Populares have won the election!"

The victory of the Populares was not a landslide, but it was a triumph. The party that had fought its way into the forefront of Puerto Rican politics was exuberant. The opponents who had worried over its progress only in the latter days of the campaign were amazed. The electorate, on both sides, was aroused by the drama that Muñoz Marín had wrought by his own sweat, his own aching muscles, his own tired lungs.

The balloting had awarded 224,423 votes to the coalition, 214,857 to the Popular Democratic party, 130,299 to the Tripartite party. Bolívar Pagán, of the coalition, had been elected resident commissioner. The coalition had also placed nine senators and eighteen representatives. The Populares had been awarded ten senators and also eighteen representatives. The Tripartites had the apparent balance of power with three representatives. There were sidelights for the newspapers and the café gossips. The Populares had elected a woman representative, María Libertád Gómez, little heard of before the campaign. They had also chosen as a representative the only American born on the continent ever placed in elected office in Puerto Rico. This was Elmer Ellsworth, a wealthy idealist, fighter for the rights of the common man, and, as detractors said, for the common woman. Another bit of byplay was the defeat in Ponce, still the center of Spanish traditionalism, of Don Pedro Juan Serrallés, patriarch of a wealthy sugar family, by a worker candidate of the Popular party. Almost unnoticed was the loss of the mayoralty of Ponce by Luis Ferré, rich industrialist, to another proletarian Popular contender. Serrallés withdrew to the comforts of his fortune, but more was heard later from Luis Ferré.

For the moment Muñoz, having received the largest vote of the candidates for senator at large, was concerned with his position as president of the Senate. After the governor and the resident commissioner, he held the most influential position in the Puerto Rican government.

He was quickly aware that he had won the responsibility that he sought, and only half of the authority; perhaps less, for after sharing voting power with the coalitionists and the tricky three representatives of the Tripartite group, he had Washington to confront. And the fulfillment of many of his promises depended on American complaisance.

Regardless, Muñoz assumed the role of leadership. The anguish that had been his philosophical burden immediately hardened into almost a physical load from which he would never be relieved. He had assumed the task of saving men's homes without losing their souls. He would never be certain that this could be done, but he would never be able to consider another course. His commitment was made.

Muñoz Marín's triumph in 1940 and the campaign that preceded it were accompanied by a major change in his personal life. Inés Mendoza had taken the place of Muna Lee, and Muñoz had replaced the painter Palacios, who had been Inés' husband. Their home in Isla Verde, the palm grove bordering a sandy cove on the outskirts of San Juan, had already witnessed the birth of a daughter, Viviana. Now another girl was born, and to honor the successful Popular campaign, she was named Victoria.

Inés, the schoolteacher cited for dismissal in 1937 by the committee investigating the island policy on language instruction, had come from the hills of Puerto Rico. She was destined to share the remainder of his career with the man who had dedicated his future to the people of the hills and to all their cousins on the island.

Muna Lee, Muñoz's partner of the twenties and thirties, returned to Washington to continue a career of public service devoted principally to the cultural joining of the peoples of the Americas. When her divorce from Muñoz became final in 1947, he married Inés Mendoza. From a distance, Muna Lee has never ceased to be Muñoz's devoted follower.

ELEVEN

The Tightrope Walker

As HAVE SO MANY public figures, Luis Muñoz Marín became a publicly defined personality during a limited and particular segment of his life span. Prior appraisals were solidified, altered, or negated. Subsequent assessments, though affected by his later performance and statements, stemmed from the continuous praise, vituperation, and analysis that were voiced, written, rumored, and otherwise recorded during the first four years of Muñoz Marín's elective leadership of the Popular party and the Puerto Rican Senate.

The boldness with which he espoused revolutionary economic solutions to the island's problem incited the opinion that he was either a Socialist or an irresponsible bohemian playing with the tools of government. The earnestness he applied to implementing his campaign promises convinced his humble followers that he was a father of the people, a saint, a beloved friend, while persuading his opposition that he was a vengeful devil bent on its destruction. One description of Muñoz made him a sly and hypocritical politician who was eluding the issue of political status until he should have achieved sufficient power to take Puerto Rico out of the American orbit. His patriotic declarations of full adherence to the American cause as the war came closer and his caution in the application of reforms caused the more separatist of his supporters to whisper that he was a timid, worried, and unsure man. His eloquence and rhetoric brought out denunciations of demagoguery. He had even mentioned the criticism obliquely in a post-campaign speech, saying, "How many times have I heard educated and normally sensible people leave Popular party meetings saying: 'I am going because if I stay,

I
La Fortaleza, at the gateway to San Juan harbor, guarded the Spanish city and housed governors from Spain, the United States, and now Puerto Rico.

2
Luis Muñoz Marín, first elected Puerto Rican governor, in 1949 moved into the Fortaleza, within sight of Ponce de León's castle, later residence of U.S. military commander.

3
Winner of Puerto Rican
autonomy from Spain—
Luis Muñoz Rivera,
father of Luis Muñoz
Marín.

4
Práxedes Mateo Sagasta,
Spanish Liberal leader,
ceded to Muñoz Rivera's
demand for Puerto Rican
autonomy on
November 25, 1897. The
next year the American
landing again made the
island subservient.

5
Dr. José Celso Barbosa greeted
the first American landing in
San Juan, founded the Puerto
Rican Republican party.

6
After his father's death Muñoz Marín (left) joined the island's Socialist
party, led by Santiago Iglesias Pantín (right).

7
A *jíbaro*, Puerto Rico's countryman, wears a U.S. infantry hat, carries Christ figurine in his breast pocket.

8

Jíbaro girl shows Spanish, Negro, Indian traces. Her man's guitar and change of clothing hang inside hut.

9
Muñoz in his 100-cigarette-a-day period, before he stopped smoking entirely, worked daylight hours in his garden at Isla Verde.

10
Jíbaro delegates brought their problems to Muñoz Marín's home, discussed them in his garden.

11
Throughout the countryside, *jíbaros* joined the new Popular Democratic party, displayed its banner on the walls of their shacks.

12
Calle Cristo, in old San Juan, still evokes memories of Spanish colonial days.

13
Puerto Rican labor leader confers with the governor over program to improve working conditions.

14
Muñoz Marín carries the Popular
party campaign to all parts of the
island, combines modern
microphone with old-fashioned
shelter.

15
End of the campaign. A triumphant Muñoz Marín casts his ballot for the
Popular party.

16
At the Capitolio. The governor with party leaders Samuel Quiñones,
Senate president (left), and Ernesto Ramos Antonini, former House speaker
(right).

17
Muñoz and Conrad Hilton discuss
Caribe Hilton Hotel's launching of
Puerto Rican tourism promotion.

18
Surge of tourist interest
spurs success of Operation
Bootstrap, encourages new
hotel construction lining
San Juan's beaches.

19
New San Juan low-income housing development sets standard followed throughout the island.

20
Commonwealth Oil Refining Company, near Ponce, cuts island costs for fuel, aids industrial development program.

21
Teodoro Moscoso
(right), former
administrator of
Operation Bootstrap,
proposes new
development plan to the
governor. Moscoso later
became U.S. ambassador
to Venezuela, then U.S.
coordinator for the
Alliance for Progress.

22
The governor with daughter
Mela and grandchildren at a
birthday party.

23
Muñoz kibitzes a pinball
game in a Puerto Rican café.

24
In the stands at a Commonwealth Day parade.
Left to right: Senator J. W. Fulbright, Governor
Luis Muñoz Marín, Doña Inés Mendoza de
Marín.

25
A state visit to the Fortaleza. Left to right: Rómulo Betancourt, former
president of Venezuela; Doña Felisa Rincón de Gautier, mayor of
San Juan; Governor Luis Muñoz Marín.

26
Musicale at the Fortaleza. Left to right: Jesús María Sanromá, Puerto
Rican composer-pianist; President John F. Kennedy; Governor Luis Muñoz
Marín; Mrs. Kennedy.

27
Luis Ferré, leader of the island's Republican
Statehood party, election adversary of Muñoz
Marín.

28
Luis Muñoz Marín, leader of the Popular Democratic party,
guardian of Operation Bootstrap, proponent of commonwealth
status for Puerto Rico.

this man will convince me.' As if anyone in this world would be damaged by being convinced of the truth!"

Because of his brilliant contributions to the program initiated under Muñoz Marín's leadership, Guy Rexford Tugwell's comments about Muñoz have had special value. Tugwell, a professor of political science, was one of Roosevelt's first "brain trusters" as undersecretary of Agriculture, was associated with Mayor La Guardia as chairman of the New York Planning Commission, and was appointed governor of Puerto Rico in August, 1941, less than a year after Muñoz assumed his office. A man of extraordinary intellectual and educational equipment, Tugwell, while becoming an effective administrator, never stopped being a professor who looked upon his colleagues as students. Adversaries were either fools or businessmen, usually both. His cold concentration on techniques rather than people clashed persistently with Muñoz's humanity and with his subtle political sense.

Though recognizing the burden that Muñoz had assumed, Tugwell thought him unable to face it with proper sternness, and he listed as evidences of weakness some characteristics that humbler commentators have called manifestations of strength:

"It was Muñoz's task to check this downward spiral and to start it upward," Tugwell wrote. "It was a heroic work, requiring resolution, ruthlessness, and persistence. He had the resolution—but I was afraid that he lacked the requisite toughness. And I wondered whether he had the persistence. . . .

". . . He would not control his subleaders; he would not require discipline; he was infected with *ay, bendito* (the Puerto Rican shrug for 'what can you do, poor thing?'); he was soft when he needed to be hard. . . .

"He was the kind of person who never really believed that others' motives were self-interested and so inimical to the public good. It seemed sometimes that he always thought everyone but me at least partly right, and probably his rejection of my advice was because it was hard. This trait of his was so overmastering that he always found excuses even for those who betrayed him." *

* Rexford Guy Tugwell, *The Stricken Land* (New York: Doubleday & Company, Inc., 1947), p. 9.

This Tugwellian interpretation, though highly personal, did stem from some of Muñoz's more apparent characteristics. But the viewpoint of an opposition that came close to hysteria as Muñoz and Tugwell pursued their reforms took little note of the softness and sweetness in Muñoz that Tugwell decried. An article in *El Mundo* written by the secretary of the Tripartite party was in considerable conflict with Tugwell's views:

> Hitler, speaking against Czechoslovakia in the Munich beer hall, did not express himself with more vitriol, with more petulance, and with less sense of justice, democracy, and political diplomacy than Luis Muñoz Marín over the radio last Saturday.

This article alluded to Muñoz's appeal to the people to force its representatives to approve the budget for the fiscal year 1940–41. The Tripartite group had been uncooperative because it had not been able to obtain the commissioner of labor post in return for its parliamentary support. The article went on to announce the withdrawal of the three Tripartite votes from the Popular program, leaving Muñoz without a voting majority in the House, and to denounce "the chloroforming propaganda about social justice of this Puerto Rican Goebbels."

The insult did not draw Muñoz into personal controversy. The Spanish blood that had led his father into a number of duels and other personal encounters of a less dignified nature was tempered in Muñoz by humor. This, of course, further infuriated his enemies, but American congressional committees came to enjoy their tilts with Muñoz for the crackle of his wit and the kindness of his humor. *The Congressional Record* preserves his statement when once twitted about his predilection for Puerto Rican independence: "Without in the least wanting to belittle the memory of George Washington, I must say that I am unalterably opposed to the use of violence for the achievement of independence."

His dispute with the coalition resident commissioner, Bolívar Pagán, during a congressional hearing, caused merriment in Washington and Puerto Rico. Pagán had been insistently playing on the conservatism of the committee by asking Muñoz if the Popular party were not socialistic. Muñoz finally stated that it was shaped, without doctrine, to the needs of Puerto Rico, but as to its being socialistic, he would have to refer the matter to Pagán, since he was the head of the Socialist party on the island.

Those who knew Muñoz, and those who are close to him now, have seen him as a man of great compassion who in 1940 had been given the trust he had asked for, and who was driven by a compulsion to redeem the pledge he had made to the electorate. The greater part of the opinion of Muñoz formed in the early forties reflects the anguish he felt for suffering, the essential tenderness of his spirit, and a dedication able to use the resources of political power to induce a people to work out its own solutions to its own problems.

The machinations of politics, without this motivation, were distasteful to Muñoz. Soon after the 1940 election he fled from office seekers to the repose of Elmer Ellsworth's country home, partly also to recover his exhausted energies. He asked that no one be admitted to see him but members of his family and any *jíbaro* who might call. Earl Parker Hanson has recorded the story of the aged *jíbaro* who sold two chickens to raise the bus fare to Muñoz's hideout. The old man said that he had promised the Virgin that he would make the trip and kneel to her in the presence of Muñoz if he were elected.

Muñoz responded, "A man must keep his promises. . . . And there is no reason why I should not kneel too. Let us kneel together."

When the *jíbaro* was ready to leave, others in the party told Muñoz how he had sold the chickens to pay his way and now had no return fare. They suggested that Muñoz pay for his round trip. Muñoz's answer was, "When a man offers you his soul, do you give him change?" Then he sent the countryman home in his own car.

The ingenuousness of Muñoz has surprised even the most prepared of his contemporaries. Many have described an intense meeting joined by the children of the family. In the midst of a profound discussion over political or economic issues, a child may wander into the room, happily climb on Muñoz's lap, and sit there wide-eyed while he continues the conversation, one hand waving in the air, the other caressing the infant.

The poet in Muñoz has found many expressions, the major one politics. But many of the surprises best remembered by his almost idolatrous friends go back to the tumultuous years of the early forties. This was a time when Antonio Colorado, who had designed the Popular symbol, was often with Muñoz when he attempted to escape the battlefield. On one of these walks in the country, the

talk led to the question of God's existence. "Let's not be so preten-
tious as to question it," suggested Muñoz. They walked on.
Muñoz stopped by a tree and gently rubbed its bark. "I wonder if
it is alive like us," he mused. Then he looked at Colorado. "Maybe
it sings," he said.

Another time, the two friends went fishing. Neither was much of
a fisherman. They wanted only to loll in the hot Caribbean sun
and watch the blue waves slosh rhythmically against the small boat.
They had brought a fisherman along to perform the function jus-
tifying the trip. He soon caught a barracuda. The three men brought
him into the boat, shouting while they stumbled about to avoid
the slashing teeth of the killer fish. The gnarled fisherman found a
club and crashed it against the barracuda's head. Colorado turned
to see Muñoz, the fighting leader of his people, crouching at the end
of the boat, unable to watch the blows rain on the barracuda.

Muñoz's sense of personal honor was so great that he did not
feel the need for formal manifestation of his dignity. Nor was he
impressed by the trappings of office. He wore a necktie only when
required and took it off as soon as relieved of the occasion. Money
has never meant anything to him, his own or anyone else's, except
that necessary to maintain a decent standard of living in Puerto
Rico. His man-of-the-people image was so genuine that critics com-
pounded it with his eloquence as part of a demagogic pose.

The compelling force that drove Muñoz relentlessly toward his
distant objectives often blinded him to the personal desires of those
working with him. If they were allied with him in the effort to
bring dignity and comfort to the people of this island, they must be
joined in his utter forgetfulness of food, sleep, family, and money.
His associates were expected to share his sixteen-hour day and his
obliviousness to material reward.

In later years some associates tired of the strain of giving their un-
remunerative love to Muñoz's cause. He could never understand
their desire for rewards more immediate than the building of the
Puerto Rican people. Raul Gándara, the burly companion of his
first campaign, was later appointed insular fire chief and, unofficially,
stage manager for public political appearances. His loyalty was eventually tried when another branch of the government, one of the
bright, prosperous new agencies, offered him a post at twice his
salary.

Gándara accepted, then called on Muñoz to tell him of his decision. Muñoz listened quietly, looking over his huge desk. Then, wiping his face with one hand, he replied, "I am annoyed because they made you the offer without consulting me. Of course I know it is an autonomous agency, but I think they owe me the courtesy."

"I thought they had told you," said Gándara nervously.

Muñoz shook his head. "No. But that does not matter. And if you want to go—" He began to shuffle papers on his desk.

"It isn't that I want to go," pleaded Gándara, "but it is twice the money. I've worked for you long and hard. I have a family. And I will still be working for you in the other agency."

Muñoz nodded. "You are right. I know you will do well at the job. I hope you will be happy in it."

Gándara rose and moved toward the door of the office. His hand on the knob, he turned. "Well, good-bye, Don Luis. By the way, who will you get to replace me?"

Muñoz gazed up at Gándara with the eyes that so few have been able to resist. "I don't know," he said. "You leave me with another problem."

Gándara hesitated, then moved back to the desk. "Never mind, Don Luis," he said. "I will solve that problem for you. I will stay."

"Thank you," said Muñoz simply.

Raul Gándara is still insular fire chief of Puerto Rico. He has, however, filled out his income, at times by writing radio soap operas for the island's advertisers.

Back from his respite in the country, Luis Muñoz Marín, president of the Senate of Puerto Rico, served notice on his people that their lesson in democracy had not been terminated by the act of his election, advised the Senate of Puerto Rico that its course in political science was just beginning, and warned whatever governor Washington might send him that he would be expected to share the responsibilities the electorate had placed upon the island's government. He made it immediately clear that his campaign words were not to be taken lightly.

"Basic economic and social problems of our country were taken up in the course of the public discussion that preceded the election," he stated in his discourse at the opening of the legislative session on February 10, 1941. "What has given vital importance to that discussion . . . is the apprenticeship, unbelievably short, by our people, the mass of our people, before it came to share in the consideration of the problems, give its decision, and establish its mandate. . . ."

Realizing that he had only a one-vote majority in the Senate, that the balance of power in the House rested with the three Tripartite delegates, and that a new governor would soon be coming to the island, Muñoz rolled his words sternly through the great Senate hall. There should be no misunderstanding that all legislators were joined in the view of the Puerto Rican people:

The land problem was specifically discussed before the people. The people were asked if they wanted the breaking up of concentrated landholdings. . . . The people were clearly told that on their votes depended the decision as to whether this land policy be followed or not.

Relentlessly, inexorably, item by item, Muñoz tolled the pledges to which he meant to bind his hearers:

. . . The resolve to lower the price of staple foods and raw materials was explained to the people. The people, by their votes, directed that this policy be followed. . . .

There was expressed the intention to establish general minimum wage legislation. . . . The people, by their votes, ordered . . . that this public policy be carried out. . . .

There was expressed the intention to abolish the salt tax. . . . The people, by their votes, directed that the salt tax be abolished.

It was proposed that the tax of two percent that burdens both trade and consumers be likewise abolished. The people, by their votes, directed that such tax be abolished.

And to the repeated applause of his supporters and the nervous squirming of his opposition, Muñoz continued through the program, concluding: "For these purposes, and subject to these orders, the people have elected us. Here we are."

Finally he added his warning to the new American governor. "The governor, likewise, when considering whether to sign or to veto a bill, gives decisive consideration, according to the principles of democracy, as to whether that bill represents the will of the people as expressed in the election."

He then summarized the simple spirit of his goals:

> Behind the purposes clearly ordained by the people at the election; behind the specific legislation that seeks the way to attain these purposes; behind the travail of the spirit and the mind in the exercise of democracy, what the people of Puerto Rico require, what they demand, what they will be satisfied with can be reduced to these two words: work and live.

The words were left with Muñoz's listeners, and their comments filled the cafés of Puerto Rico. He was the greatest of patriots. He was a demagogue. He was a saint. He was a master politician.

But Muñoz was already at work. His first major legislative accomplishment was the passage of the Land Law and its establishment of the Land Authority. Muñoz was the architect of this law. In obtaining its sanction in April, 1941, he displayed a combination of boldness and sagacity that only his most ardent followers had ascribed to him. Land had in various parts of the world been the symbol of revolution. Its confiscation had been dramatically a part of the Russian Revolution; its redistribution in Mexico had been associated with the firing squad; the lands of the aristocracy and the Church in Spain had been an incitement to a cruel civil war. In the American mind land as private property was part of a sacred system. Overlooked was the historical American solution. Our government had asserted ownership, then had parceled it out to homesteaders.

Now Muñoz proposed to enforce the law placed on the books at his father's instigation by the Foraker Act in 1901, limiting individual land ownership to five hundred acres. Muñoz's statesmanship in devising the Land Law provided a later example for emerging nations. His project was based on respect for the rights of property holders. It was designed neither for vengeance nor control. Its motivation was the creation of incentive for the mass of agricultural workers. The structure of the law surprised the critical Tugwell for its "inventiveness," frightened many among the wealthy class for its assertion that Muñoz was determined to proceed with his program, and through its skillful application of economic realities won the respect of those whose interest in Muñoz had been checked by caution.

The Land Authority was empowered to purchase for just compensation lands held in excess of the five-hundred-acre limitation. But since sugar could not be cultivated profitably by small landowners, the new tracts were to be held and administered by the government. To the extent feasible, the sugar mills would remain in private hands. Managers and laborers on the government fields would be paid wages, and to those wages would be added proportionate shares of the profits.

Adjacent to the large tracts operated by the government, small plots would be parceled out to homesteaders for subsistence farming. Their proximity to the government estates would provide the small farmers some extra work and income. The small farms would be clustered into villages supplied with electricity, water, and sanitary facilities.

The pace of the operation would be set by the funds the government could make available for its financing. In a very short time these funds would come from a source undreamed of, even by Muñoz, and would be ready by the time the administrative paraphernalia had been established for implementing the law.

The steady progress of the Land Authority's work was not without problems. Within seven years it owned and leased (putting many private entrepreneurs back on the land) over 110,000 acres of cane, one third of the island's sugar land. It employed twenty percent of the sugar workers, owned two sugar mills as a control over the privately owned mills, and had established 143 rural villages settled by 17,631 subsistence-farmer families. Its own forty-eight proportional-benefit tracts had paid out $1,244,000 in profits to their workers. In four of the projects production had risen 78.4 percent, against the average insular increase of 19.4 percent.

A major worry to government land administrators was the competition of the still privately held properties with their increasing use of laborsaving machinery. The government had to decide whether to mechanize and reduce employment or spread the labor and reduce proportional benefits. The decision to do the latter somewhat negated its hope to increase average income and subjected the government operation to the jibes of the private sector. It was disappointed, too, by the tendency of workers to consider that they had merely exchanged employers rather than become involved in the management of a project.

Another concern was the slumlike nature of the new villages. Not until years later, when an executive of the Social Programs Administration, Luis Rivera Santos, devised a method of building simple concrete bungalows with outside latrines for $300 each, was the problem largely solved. The method was for the government to put down the foundation and provide the materials for the family to finish the job with the help of its neighbors, making a down payment of $30 and the remainder at $2.25 a month.

Even rabid opponents of the plan had to admit that its invention was Puerto Rican, that its administration was Puerto Rican, and that, as it turned out, its financing was Puerto Rican.

On May 28, 1941, Luis Muñoz Marín stood before the graduating class of the University of Puerto Rico and made some remarkable statements. The leader of a new political party on a small Caribbean island revealed a prescience of world affairs to be expected of a practiced statesman. He spoke as though the United States were already fighting on the Allied side in World War II. He clearly indicated that the war was releasing the forces of social revolution throughout the world. He pointed to the position to be sought for Puerto Rico in the coming realignment of social responsibilities.

In his rumpled white suit, the tall, black-haired legislator spoke softly to the youthful audience on that steaming day in May.

"This is a time," he said, "when civilization will be graduated or be hanged. You have graduated. The joining of the immense reality with your personal reality will form the framework of destiny for each of you. . . ."

After describing the mobilization of peoples under two major ideologies, Muñoz said of those on the side of democracy: "The people in the democratic area of the world do not believe it sufficient to return to the democracy that existed before. . . . The extension of the democratic concept, I believe, has to be translated into two words. . . . These words are: social security." He was not referring to the specific legislation. He said that social security is "that which makes man free of hunger, of the misery of his children, of fear for his own old age, of fear for his own liberty, free for the most noble expression of his own life."

As he developed this theme, Muñoz seemed to give proof to the adversaries who accused him of being a socialist at heart. "The old concept of economic democracy to the effect that a great many people have an equal opportunity to convert themselves into a few millionaires no longer satisfies or appeals. . . . The objective is not opportunity for a few among many. . . . The object is that no one become a beggar or a slave to extreme poverty."

Muñoz also seemed to say that although he had foregone the issue of Puerto Rico's political status in order to embark on an economic crusade, he meant to return to it at the proper time. "Puerto Rico defends democracy and practices democracy, without having it entirely. . . . The world could call us 'the servants of liberty,' those who serve liberty without being a clear part of it."

He was willing and anxious that Puerto Rico should give its labor and its lives to the cause for which he presumed the United States would fight, but he expected something in return. "I assume that on the day of victory, the victory will be the same for Puerto Rico as for all the sectors who comprise the corps fighting for democracy in this world."

In a short and simple address, Muñoz again seemed to combine the seer and the politician. He anticipated the Atlantic Charter, which President Roosevelt and Prime Minister Churchill would announce three months later as a pledge to worldwide social revolution. He appeared to expect the American entrance into the war, which occurred before the end of the year. He restated Puerto Rico's demands for a greater measure of self-government, which he would support aggressively within two years.

His legislative action was a race with the looming event that would finally establish the United States as a belligerent. A parade of bills was shoved through the legislature to assure the base of Muñoz's program: social progress. Minimum wages, shorter hours, elimination of the salt tax and sales tax, social-security provisions—all were moved past the dazzled legislators, by force when Muñoz had it, by wheedling and cajoling when he did not. The three Tripartite representatives in the House were his teachers and his curse. If he had not been before, the three made a politician of Muñoz. Compromises and the prospect of jobs for their constituents were Muñoz's weapons in seeking these crucial votes. When the Tripartites attempted to extort too much for their support, Muñoz foraged among the coalition group for defectors and found them just often enough to meet his needs.

The necessity for balance among these prickly politicians accentuated Muñoz's demand for absolute loyalty from the Populares. Not one man could be spared from a voting session; not one defector could be condoned. Such control was challenged, however, by the tendency of the Popular party to fall into three groups. The old-line politicians inclined toward Francisco Susoni, vice-president of the Senate and political boss for Muñoz. Susoni handled most job requests, keeping the file of applicants in a shoebox that he carried between his home and the senate office.

The second sector of the party tended to follow Ramos Antonini, the gay and brilliant lawyer who had become the leader for organized labor on the island. Ramos Antonini obtained a federal stipulation of minimum wages in Puerto Rico, then successfully sued the sugar interests to force their compliance with the law. He was to become a notable figure in labor congresses in many countries. In Puerto Rico he was the nemesis of the employer class, long feared as the "demagogue" who might, upon succeeding Muñoz, lead Puerto Rico toward independence.

The third group of Populares were primarily influenced by Samuel Quiñones, speaker of the House, Vicente Géigel Polanco, writer of much of the party legislation, and the indefatigable Felisa Rincón, who later, in 1946, became mayor of San Juan and eventually the most famous lady mayor in the Americas. Behind this trio was an assemblage of writers and intellectuals whose passion for the island's independence often shook the tightrope along which Muñoz was striving to balance his way to the 1944 election.

Muñoz rapidly concluded that his strongest weapon for keeping this spirited assortment of followers within the bounds of party discipline and for overwhelming a stubborn opposition outside was the support of the people. The continued publication of *El Batey*, recourse to the radio, and as many personal visits to the villages as his time would permit were continuous techniques of communication with a growing mass of constituents.

However, the political strategist in Muñoz warned him not to leave a flank exposed, and when the first legislative session of 1941 closed, he went to Washington and New York. Almost by chance, his visit met immediate success. On Saturday, August 30, when he was leaving his hotel in New York to spend a weekend with friends in Connecticut, he received a letter from Eleanor Roosevelt inviting him to lunch at Hyde Park. There Muñoz found an assembly of notables and an audience of the Roosevelts' neighbors gathered to hear the President's annual Hyde Park message to the nation.

At the end of the discourse, the President turned to Muñoz and announced, "We have with us a very distinguished visitor. I can almost call him Prime Minister of a part of America which is also part of the United States. Mr. Muñoz Marín is president of the Senate of Puerto Rico." The statement was immediately flashed to Puerto Rico, where it evoked memories of the brief period when Luis' father, Muñoz Rivera, had been known as "Premier." It also aroused fury on the part of the opposing coalition, which had won the majority of popular votes in the 1940 election. The Popular party leader was acting like and being received as the chief of a majority party.

Upon his return to Puerto Rico for the fall legislative session, Muñoz realized that he had quickly to utilize the forces favorable to him because some of them contained the seeds of their own possible destruction. Predominant was the new governor. Rexford Guy Tugwell brought to the insular administration a sincere sympathy for the Popular party program, brilliant administrative ability to advance its operation, but also an arrogance and lack of political deftness guaranteed to create enemies. The strong Republican block in the United States Congress envisioned Tugwell as the most radical of Roosevelt's team. It was not long before it characterized his support of the Popular plan as the implantation of socialism under the American flag off continental shores. Congressional mulishness could block federal funds for the island's social and economic reforms, while Puerto Rican antagonists used the courts to delay the functioning of new legislation. Meanwhile any pro-independence expression by members of the Popular party would play into the hands of the American congressional opposition. Although Muñoz might keep his party in check, he could foresee mounting hostility in Washington. His fears were later justified by congressional committees sent to Puerto Rico to "investigate" conditions; their avowed purpose was to force the removal of Governor Tugwell.

To hold Popular party support, Muñoz felt required to obtain gubernatorial appointments for his own candidates. But Tugwell was concerned only with the competence of officeholders, not their party affiliations. He found it impossible to understand Muñoz's desperate need to develop a strong political machine. Tugwell read the party voting strength only in the legislature, but Muñoz remembered that the Populares had won only thirty-eight percent of the public vote.

Muñoz trod the line between the coalition and the Populares, between the Tripartite balance of power and the other two parties, between Tugwell and all parties on the island, and between Tugwell and the Republicans in Washington. During the fall session he rushed through forty-three bills. His program was in place. It needed only money and an administrative structure. Tugwell was ready to provide the latter. On December 7, 1941, the Japanese bombing of Pearl Harbor supplied the former. A shocked nation was at war.

No part of the United States was more involved in the conflict than Puerto Rico. During the early months of the war when German submarines were still roaming freely, some five hundred merchant vessels were plunged to the ocean bottom in the Atlantic and the warm, shark-infested waters surrounding Puerto Rico. Within ten months the island's normal 100,000 tons of monthly shipping was reduced to 7,000. Hospitals were filled with gasping seamen fished out of the tropic sea. The airlift of medicines and vital foods was barely adequate to serve military needs.

The pattern of life on the langourous island changed swiftly. The streets of San Juan were filled with soldiers and sailors. Clubs and civic groups organized activities to entertain the servicemen and to raise funds for war charities. Night life was adjusted to the code of the blackout. People either sweltered in closed rooms or turned out the lights and opened the windows. Air conditioning was unknown. Rationing was extended to all necessities. Midst Muñoz's drive toward abundance, scarcity was forced on the island in a manner never before experienced.

Other patterns changed also, not only in Puerto Rico, but throughout Latin America. The United States and her allies became an insatiable market for food and raw materials. Since imports of Scotch from Britain were cut off, Puerto Rican rum found ready acceptance. Prices rose for this product, for sugar, and for tobacco. Excise taxes collected by the federal government were turned back to the island treasury, giving the insular government $160,000,000 above its budget. Dollars spent by the armed forces on the island also added to the income taxes paid by insular citizens.

The same type of prosperity was reaching into the other countries of Latin America. Argentina's coffers were swollen from sales of wheat, other cereals, and meat. Brazilian millionaires became almost as numerous as her coffee beans. Venezuela fattened on oil exports. Colombia, Peru, Mexico, Cuba, Uruguay, every Latin-American country, had food and raw materials to sell to a buyer who was almost unconcerned about the price. Many of those who have called the open American marketplace a special advantage for Puerto Rico have had short memories for the years when the Allies were insatiable buyers for nearly every product all Latin America could offer.

This was the era of the ant and the grasshopper. Muñoz Marín and his team insisted on reinvesting the government surplus in a program of social projects to build the spirit, the health, the education, and the working capacity of the Puerto Rican people. They also initiated a program of industrial development to provide postwar employment. Most Latin-American nations concentrated the benefits of their gains within a limited sector of wealthy families who used the new wealth to buy land, political influence, and the protection of a series of praetorian guards for captive governments. Close to Puerto Rico and leading the "dance of the millions" was Cuba, whose capital city had become a brilliant metropolis of splendid avenues and parks, palaces for the wealthy, scores of clubs for weekend pleasure, and some of the world's most lavish gambling casinos. Far to the south, Argentina took pride in the splendor of Buenos Aires, with its cathedrallike Jockey Club and the magnificent *estancias* outside the city. In both countries the man with the hoe was forgotten—until the day he should exchange it for a gun.

In the wooden house hidden in the palm grove of Isla Verde, Muñoz's plans were discussed as often with Inés Mendoza as with his political confreres, but the conversations often became more heated. Inés had never given up her passion for Puerto Rican independence, her wariness of American intentions, her almost religious attachment to the Spanish residue in the island culture. Muñoz's patient explanations of his policy did not always satisfy the fiery Inés.

Added to political differences were personal disagreements. Inés was a woman of discipline; Muñoz, a man indifferent to detail, impatient with the rigors of doctrine, dress, or time, tended still to lose himself in midnight conversations in downtown cafés. He was not an easy subject for reform, but Inés was not one readily to accept habits or vagaries that might dissipate the energies of her man.

One night Muñoz was seen brooding alone in downtown San Juan. He had stormed out of the house in Isla Verde after an especially lively quarrel with Inés.

When he returned home Inés was not there.

Their separation continued, to the distress and amusement of their friends. The lovers were obviously miserable. No conversation with either one was possible without the name of the other being anxiously brought up for comment.

"We must get them together," said a friend of Muñoz. "Don Luis is acting like a lovesick boy. He can't even do his work properly."

"But how?" asked a friendly conspirator.

"Let's ask each one to a party without telling the other."

The party was an outdoor affair, focused on roast pig and a generous supply of rum. Muñoz was mooning about the garden, talking sparingly with the guests when Inés arrived. He stopped his conversation and looked steadily at her, and her gaze did not move from his eyes. Then the two fell into an embrace and began to babble somewhat incoherently as the other guests sighed with relief.

The party continued, but in a few minutes someone noticed the absence of Inés and Luis. They were in a car headed out of the city. Inés was telling Muñoz about the charming home she had found in Trujillo Alto. They never returned to Isla Verde.

Now Muñoz Marín turned his full attention once again to the tasks involved in cajoling a suspicious legislature to provide operating funds for Governor Tugwell's rapidly expanding administrative structure—the new agencies making up a system that *Time* magazine once called "undeniably socialistic."

Within a period of twelve months, 1941–42, there were established the Water Resources Authority, the Communications Authority, the Transportation Authority, the Puerto Rico Industrial Development

Company, the Government Development Bank, and the Land Authority. To coordinate the functions of these and other bodies there was also established the Puerto Rico Planning Board.

While Muñoz Marín labored to keep the political channels open for the task of these agencies, Rexford Tugwell sketched out their functions and recruited their managers.

Most of the men Tugwell attracted to top posts were in their late twenties or early thirties, more than ten years younger than Muñoz and markedly ahead of him in academic development. Muñoz had captured their imaginations with his philosophic approach to the island's needs, and Tugwell reached their minds with his incisive knowledge of public administrative practices. Contrasted with the politicians who aided Muñoz in building the party machine, they were a set of bright-minded young Puerto Ricans, somewhat scornful of politics but enamored of the techniques of management and clamorous for results. One of them referred to Susoni and his cronies as "the political crowd" and said, years later, that at the time even Muñoz "didn't know a planning board from a parole board." With this talent suddenly urging him, Muñoz was forced into a cram course on economics. Perhaps one of his greatest accomplishments was in not forgetting the goals that economics serves.

Most of the young team stayed in Puerto Rican government affairs for the rest of their careers. They embarked on an endless crusade. Among them was Roberto Sánchez Vilella, the tall, handsome civil engineer from Ohio State University who took over the Puerto Rico Transportation Authority. Another was Rafael Picó, University of Puerto Rico graduate and Ph.D. from Clark University in Massachusetts. He had returned to the island as professor of geography, became a member of the Land Authority, then the first chairman of the Puerto Rico Planning Board. Antonio Fernós-Isern, Muñoz's contemporary and an M.D. from the University of Maryland, who had made a name as a leader in island medical circles, became commissioner of health. Jaime Benítez, with a master's degree in political science from Georgetown and experience on the local faculty, was appointed chancellor of the University of Puerto Rico. Rafael Cordero, university professor, became government controller. There were others—Luchetti, Cuevas, Fernández García, Buscáglia, and the somewhat monumental representation of animal energy that was Teodoro Moscoso.

Moscoso had attended the Philadelphia College of Pharmacy and Science and the University of Michigan. He was in the drug business in Ponce when government service attracted him to the Housing Authority of the southern city. Tugwell and Muñoz agreed he was the man needed to run the key Industrial Development Company. Dedicated, intelligent, hard-driving, possessed of great physical energy, this massive young man quickly became the pivot of the island's new economic machine. Teodoro Moscoso was one of the few men on the island who could work Muñoz's hours and emerge as fresh as the Popular party's leader. Blunt, abrupt, hard-hitting Moscoso became a master administrator whose sincerity salved the wounds his impulses might cause.

The eagerness of these dynamic young men was its own insulation against the doctrinaire quarrel aggravated by the establishment of the new government agencies. The decision of the government to reinvest its surplus in an income-generating program was largely considered a challenge to the free enterprise concept. Until the program had provided light, power, transportation, communications, and financial resources and placed them at the service of private industry, businessmen feared its success and doubted its purposes. Only later was there an appreciation of the care with which the public corporations had been planned to keep them free of political control. The insular government was represented on their boards but not their managements. The island's controller had accesss to their books but not to their policy development.

Tugwell and Muñoz absorbed the political shock of the opposition's attacks. Although they were able to hold steady against direct charges on the program, Muñoz was shaken by strong recurrences of the status issue, fearful that it might blunt the spirit of the mass of voters, who perhaps did not understand the complexity of the economic program. Muñoz never divorced the need for political identity from the struggle for material well-being. One might take the lead at a certain stage of affairs, the other at a different time.

Millard Tydings kept the fire warm with another attempt to introduce an independence bill in Congress. This was fended off, but it encouraged Bolívar Pagán to make public a letter to President Roosevelt citing the Atlantic Charter as justification for Puerto Rico's right to elect her own governor. On February 2, 1943, Muñoz Marín signed, with the leaders of all parties, a petition to Congress in support of Bolívar Pagán's demand. The Puerto Rican legislature unamimously passed a resolution endorsing the request that the island elect its own governor in 1944.

The next month Franklin Roosevelt recommended that Congress pass the necessary amendment to the Jones Act. A special commission from the island, including leaders from all parties and Rexford Tugwell and Harold Ickes, was formed to negotiate the new law in Congress. The law never emerged from committee deliberations. Congress was intent on another investigation of Tugwell's "socialism" in Puerto Rico. Obviously no major concession could be won from a congress so adamantly hostile to the most effective servant the United States had yet sent to Puerto Rico.

While Muñoz was engaged in this and other matters, a bill was passed in the Puerto Rican House that exempted petroleum companies from certain tax payments amounting to four million dollars. Enraged, Muñoz attacked the measure in the Senate, imputing bad faith to its supporters, including some members of his own party. The incident solidified the opposition against him and nearly brought a split in Popular party ranks.

In August the insistent independence group in the Popular party called a meeting of eighteen hundred delegates to a congress for independence, attended by fifteen thousand private citizens. Although not a participant, Muñoz sent the meeting this message: "I wish the congress all success in expressing before the people of the United States the ideals that indisputably are those of the majority of the Puerto Ricans."

Many have questioned Muñoz's motives when he wrote that message. In view of later events, he may since have wondered what had pushed his hand.

TWELVE

Metamorphosis

THE SOUTHERN COAST of a Caribbean island is rarely its moderate side. Usually the capital is in the north, where sea breezes originating in the Atlantic tend to cool tempers. The second city boils on the southern coast, its populace steaming the year around, its people traditionally divided between wealthy landowners and miserable workers of the fields, all subject to the first hammer blows of the hurricanes that roar out of the South Atlantic. The revolutionists of Cuba have often stormed out of the frying pan of southern Santiago; the extremists of Puerto Rico often came from Ponce, where Muñoz Rivera wrote his most vitriolic editorials against Spanish domination and found his fiery bride. Here, in the slumbrous colonial town, sizzling in midsummer Caribbean heat, the locale of the Ponce Massacre of 1937, Luiz Muñoz Marín confronted the first rebellion within the ranks of his Partido Popular Democrático.

He had called the preelection meeting of the party in Ponce for August 20, 1944, to affirm his leadership. After a welcoming speech by the mayor of Ponce, nominations for 1944 election candidates were opened immediately. For the principal post of resident commissioner, Antonio Fernós-Isern and Rafael Arjona Siaca were proposed from the floor of the Teatro La Perla, traditional theater of Ponce. Arjona Siaca was one of the leaders of the Congreso Pro-Independencia, the insistent independence group in the Popular party. Fernós-Isern was Muñoz's candidate.

The assemblage received the announcement of Fernós-Isern's name with cool courtesy. As the candidacy of Rafael Arjona Siaca was called out from the floor, the Populares burst into tumultuous applause. Muñoz, frowning at the speaker's stand, may have remembered his father's efforts to keep the independence seekers of the Unionist party in check when he was negotiating the Jones Act— and he may have forgotten his own rebellion against the conservative Barceló when the *independentistas* followed Muñoz out of the Liberal party. Muñoz spoke against Arjona Siaca's proposed nomination in controlled, measured tones, then found he had challenged a tiger. Arjona Siaca rose before the assembly and passionately demanded that the party of democracy follow its own principles in allowing free deliberations in its own meetings and subscribing to the democratic policy of an undirected vote.

For a moment the history of Puerto Rico balanced on the scales of a party schism. Then Muñoz, accepting the challenge, demanded that the assembly place into nomination for the resident commissioner's post either himself or the man he would propose. With his chair and whip, Muñoz forced the lions back into their cages as they accepted his suggestion. Then he threw them their consolation. He endorsed the candidacy of Jesús Piñero, which was swallowed. Fernós-Isern went back to his job as commissioner of agriculture. The breach with Arjona Siaca was never healed—even when, years later, young Luisito Muñoz Lee married Arjona Siaca's daughter.

In Ponce, on August 20, 1944, only Muñoz Marín understood the change that he was undergoing and the transformation that he would be required to effect in the Partido Popular during the coming four years. For he was certain that his party would be asked to carry the responsibility for the island's destiny at least until 1948.

Just twelve months earlier Muñoz had sent a message of encouragement to a meeting of the Congreso Pro-Independencia. But during those twelve months the vague profile of the new Puerto Rican economy had come into sharper focus, and the obstacles to Muñoz's aspirations for his people had become more clearly defined. The Puerto Rico Industrial Development Company now owned and operated four factories. It was a manufacturer of glass containers for the burgeoning rum business, of paperboard containers for shipment of rum to the mainland, of cement, and of structural clay products and sanitary ware. And it was doing rather poorly at all these projects, since they provided minimal employment and yielded more losses than profits. There was little indication that government in business would provide the employment that private enterprises had failed to generate.

Meanwhile the United States, sensing the twilight of colonialism, and grateful to the Philippine people for their gallant struggle during the war, was preparing to comply with its long-standing promise of independence for its Pacific associate. Muñoz Marín's growing doubt that Puerto Rico could sustain herself alone was further burdened by his observation of the negotiations by which the United States attempted to assure the Philippines, with their wealth of natural resources, that they would not fall into an economic mire. With the bitter poverty of his island thus highlighted, this compassionate ally of the *jíbaro* saw the price of the ideal of independence marked on a death's-head. Yet the poet and the man in Muñoz still required the hope of independence as a pledge of dignity for his people. There must be some way out.

One night, some time prior to the Ponce convention, at the Escambrón Beach Club, seated alone at a table with an American visitor, Muñoz put his conflict to trial. His protagonist was Ben Dorfman, a tariff expert who had worked on the plans for the economic separation of the Philippines from the United States and who was engaged in a study of the economy of Puerto Rico. Muñoz, urging his polemic powers and lashing his imagination, attempted to find the formula that would allow Puerto Rico the dignity of her own sovereignty without sacrificing hope for a decent minimum of prosperity.

Patiently, neatly, objectively, Dorfman explained to the disturbed Muñoz why an independent Puerto Rico, competing as the Philippines would have to compete for the American market, would starve. Against Muñoz's objections he ranged the American most-favored-nation policy, which would prohibit considerations for Puerto Rico not granted to all other nations. As the evening wore on, Dorfman met Muñoz's every thrust, relentlessly cutting back his arguments with the facts of American international obligations and Puerto Rico's limited resources.

"It was like a surgical operation," a colleague of Muñoz has said; and before dawn it left the Popular party leader a weary and anguished man.

Those who were amazed then at his infuriated reaction to the challenge of Arjona Siaca's followers in Ponce were unaware that something other than the compulsion to dominate the Popular party was driving him into a towering rage at the convention that August night. They had brought to the surface a grief of spirit that he could share with no one.

The party platform adopted at Ponce reiterated the claim that the island's political status was not now an issue, with the qualification that colonial status was unsatisfactory. This problem, it stated, would be faced when the war had ended, but no decision would be taken without a vote of the people.

The objectives of the party were much the same as those presented before the 1940 elections. And added to the program were the aims of fully developing the resources of the country and of promoting through private enterprise the growth of industry on the island. The proclamation closed with an endorsement of the administration of Governor Guy Rexford Tugwell.

All other parties were opposed to such approval. In the platform statement of each was a condemnation of Tugwell, to the extent that one party chose to designate him as "an enemy of Puerto Rico." The role was not new for an American governor of the island; it was an innovation, however, that he should be acclaimed by the most powerful party contending for election.

Recognition of the expanding influence of the Populares moved other parties to new positions: first, by their inclusion of social reform measures in their platforms: second, by their decision to form a common front against the Popular party. Nothing could have been more encouraging to Muñoz. And nothing could have been more amusing than their method, since no party was able to submerge its own ambitions for the cause they jointly claimed. All these parties maintained their own identity and divided up the leading candidacies. The Liberals would propose the single opposing candidate for resident commissioner. The Senate leader would be a Socialist; and in the House, the speaker would come from the Union Republican party.

Meanwhile, in another reminder to the electorate that politics was their business, the opposition in the month before the elections, with the help of the three dissident Tripartite votes in the House, held up an appropriation of fifteen million dollars for public works, the main purpose of which was to provide employment during the difficult later years of the war. Tugwell and Muñoz decided that since the funds were of federal origin, and the need called for courage, the money should be spent; and they put it to the uses designated.

Opposing court action was successful. Judge Marcelino Romany ruled the action illegal and jailed the governor's cabinet, the executive council, for misuse of funds. The photograph of this leading group of reform leaders behind bars appeared in all newspapers and greatly aided the Popular party cause. Americans have since remembered Marcelino Romany as the Puerto Rican delegate to the 1952 Republican convention who convulsed a nation of television viewers by insisting on a roll call of the Puerto Rican delegation by an Irish chairman unable to pronounce the names. Populares have remembered him as a helper of their 1944 campaign.

Muñoz, never alluding directly to the court action, let it come easily to the forefront of listeners' minds with dramatic pleas for only "one more vote" in the House to allow his program to be enacted without threat to the financial resources it should require. The Populares had obviously kept their promises. Muñoz had only to insist that they would have done more had they held full political control.

The people accepted the thesis. They gave the Populares 383,280 votes against 101,779 for the second contending party, the Unión Republicana—seventeen senators against two opposers, and thirty-seven representatives against two for other parties. Jesús Piñero was elected resident commissioner, to replace Bolívar Pagán, and joyous wags spread the story of Muñoz's power by saying that he had caused "Jesús to replace the Pagán" in Washington.

Perhaps the most important occurrence in Puerto Rico as part of the 1944 election was the downgrading of power as an absolute goal. Power was sought in order to serve ideas. The idea of social reform promulgated by the Populares had been accepted by the great majority of voters and included in opposition platforms. At a time when militarists and manipulators were seeking access to temporarily swollen treasuries in many other Latin-American countries, Puerto Rico was able to vote on differing proposals for accomplishing the public good—when its wartime treasury was diminishing rapidly.

Another challenge of ideas came almost immediately after Muñoz took office again as Senate leader. A Congreso Pro-Independencia meeting demanded that Muñoz express his ideas on the political status of Puerto Rico.

By letter, in response to the congress' resolutions, Muñoz reiterated that the Popular party was pledged to act in reference to the island's status only as instructed by the people in open referendum. And he took the opportunity to say publicly that this vote should occur as soon as possible and that the closest conceivable date would be at the close of the war. The vociferous claimants of independence were unimpressed. Muñoz was forced, even as he had provoked Antonio Barceló, to express disapproval of a splinter wing of his party for launching its own campaign for independence.

Muñoz was now embarked on his attempt to convert the bulk of his supporters from a desire for independence, which he had once encouraged, to willing acceptance of a status in continued association with the United States. But he had not fully disclosed his purposes, and the challenges of his most idealistic adherents were a trial of his explosive temper. But it was Millard Tydings, the American senator so closely associated with American sugar growers, who finally flushed Muñoz out of the incubator in which he was trying to hatch a new solution to Puerto Rico's problems. Tydings had put his name on the bill for Philippine independence that would eventually reduce offshore competition to American sugar. In 1945 he was again the progenitor of a proposal for a Puerto Rican nation.

Muñoz Marín and other members of a Legislative Commission on Status created by insular law in 1943 were called to Washington to testify before a Senate committee considering Tydings' bill. Since the bill contained an offer of a twenty-year period of graduated reduction of tariff concessions, it appeared to answer the violent objections to Tydings' first effort. It also was rapidly reinforced by the full endorsement of a sizable group of Popular party legislators whose names were registered with the Congreso Pro-Independencia. Muñoz was placed in a trying situation. His effort to evolve away from the banner of independence without losing his followers was mined with obvious traps.

This was a stage in Muñoz's steady climb toward the crest when the boulder shook recklessly in his grasp. The foot of the hill suddenly seemed closer than the top. A misstatement or a misjudgment could lose the whole game. In Muñoz's view the program that was improving the life of Puerto Rico's masses was in peril. The philo-sophical issue of their spiritual dignity had to be put off until the cramps in their stomachs were stopped, and then it must be re-solved in a way that would not bring back the hunger.

Perhaps Muñoz, at forty-seven, driving toward goals he was able clearly to locate in order of their priority, reached the height of his powers before this last challenge of Millard Tydings.

He emerged from the hearings with a triumph conceded even by his most hostile adversaries. Muñoz agreed with the spirit of the bill in declaring that the colonial status of Puerto Rico was intolerable. All parties, and Congress, were in agreement. He also stated that the bill should be amended to permit the Puerto Rican people to choose between the two political alternatives of statehood and inde-pendence. In this thesis too his adversaries and his followers found themselves, perforce, in agreement, with Congress nodding to its logic.

Muñoz then suggested that the responsibility of the United States toward a territory it had acquired forty-seven years ago called for cer-tain guarantees: (1) free trade between the United States and Puerto Rico, on terms to be qualified by mutual agreement; (2) no tax on Puerto Rican goods sold to the United States, with Puerto Rico free to collect export taxes equal to U.S. export imposts; (3) continuation of sugar quotas; (4) continuation of other agricultural-support benefits; and (5) continuation of other federal subsidies and supports until the Puerto Rican economy should reach an agreed-upon level.

With Congress listening and Puerto Rican opposition unable, for political reasons, to object, Muñoz then stated that Congress should offer to Puerto Rico only those political alternatives that it could de-liver, since there was no use in a referendum on proposals that could not be realized. He pointed out that the island could not vote itself into statehood, nor could it select independence under five condi-tions that only the United States could concede. The Legislative Commission, of course, acquiesced, and Tydings amended his bill to include the five conditions Muñoz had requested. At this point Ty-dings, who was stumbling now, was given a final push by resident commissioner Jesús Piñero, who asked that dominion status also be considered. The bill was killed in committee.

Muñoz's masterful performance attracted the attention of American journalists. In August of the same year, 1945, *The Reader's Digest* ran a piece by J. P. McEvoy, titled "Unhand Me, Uncle!" With American attention focused on colonial problems represented by India, Burma, the Philippines, Indochina, and other sectors, McEvoy wrote, "the future peace of the world will largely depend on finding a satisfactory answer to the colonial question—satisfactory, that is, to the colonies." He then quoted Muñoz Marín as saying, "The American people do not wish to exploit Puerto Rico. . . . Granting our pleas for self-determination would give concrete proof of sincerity to all peoples, especially in Latin America; it would suggest one workable solution to the complex colonial problem; and it would provide a model of trusteeship for the whole world. . . ."

The full effect of Muñoz's logic and tactics during the congressional inquiry on the Tydings bill reached its culmination in a statement from the White House. On October 16, 1945, President Harry S. Truman sent the following message to Congress:

It is the policy of this government to promote the political, social, and economic development of people who have not yet achieved their own government and to make it possible for them to form their own type of government. It is our pride that this policy has been loyally followed in the case of the Philippines. The Philippine people determined that it desired political independence, and the government of the United States made arrangements to that effect.

It is now time, in my opinion, to determine on the part of the Puerto Rican people their desires regarding the final political status they prefer and—within the limits to be set by Congress —to concede to them the type of government they desire. It is apparent that the present form of government on the island is unsatisfactory to a great majority of its inhabitants. There are different possibilities: first, the right of the Puerto Ricans to elect their own governor, with a large measure of local self-government; secondly, statehood for Puerto Rico; third, complete independence; and fourth, government in the form of a dominion.

Each one of these propositions is being urged among the people, who remain ignorant of what precisely will be the future of Puerto Rico. These uncertainties should be clarified at an early date. To this end, I recommend that Congress consider each of the propositions and that it approve legislation to submit the various alternatives to the people of Puerto Rico. In this way, Congress can discover what the Puerto Ricans most want for their political future.

However, in the interest of good faith and the good will between the people of Puerto Rico and those of us who live on the mainland, Congress should not submit any proposals to the Puerto Ricans which it is not prepared to promulgate finally into law. We must be prepared to carry out any option submitted to the people of Puerto Rico, once the Puerto Ricans have demonstrated their preference. . . .

Muñoz was clambering up the hill again, the rock firmly on his shoulders.

Despite his extraordinary compassion, Luis Muñoz Marín has been likened, as a politician, to a boxer with the "killer" instinct. Probably he has never wanted to harm any living thing. In his most vigorous battles against dogma, he has sought always to overwhelm the concept, not its apostle. Yet he has had an almost magical perception of the weakening of opposing power, an intuition for the moment that could carry him to another victory—if he should press home the attack.

Early in 1946 Muñoz discerned the forces that could be rallied to his cause and sensed the desperation on the other side of the lines. With a series of four articles in *El Mundo*, now Puerto Rico's leading newspaper, he set the stage for the knockout blow he now held ready for delivery.

The first article was a dispassionate assessment of Puerto Rico's economic situation. It described how the economy of Puerto Rico, poor as it was, had developed at a pace equal to the growth of the population until the year 1934, when economic growth reached a low plateau but population figures continued to increase and aggravate the island's misery. He pointed out that since that date the island had survived on the artificial aid supplied by the United States and the Second World War. He then sternly reminded his people that they must create their own replacement for charity and lucky accident by laboring for an increase in agricultural and industrial production.

"Puerto Rico by, let us say, 1960, will have to have increased her production," he asserted, "to the point in which the minimum standard of living of its population will reach a level at which its birthrate will decrease . . . or, if not, Puerto Rico is lost. The people of Puerto Rico, and their civilization, will disappear like a brief, bright light smoking in the shadow of time.

"What must be done to save Puerto Rico must be done under whatever political status," he declared. And government had to provide a lead. This was his answer to accusations of socialism in his administration.

His second article states: "The essential propositions of the Popular Democratic party are, as they were, to distribute justly what is produced, and to work for increases in what is produced. The means . . . are laws administered by departments and agencies of the government, and the creation and functioning of public corporations to provide the greatest advance and stimulus possible to the urgent needs of the program."

Directly facing the issue of doctrine, Muñoz stated that the government "sustains absolutely neither the theory of public initiative nor that of private initiative in the process of increasing production. . . . We cannot allow ourselves the ideological luxury of losing the constructive factors of one or the other. Puerto Rico needs them both. . . ."

He also attempted to put aside the Nationalist arguments against rising American investment, declaring: "Just as I say about public and private enterprise—that we cannot permit ourselves the luxury of choosing one and discarding the other, because we need them both—I say the same about assistance from within or from outside Puerto Rico."

Muñoz was ready now, in his third article, to attack the dissident Independents within his party. He was particularly bitter about those who maintained party membership while conducting a separate pro-independence campaign. "A political movement has a perfect right to attack another political movement," he wrote. "But the same person cannot belong to the two political movements."

Muñoz closed the series with a long essay that faced the political issue with a demand for autonomy under economic protection. He contended that, to the extent possible, the island should be relieved of the burdens of colonialism, but should not be abandoned to the risks of complete political freedom until it should have developed a sufficient measure of economic hardihood.

"The problem of status," he wrote, "must always be difficult—for economic, not for political, reasons. However, this moment of time in the world seems most appropriate to confront it with prospects of success."

The moment in time was swollen with history-making action around the world. The Security Council and the General Assembly of the United Nations had initiated their maiden sessions in London. They had decided on New York as headquarters for the new world organization. A new Labor government had been swept into office in England to replace war hero Winston Churchill with Clement Attlee as Prime Minister. Bowing to the insistence of Mahatma Gandhi, leader of India's independence movement (also idol of Muñoz Marín), Attlee now offered terms for Indian freedom from her colonial state. Other colonial demands for independence were being pressed upon the great European powers from all corners of the globe.

Anticolonialism was a rising sentiment in the United States. The nation was headed toward antagonizing old friends by urging Britain to divest herself of colonial possessions, by shouldering the Netherlands into a decision to renounce control of Indonesia, by withholding aid to the French in their war with embattled Indochinese seekers of freedom.

This rising tide could sweep Puerto Rican aspirations further toward the autonomy briefly enjoyed before the Americans had landed on the tropic shores. But in the United States political reversals were visible. Muñoz was worried about the Republican Congress that was impeding much of President Truman's Fair Deal program. Like other political observers, he was convinced that Truman would be voted out of office in 1948.

Close at hand, Muñoz could also view a new threat to balanced action: the return of the Puerto Rican soldier veterans of World War II. The first crop of islanders ever to be toughened in the crude school of war, they were also the first to encounter the brutal prejudices of the United States. Those that were dark of skin were immediately placed in Negro regiments. Others, who were lighter, were classified as Negroes simply because they had come from Puerto Rico. Soldiers and officers alike were now returning to their village homes with dollars in their pockets, a new toughness in their spirits, and bitterness in their hearts. Many of them would welcome the return of Albizu Campos, soon due to be released from his stateside prison, and would be the first to take up the arms that he claimed could alone bring justice to Puerto Rico.

Alleviation of Puerto Rico's strictly colonial status had to be accomplished quickly, had to be achieved in this moment of time. Rexford Tugwell, who had done more to advance the ability of Puerto Ricans to solve their own economic and administrative problems than any other American governor, now prepared for his final gesture toward the islanders. Having come to the conclusion that congressional cooperation to further either economic growth or political development in Puerto Rico was impossible so long as he remained in the Fortaleza, Tugwell quietly let Muñoz and the President know that he was prepared to resign. When his retirement occurred, Puerto Ricans and Americans who had criticized his administration so bitterly failed even to credit the altruistic motive behind his decision; they claimed that his resignation was forced by the growing protests against his regime. It took all of Tugwell's self-assurance to overcome these appraisals.

Now Muñoz took the offensive, making use, for probably the last time, of journalistic communication to urge a major point. Thereafter, oratory would be his weapon. In two carefully written essays for *El Mundo*, published in June, 1946, and titled "New Solutions for Old Problems," Muñoz proposed for the first time—though he did not use the exact term—a commonwealth status for Puerto Rico.

His first article opened abruptly. "I am going to define clearly what I think about political status," it announced. "I will first briefly make some observations about the state of the world, and then I will make those pertinent to the specific case of Puerto Rico."

Swiftly describing the massive changes world structures had undergone, he declared, "We have to modernize our concept of the problem. We have been arguing traffic rules for victorias and buggies in a time of automobiles and airplanes. . . .

"One of the things that was altered profoundly is the understanding of what sovereignty means. Another is the comprehension of liberty. . . ." Pointing to the need of nations to sacrifice some sovereignty in a world order adjusted to peace, Muñoz continued: "If sovereignty is one form of liberty, and freeing oneself from the threat of war is another form of liberty, humanity must choose which of the two forms of liberty it prefers, because one is clearly incompatible with the other."

He then returned to a view of liberty that he had started to define during his first campaign with the Popular Democratic party.

"If liberty from the fear of hunger is one liberty, and the freedom to govern oneself without the economic means to eliminate the fear of hunger is another liberty, then we must find how to avoid that one such liberty should destroy the other . . . we have to seek the means of self-government without slavery under the threat of hunger."

The article then attempted to set aside the existing shibboleths concerning independence and statehood: "The classic words 'independence' and 'statehood' do not by themselves have any meaning. . . . In its intrinsic aspect, independence may function and subsist under certain conditions related to the economy and can destroy itself under other conditions of economic relationship. In the political aspect, statehood for the forty-eight states of the American Union contains today much less authority before the federal government than it did fifty years ago."

On this base, Muñoz's second article built the case for commonwealth. It stated that statehood was impossible for the current economy of Puerto Rico and that independence without special economic conditions (which the most-favored-nation policy of the United States made unavailable) was also impossible. This led to a call for action of a new type.

Three proposals were offered: self-government under current conditions until the level of the economy should permit a plebiscite on independence or statehood; an immediate plebiscite, conditioned on granting the chosen status when a certain economic standard should be achieved; full, irrevocable autonomy (commonwealth), with the proviso that the Puerto Rican legislature could, when it so chose, conduct a plebiscite on statehood or independence.

Nowhere did the word "commonwealth" or the term "free associated state" appear in these articles, but the road to the new idea had been opened.

Meanwhile Muñoz's proclamation was quickly followed by the most dramatic events in the island's political history since the Jones Act: Governor Tugwell's resignation was announced; and on July 25, 1946, forty-eight years from the day of the American landing at Guánica, President Truman announced the appointment of the first Puerto Rican governor, Jesús Piñero. The Popular party assigned Dr. Antonio Fernós-Isern to replace Piñero as resident commissioner in Washington.

On the same July 25, the dissident splinter of the Popular party made its final break and announced formation of the Independence party, under the leadership of Gilberto Concepción de Gracia.

Governor Piñero was inaugurated on September 3, 1946. A few months later, on May 2, 1947, the United States Congress, acting on a bill sponsored by Fred Crawford, Republican representative, and Hugh Butler, Republican senator, accorded Puerto Rico the right to elect her own governor, beginning with the election of 1948.

Puerto Rico's moment in time was at hand.

Muñoz Marín had been the dominant figure of Puerto Rican politics for ten years when the island prepared to elect, for the first time, its own governor. This was long enough for the populace to tire of him. It was long enough for him to have promised much, to have made mistakes, to have created enemies. It was also long enough for him to achieve a great deal, score some dramatic successes, and attract a horde of adorers. It was long enough too for the nature of Puerto Rican society and the economy to have changed markedly, and for major issues to have altered importantly. But Muñoz had learned that the leader who stays ahead of the issues is on the ascendancy; the man who falls behind them has begun his decline.

Improvement had been promised on two interlocking fronts— social and economic. Muñoz was primarily responsible for the former; Tugwell, Moscoso, Picó, and the team of economists carried most of the latter responsibility. Muñoz, the Popular party candidate for governor, emphasized the social reforms his party had accomplished since 1944. They constituted an impressive record:

1. Sugar workers employed by the Land Authority had earned a total of five million dollars, half a million in profit sharing.

2. Over ninety thousand former tenants now lived in their houses on their own parcels of land.

3. Increased medical aid was available through eighty-nine new medical centers and an increase of fifteen hundred beds available in general hospitals.

4. New educational facilities were represented by two thousand additional schoolrooms and the employment of three thousand more teachers.

5. Nearly two hundred thousand schoolchildren were receiving free school lunches.

6. Urban public housing was under way in a program to move thirty-two thousand from the slums to new apartments by 1948.

7. Electricity had been brought to 150 formerly lamp-lit rural districts.

8. Physical fitness had been further promoted by the installation of thirty-four sports fields throughout the island.

9. Highways and roads had been extended from the former 1,563 miles to 2,000.

10. A program of aid for the aged was supplying monthly funds to thirty-two thousand indigents.

While barraging the public with these figures, Muñoz quickly admitted that not enough had been done, and the record of the Industrial Development Company seemed to underscore his claim that the battle for production had just started. The government-owned factories had been beset by strikes that a labor-oriented government met ineffectively. The paperboard mill operated at a loss, there were no impressive profits, and the rum bonanza had ended as Scotch again flowed freely into postwar America. A commitment of nearly twenty million dollars over five years, directed toward a need for one hundred thousand industry-created jobs, had provided work for only two thousand laborers. Furthermore, the government's ownership of five factories had balked its efforts to attract private investment in industry. Private business was cautious of coming into an economy dominated by a public entrepreneur. At the end of 1947 only thirteen plants of United States origin had been built.

Operation Bootstrap, as it came to be called, was displaying many of the attributes of the first years of the Alliance for Progress in the sixties. Both faced the need for industrial development and land reform. Both projected a double-pronged plan for economic development paralleled by improvement of social conditions. Both were based on the concept that accomplishment could not be imposed but must be achieved by the people involved. Both faced the same line-up of adversaries: large landowners and industrialists unwilling to contribute toward social reform, reluctant to cede economic power, and suspicious of state action. In the case of Bootstrap, the dramatic force of Muñoz's personal leadership and effective communication with his people finally prevailed.

The program of social rehabilitation and economic reconstruction that the Popular party had launched in 1940 came to a turning in the road. Muñoz and his colleagues had decided in 1947 to seek the support of private business for the industrial-development program and to channel government funds toward the promotion and assistance of private firms rather than into direct investment. This change in policy brought in the name "Operation Bootstrap," which thereafter has referred to all the development programs set in motion since 1940. The first move was passage of the first tax-exemption law in 1947, freeing eligible new businesses from insular and local burdens for a period of years after their installation. The bill was amended in 1948 to make the ten-year tax-free period effective. It was extended and amended again in 1954, and again in 1963.

More important was the decision to offer the government factories for sale to private buyers. The last one was not disposed of, however, until 1951. All were bought by Luis Alberto Ferré Aguayo, wealthy Ponce industrialist, stern opponent of Muñoz's programs, and good citizen of Puerto Rico. Ferré has since said that although he opposed the public concept of Operation Bootstrap, "I really put the program on its feet."

The transitory stage in 1947 was dramatized by government construction of a textile mill to be operated privately and by the signing of a contract with Conrad Hilton for operation of a luxury hotel to be built by the Industrial Development Company. When the government was casting about for a private operator of the project, it received a letter from Hilton written in Spanish. The incipient nationalism in every Puerto Rican came to the surface and Hilton was immediately invited to negotiate. With plans for the luxurious Caribe Hilton, Puerto Rico was launched into the tourism industry and Hilton was embarked on a new career as innkeeper for the world.

Had nationalistically inclined Puerto Ricans visualized how successful this project would be, their protests would have become a campaign issue. It ultimately changed the face of Puerto Rico more than any single action in the island's history, probably including the American invasion in 1898. Until the Caribe Hilton opened its doors in 1949, Puerto Rico had never received more than 60,000 tourists a year, and their expenditures on the island had never exceeded $6,500,000. Within ten years the annual tourist inflow rose to 350,000, spending over $53,000,000. New hotels were eventually added to line San Juan's seaward shore, and others in Ponce, Mayagüez, Fajardo, and the interior. A new way of life was implanted on the tropical island, and with it a new measure of prosperity.

But in 1947 there were already expressed misgivings about the Americanization of Puerto Rico. Pablo Morales Otero, essayist, writing of *Nuestros Problemas* (Our Problems), said that "we are learning English, swearing allegiance to the Stars and Stripes, and singing 'Old Black Joe,' 'My Old Kentucky Home,' 'Swanee River'!" Although many *jíbaros* still walked unshod, frequented cockfights, ate rice with cocoa, liked their shot of rum, fought at dances, and when in love "carried off the girl," the folklore of Spain was submerging under the wave of American influence. The intellectuals who had joined the new Independence party abetted such conservative resistance to the island's transformation. The returned war veterans were more vehement and less poetic in their feelings.

But Muñoz was in the forefront of change and reaffirmed that posture on July 4, 1948, in the clearest statement to date of his political views. What he said convinced the most fanatic nationalists that their cause depended upon the destruction of this man. Muñoz and Inés, knowing this, soon after the speech commended their children to certain friends if Nationalist violence should reach the party leader.

"The idea of independence," Muñoz said, "is respectable." Again spelling out the economic consequences of such liberation, he continued, "But to this destruction would you give the name of independence? The idea of statehood is respectable. To this destruction would you give the name of a state in the great American union?"

He then proposed that "the people of Puerto Rico should vote to authorize . . . that Congress by law should complete self-government in Puerto Rico to the point possible without being a state in the constitutional structure of the United States—the point that at times under the name of autonomy, at times under the name of dominion, at times under other names, has been one of the solutions historically promulgated in Puerto Rico."

Thus, in Puerto Rico's first campaign to elect her own governor in 1948, the issues were joined. The Independence party entered the electoral battle under the guidance of its gubernatorial candidate, Francisco M. Susoni, and its candidate for resident commissioner, Rafael Arjona Siaca. The coalition parties came forth with candidates who reflected the rising level of Puerto Rican politics. For governor they proposed the highly respected supreme court judge Martín Travieso, and for a resident commissioner Luis A. Ferré, Ponce businessman graduated from the Massachusetts Institute of Technology. Travieso, although a key figure in the Republican party, had been known to be sympathetic to the social-reform concept spearheaded by Franklin D. Roosevelt and had highlighted in the party's platform a commitment to submit the question of political status to a plebiscite in Puerto Rico. Ferré, son of a wealthy family of purely Spanish antecedents in the feudal atmosphere of Ponce, was chief administrator of his family's industrial enterprises. He was demonstrating his attunement to the twentieth century through his intelligent management of the Porto Rican Iron Works, Inc., and the Ponce Cement Corporation within the framework of personnel policies more liberal than those legislated by the Popular regime.

Muñoz was not to be headed off by such sturdy challengers, because he still led rather than followed the issues. His party platform no longer insisted that status was not an issue. It stated that it would request the right to formulate a Puerto Rican constitution based on self-government and containing the right to convoke a plebiscite, when proper, on statehood, independence, or continuation of the political structure.

Before a mass rally of Popular adherents in San Juan, Muñoz reiterated his faith in the party's economic program, saying, "We have done a great deal. . . . But there is still much for us to do. When I look at the bottom of the hole, I see that we have climbed far. But when I look toward the crest of the hill, I see that we have to clamber still much more to reach our goal." The slogan of the party was still *Jalda Arriba!*—Up the Hill.

A sense of the world's great problems had permeated Puerto Rico. A feeling of pride had moved into the hearts of people formerly seized by despair. Except for the small but dangerous minority that called him a turncoat, even Muñoz's opponents admired the statesmanship of his move away from the emotional appeal of independence toward the pragmatic solution of commonwealth; and many had approved the empiric change from public leadership of the economy to a policy of government support of private efforts. The election was the cleanest in the history of the island.

The vote was a landslide for the Populares. Against their 392,-356 votes, the Republican Statehood group registered 89,441, followed by the Independents, with 65,351; the other parties were lagging in the list. Dr. Antonio Fernós-Isern was reelected resident commissioner, Samuel Quiñones was the new president of the Senate, Ernesto Ramos Antonini became speaker of the House. The first elected governor of Puerto Rico was Luis Muñoz Marín.

THIRTEEN

View of the Crest

HIS ELECTION to the governorship sent Muñoz Marín rushing toward his goal of the commonwealth in a dynamic surge surpassing all his previous efforts, and leaving many colleagues gasping by the wayside. His absorbing dedication to his campaign promises clashed immediately with the Fortaleza's distracting formalities. The new governor was impatient with ceremony, distressed at protocol. His dissent was symbolized by his complaints at having to wear a necktie as he sat at the huge mahogany desk that overlooked the Fortaleza's magnificent Throne Room. He saw no good reason for a police guard on this home rather than any other, or any reason why detectives should follow him if he chose to meet a friend at a bar at midnight.

He found it difficult to understand why associates should want, at the end of the day, to go home to their families instead of staying at their desks to work for the people of Puerto Rico; nor could he comprehend his subordinates' concern about their own incomes. Their jobs were to raise the island's, not their own, standard of living. Yet nearly all these associates stayed with Muñoz, devoted to his causes, inspired by his passion, enchanted by his warmth.

The long hours of work and an almost monastic indifference to money, already part of the growing Muñoz Marín legend, now became firmly fixed on him as governor. One tale of the many described a situation in which Muñoz was acting as host to a government official from a neighboring Latin-American country. After lunch at the Muñoz country home in Trujillo Alto—which Don Luis and Doña Inés had bought recently with the help of an

FHA loan—the two men were lounging and talking on the veranda. Up the garden path came a man whom Muñoz hailed as he approached, but the governor's ease turned to embarrassment when the man said, "I am here to collect your monthly dues to the party, Don Luis. I think—that is, I understand—that you are behind in the payment."

"How much is it?" asked Muñoz, knowing the answer as well as his own name.

"Twenty-five dollars, Don Luis," the party worker said.

Muñoz rose and went into the house. He emerged somewhat ruffled. "Look. All I have here is twenty-three dollars," he protested. "Let me pay you the rest next week."

The man touched his straw hat and grinned. "Don't worry, Don Luis. Good afternoon."

As Muñoz's guest watched this unrehearsed scene, his eyes widened. In silence he watched the man walk to the garden gate, then he turned to Muñoz and exploded. "You—the governor of Puerto Rico! And you don't have twenty-five dollars? What kind of a Latino are you?"

The Congress of the United States was discovering that Muñoz was the kind of "Latino" who intended to comply with his promise to find for Puerto Rico a political status free of the humiliating yoke of colonialism, yet adjusted to the island's economic needs—which required access to the American market, unavailable through independence; and freedom from federal taxes, impossible under statehood.

The proposal for such a status was offered to the House of Representatives on March 13, 1950, and to the Senate on the last day of the same month. Fundamentally, these bills suggested that the terms of the Jones Act of 1917 be replaced by new ones reaffirming Puerto Rico's commercial relationship to the United States—mutually open markets, joint trade and tariff structures, return to the Puerto Rican treasury of federal imposts on island exports to the United States. This also included confirmation of certain areas of federal jurisdiction over insular affairs—defense, currency, coastal shipping, the quotas on sugar production and limitations on its refining that were stipulated in the Jones-Costigan Act of 1934. In return for her economic privileges, Puerto Rico would continue to yield to federal controls in these broad areas of insular life. In another exchange, since the island would continue without voting representation in Congress, Puerto Rico would still be free of U.S. taxes.

With this Federal Relations Act, Congress would offer the people of Puerto Rico the opportunity to write their own constitution, conditioned only on its compatibility with the Constitution of the United States and its inclusion of a bill of rights.

Congress offered these terms to the people of Puerto Rico through Public Law 600. The package was termed "in the nature of a compact," a phrase with various possible meanings. For Muñoz Marín and his followers it signified that Puerto Rican acceptance would complete an actual "compact." In Congress many saw it as "something like a compact."

The project had put Muñoz Marín on the high wire again: He was forced to balance between his assurances to Congress that the basic relationship of Puerto Rico to the United States was not being altered and his insistence to Puerto Ricans that the commonwealth envisioned in the Puerto Rican constitution would not foreclose future prospects of either statehood or independence. In each case he claimed that the spirit of the proposal was a change from a relationship in which a sovereign will had been imposed upon a dependent people to one of government by consent of the governed.

Muñoz must have known that the times favored the commonwealth project. The voting in 1948, with political status included in the Popular platform for the first time, had given him full local endorsement. And in the United States the State Department had summarized the need to remove the taint of colonialism. Its advice to Congress counseled:

> The Department of State believes it to be of the greatest importance that the Puerto Rican people be authorized to frame their own constitution as provided for in S.3336 [the bill that had been dropped in the Senate hopper], in order that formal consent of the Puerto Ricans may be given to their present relationship with the United States. . . .
>
> . . . Such actions by our government would be in keeping with the democratic principles of the United States and with our obligations under the Charter of the United Nations to take due account of the political aspirations of the people in our territories and to develop self-government in them.

In view of the importance of colonialism and imperialism in anti-American propaganda, the Department of State feels that S.3336 would have great value as a symbol of the basic freedom enjoyed by Puerto Rico, within the framework of the United States of America.

Though Muñoz's political creativity carried most of his people with him, his plan was denounced by the Independents as camouflaged colonialism, and by the Republicans as a covert move toward independence. And with the currents of anticolonialism broadening, with American support, throughout the world, Senator Joseph O'Mahoney was to affirm, "I think it may be stated as fundamental that the Constitution of the United States gives Congress complete control and nothing in the Puerto Rican constitution could affect or amend or alter that right. . . ."

Irwin Silverman of the Interior Department supported such a view in stating: "The Congress of the United States has the inherent power under the Constitution to annul any law in any of our territories, and never in the history of the United States has it annulled a single act. . . ."

Would these attitudes have prevailed over the pressures of public opinion if Muñoz had come out clearly to demand an irrevocable abdication of Congress' plenary power and an end to its unilateral controls over the island? Or was he excessively conscious of the shipping interests, the American beet sugar growers, the lumber industries, and other forces closer to Congress than the voice of the United Nations? Did Muñoz settle for less, rather than lose all? He seems rather to have chosen a partial gain, in hopes of later achieving the total victory.

Proof, violent and dramatic, soon demonstrated that the United States should consider seriously the effect of colonial bonds remaining in its new relationship with Puerto Rico.

Albizu Campos, freed from his term in the Atlanta penitentiary, had returned to the island. Although his Nationalist followers were few, many of them having joined the Independence party, they fanatically favored his incitements to direct action. Throughout most of 1950 Nationalists stored weapons in caches scattered over the island, as the insular police watched their preparations with growing alarm.

On October 30 the fuse reached the explosive point. While police and Nationalists engaged at dawn in a series of battles in Peñuelas, Arecibo, and Jayuya, two carloads of Campos' followers headed straight for the Fortaleza. With guns blazing, they crashed through the gate into the patio directly leading to the governor's office. Some were killed immediately. Others dived under the cars and carried on the struggle, which lasted for an hour at high noon. The governor had importunately rushed to the window of his office to see the gunfight and decide on steps to protect his family. Five Nationalists were killed, two policemen wounded. Had the Nationalists left one car to block the gateway to the Fortaleza, it is unlikely that the police could have brought up sufficient reserves in time to forestall a breakthrough to the governor's quarters.

Other flare-ups were drawing gunfire near the post office and in nearby Santurce. In all, thirty-three persons were killed before the uprising was suppressed, but for one more action. Albizu Campos had remained at home, at "headquarters." That night police besieged the house for hours before Campos hoisted a white towel on a broom.

Throughout the island the general reaction to the attack was one of revulsion. All parties except the Independentistas openly deplored the imposition of violence upon an island historically noted for gentleness and peace. The Independence party declared that the governor was responsible because of his effort to foster an illusory constitution and because the police had raided arms hideouts without a declaration of martial law.

The general Latin-American reaction to the incident contained a warning of broader troubles in store for the United States. The Albizu Campos affair was interpreted as an outraged attack on the government of the United States, the desperate lashing out by colonials still deprived of their liberty. The attitude was disclosed on the day of the attack in an immediate message to Muñoz from Prío Socarrás, President of Cuba: "In the name of the Cuban government, inspired by the traditional generosity of our peoples and the principles of human rights, I beg you to interpose your good offices to guarantee the life of Albizu Campos and his companions, thus avoiding a cause for aroused feelings throughout the continent."

Muñoz Marín, still seething in a cold fury, answered the Cuban President by cable the following day; if Congress and the American press failed to understand that the Puerto Rican issue was important beyond Washington and the limits of the island, Muñoz shared no such illusion:

I have received your message, in which you ask me "to interpose my good offices to guarantee the life of Albizu Campos and his companions, thus avoiding a cause for aroused feelings." I thank you for your message because of its good faith. It is my duty, however, to call your attention and that of all democrats of Cuba and Latin America to two errors in the information on which it is based.

You ask me to use my good offices for Albizu Campos. First, I have no right to use my good offices because my authority is derived from the votes of the people of Puerto Rico and the instructions of their laws. This is not a controversy between a group of Puerto Ricans and the government of the United States. It is a controversy between a band of less than five hundred Puerto Ricans and the people's mandate that I have the honor to represent.

In the second place, Albizu Campos represents no ideals of liberty but the fascist principles of tyranny of a small group of armed fanatics who wish with a grotesque and tragic futility to impose on two million Puerto Ricans their own interpretation of liberty. The real political discrepancy in Puerto Rico is not one between colonialism and independence. We are associated with the independence of the United States. An Independence party, not that of Albizu Campos, came peacefully to the polls and failed to elect a single delegate to our legislature, not a single mayor, nor a single alderman in the same elections in which I was elected chief executive of my country. The Albizu Campos band is much smaller still than this party, not coming nearly to a thousand people in all the country.

The immense majority of our people want to be a part, within the dynamic creation of a new form of state, of the independence of the United States in an association of citizenship. Stubborn minorities prefer separate independence. Both ideals are respectable. But in Puerto Rico, to be part of the independence of the United States has the endorsement of the immense majority, and separate independence has not. Albizu Campos is trying a violent assault on the right of Puerto Rico to have its liberty in the form that the people, who have the right, chose.

As ours is a government of laws, I need not tell you that our citizens have the full protection of the law even when they are aggressors on the people. Although Albizu Campos forty-eight hours ago ordered the assassination of myself and my family, those who know me know that he will have all the protection that a government by law owes even to its worst and most irresponsible citizens. . . .

While Muñoz's reply to the Cuban President was en route to counteract the anti-American flavor of the Southern Hemisphere's press reports of the Campos affair, further trouble was brewing in Washington. On November 1 two more Puerto Rican Nationalists attempted the murder of President Harry Truman at Blair House, where he was residing while White House repairs were being made. The gunmen were fatally shot down, and one American guard was killed. Even the pennies Puerto Rican schoolchildren collected for the man's widow could not dispel a wide Latin-American belief that the world had witnessed a rebellion against United States oppression. Nor did the merciful sentence against Albizu Campos—ten years for inciting an assault on the government of Puerto Rico—persuade skeptics in other countries that Puerto Rico was willingly associated with the United States and desired only an equal partnership in terms of political sovereignty.

The Albizu Campos incident and its repercussions in Latin America were largely overlooked in the United States; our attention was primarily directed toward Europe. The Marshall Plan and the Truman policy would be recorded as defenses against the major danger. It was not until ten years later that parallel action, labeled the Alliance for Progress and the Cuban containment, took cognizance of the nearby peril that Campos had so clearly drawn into view.

Had Muñoz been tempted to do so, he might have exploited the significance of the Campos affair. But he continued his steady drive toward the commonwealth goal. On the island he urged a smashing majority vote in favor of Congress' offer under Public Law 600. On June 4, 1951, he was gratified by a heavy turnout of voters. Of the 65 percent of eligible voters who cast ballots, 76.5 percent endorsed the negotiation.

Before the year was out, a constitutional convention was assembled; and on March 3, 1952, another popular referendum approved Puerto Rico's proposed constitution, 374,649 votes in favor, 82,923 opposed. The constitutional convention, in preparing the document for final congressional approval, passed a series of resolutions, one of which included the statement: "The people of Puerto Rico reserve the right to propose and to accept the modifications in the terms of its relations with the United States of America, in order that these relations may at all times be the expression of an agreement freely entered into between the people of Puerto Rico and the United States of America."

The statement was clear as to what Puerto Rico purported to accomplish through its approval of Public Law 600. Its eagerness to complete the negotiation accounted for only a slight show of irritation at Congress' request that the wording of the constitution's bill of rights be changed. The section had defined as "rights" education, a fair standard of living, jobs, and other social factors. These were relisted as "aims." The change dulled the bilateral concept of the agreement. It also cast a shadow over the friendship between the governor and Jaime Benítez, University of Puerto Rico rector, who had written the bill of rights.

Congress, meanwhile, in ratifying the agreement, recalled that it was subject to the Federal Relations Statute outlining areas of federal jurisdiction over the island, and to the Constitution of the United States, which contained no provision by which Congress could relinquish its plenary powers over United States territories. Obviously each side had its own idea about what was being done.

The congressional resolution of approval was signed into law by President Truman on July 3, 1952. In San Juan, on July 25, thousands of Puerto Ricans watched Governor Muñoz Marín raise the flag of Puerto Rico. The act marked the creation of the first commonwealth associated with the United States. It inaugurated what was termed the Free Associated State of Puerto Rico. This ceremony was considered the termination of Muñoz Marín's campaign to eliminate colonialism in Puerto Rico, but it launched seemingly endless years of challenge to his design and his goals.

After the anthem and the hymn, the crowd dispersed, still euphoric at the sight of Puerto Rico's single star flying in the tropic breeze. The achievement of an autonomy nearly as complete as that of the almost forgotten Pact of Sagasta had been consecrated by the public's own overwhelming vote. The margin between this new status and that which Muñoz Rivera had won from Spain was known to only a few, who, sharing the crowd's enthusiasm for the occasion, remembered Spain's generosity as greater than America's. They perceived the flaws in the agreement Luis Muñoz Marín had obtained for his people. They would wait only until the crowd's shouting died down before exposing the results of haste. But Muñoz already was planning to correct the defects in this new contract with the United States.

Meanwhile the formation of the Free Associated State and the economic growth that the rapidly developing Operation Bootstrap had stimulated helped the Popular party in the 1952 elections win a majority over all contenders combined. This was the last election for the dying Socialist party and the first for the reconstructed Republican Statehood group, which gained new strength from the candidacy of Luis Ferré, enlightened Ponce industrialist and supporter of free enterprise.

Now Muñoz Marín, alert to the vulnerable points in the commonwealth charter, seized the first opportunity to obtain the highest possible endorsement of the new state. On January 17, 1953, he wrote President Dwight D. Eisenhower to declare that the United States should no longer provide the United Nations with reports of its administration of Puerto Rico as a territory. The State Department was quick to approve Muñoz's contention but ran into stubborn doubts on the part of even friendly members of the United Nations. After debate, however, by a vote of twenty-six in favor, sixteen opposed, with eighteen abstentions, the General Assembly placed Puerto Rico in the classification of autonomous territories. One clause of the resolution "recognizes that, by choosing its constitutional and international status the Free Associated State of Puerto Rico has effectively exercised its right of self-determination."

Muñoz's speech at the commonwealth flag raising on July 25, 1952, had reminded the United States that "the Union, with its great democratic conscience, must feel gratified that the flag of a vigorous-spirited people pays it the tribute of voluntary companionship on the flagstaff of liberty." The curse of colonialism was being alleviated.

To his own people the address also recalled: "Our people come closer every day to the ideal that this flag represents. It is that of a tranquil life where there is honest work for a decent wage; though few may obtain luxury, none will live in a slum." This was not a promise of an economy of abundance, but of one in which the benefits of progress would be as broadly distributed as possible. And it was a promise that Operation Bootstrap was now helping to fulfill.

There was no hostility to free enterprise. The Bootstrap program depended upon the government's ability to create a society in which private business could prosper, but the aim was tempered by Muñoz's concept that "We value a man more for that which he intends to do than for that which he intends to acquire." The major part of the island government's expenditures was being applied to make its citizens stronger so they could work well and better educated so they could join the industrial complex the new government was building on the island.

The gains were there: nearly 200 factories, mostly new, by the end of 1952; since 1940, an increase in total product from $286.7 to $754.5 million; personal income up from $118 to $297 million; with schools and hospital care increasing, a reduction in the death rate from 18 to 10 per thousand and in infant mortality from 115.6 to 67.6.

There were other accomplishments, more spectacular in a visual way and important in building a new self-assurance. The construction of the Caribe Hilton Hotel, one of the world's most luxurious, had been met with some derision. Most Puerto Ricans had never thought tourists would want to come to their backward land. What did it have to offer? Almost everything, apparently. The Caribe Hilton became the government's most profitable single investment. Within two years after the hotel's opening in 1949, tourist expenditures on the island doubled, and new hotels were changing the skyline of San Juan. The Caribe Hilton had been built primarily to provide attractive quarters for businessmen looking at the island's investment possibilities. It was also hoped the tourism business might some day account for twenty-five million dollars. No one dreamed of the seventy million dollars it now, in the sixties, brings annually.

Yet even as Muñoz scored the advances, he worried about the corruption of the spirit that the great material success might cause. As urgently as Muñoz shared the spirit of the sign in Teodoro Moscoso's Industrial Development headquarters—"Please be brief. We are already twenty-five years late"—he could not resist the temptation, when Moscoso bustled in to see him, to push across his desk a small figurine of Mahatma Gandhi. "Will you stop pushing that damn thing at me when I'm talking?" Moscoso had exploded one day. Muñoz grinned broadly.

Muñoz kept pushing the spirit of Gandhi before all the statisticians, economists, and administrators who were on the Planning Board or otherwise responsible for the Industrial Development program. Yet he was proud of his brilliant Bootstrap team and almost immodest about its success. As head of the program, Ted Moscoso was winning the respect of businessmen in the United States and other countries. Economic observers were recording the achievements of Rafael Picó and his Planning Board, of Sol Luis Descartes, island treasurer, of Arturo Morales Carrión, who was later offered a responsible post in the U. S. State Department. As the performance of these and many other officers in Puerto Rican government agencies was winning notice in the United States press and academic monographs, the dismal contrast of most countries in Latin America became more noticeable. While the island that had only sunshine, people, and sugar land to sustain it, developed a business boom, Argentina's leaders were wasting and plundering their country's rich legacy from the war, Brazil was destroying her credit and the soundness of her currency with irresponsible fiscal management and indifference to extended pockets of misery within her borders, Chile's peso was second to Bolivia's in an apparent race toward limbo, Peru's few families still ignored the poverty of her masses, Colombia was struggling to be free of an immoral dictatorship, Venezuela's wealth was being siphoned into the pockets of a tyrant, and the tradition of robbing the Cuban treasury was being upheld by swindlers who would finally be expelled by Fidel Castro. Bright spots were few.

It was natural that American magazines should run stories about Puerto Rico's success, that American universities should see Muñoz as a candidate for honorary degrees, that foundations should undertake studies of the Puerto Rican "miracle," that over four thousand students of political science and economics—mostly from Latin

America, Africa, and Asia—should visit Puerto Rico to see what accounted for her bustling progress. And it was perhaps just as reasonable that few or none of them should perceive the changes in the Puerto Rican social structure that were troubling Governor Luis Muñoz Marín:

1. The *jíbaro*. The stoic, durable man of the hills to whom Muñoz had first carried his message of hope was changing. It was not only his search for better-paid employment in the new factories that was modernizing the legendary countryman. It was the new culture reaching into the hamlets, hills, and valleys that had quietly sheltered him for centuries. It was electricity, bringing not only light to his hut but the voices of the world crackling over the radio. It was new roads, giving him quick passage to the cities and towns and bringing the townsfolk into his hills. It was the schools, which taught his children to learn more than he could ever know so they could tell him about the new life of the island, its baseball games, the new American music, the money that was coming from the north to build new businesses.

The man who stayed in the hills awoke from the long deep sleep of centuries. He built small neat homes with his own labor and government financing for the materials. He learned that he could bring a problem to the agricultural services and they would show him how to solve it, how to build a bridge across a creek so his children could go dry to school, how to lay a pipe to the nearby aqueduct to bring water to a town. He knew that Muñoz had started all this—but would his children think the new life was anything more than a natural occurrence?

Many went to the city. One essayist, Sixto Morales Velardo, described the new migration:

> Having learned the first lessons, the *jíbaro* liked to try his luck; and he went down to the cities, congesting them in his desire to improve his lot. On the other hand, the urban workers and artisans, forced by this rude avalanche, felt obliged to find their way by emigrating.*

2. Emigration. Labor contractors and developers of new low-price air transport to the United States quickly responded to the search

* Sixto Morales Velardo, *Alma Latina*, April 9, 1949.

for work outside the island. Before 1930 the annual average of those leaving the island was two thousand, in the thirties less than one thousand; in the forties the figure rose to twenty thousand, and in the fifties fifty thousand Puerto Ricans a year came to the United States. Of the estimated eight hundred thousand living there at the end of the fifties, more than six hundred thousand were in New York City.

In a mechanized atmosphere that challenges even Americans, confronting new problems of racial attitude and language, the immigrants huddled into cheap and squalid quarters almost guaranteed to incubate rebellion and crime. They answered hostility with resentment and assimilated poorly. The Puerto Rican government, appalled at the reputation the island was gaining through the misadventures of its sons and daughters in the United States, set up an indoctrination and employment office in New York, as well as a predeparture preparation center in San Juan. It was also forced to review its policy of teaching English in Puerto Rican schools only as one subject in a curriculum.

The Puerto Rican communities in New York and later in New Jersey, Chicago, Philadelphia, and Boston, were beginning to exert great influence back on the island. In money sent and brought back to Puerto Rico, they were contributing in a range between thirty and forty million dollars to the island's economy. In their messages to families and friends, many were underlining their feeling that in the United States they were considered second-class citizens, that only statehood would give them equal status in America.

3. Labor. The new industries soon attracted the notice of mainland labor organizers. They were met coolly by the Puerto Rican worker, but their claims that he was underpaid were attentively heard. Embarrassingly, the Industrial Development program depended in part upon its ability to supply American investors a less costly labor force than they would find in the United States. There was even a special differentiation for Puerto Rico in the federal minimum-wage laws. It was fortunate for the program that Puerto Rican workers were not attracted by the Yankee organizers' methods. But Luis Ferré, growing in political importance as leader of the Republican Statehood party, lost no time in attacking the government's policy and emphasizing the higher wages paid in his own industries.

4. Religion. Born and baptized a Catholic, as José Luis Alberto, Muñoz Marín had never been close to the Church. Furthermore, he was a divorced man remarried to a divorcée.

Most Puerto Ricans are not devout. The Church is part of their lives, but not a dominant force. The Catholic faith has always attracted the large majority of the islanders; some twenty percent profess Protestantism. There are sizable groups of Spiritualists. Perhaps one reason why formal worship has so little appeal on the island is that the churches, formerly dominated by a Spanish clergy, are now largely administered by American bishops and priests. Another is that the services and sacraments of the Church represent expenses beyond the purse of most Puerto Ricans.

It was a facet of change, then, that brought the Church into the area of political activity. In the 1940's Muñoz had stated that a basic obstacle to the island's achievement of an acceptable standard of living was its excessive and rapidly increasing population. He had stated that wealthier economies had smaller families, and Puerto Ricans, by working hard, might reach that level of comfortable moderation. This had not occurred. Rather, the beneficial effects of better public health services, reducing the mortality rate, had aggravated the problem. Not even the new emigration to the States could overcome the speeding treadmill. And talk about birth control became more frequent and more open. Muñoz gave the idea his discreet, if unwavering, support. Public health services gradually included birth-control education in their portfolios.

Catholic ire was aroused. It may have been further goaded by followers of Luis Ferré, a devout and wealthy adherent of the faith. It may have been encouraged by the superstitions of hillmen and their women. The resentment was not appeased by women devotees, who had never become accustomed to Muñoz's somewhat irregular past. The Church's hostility to Muñoz increased. And since Muñoz *was* the Popular party, as well as governor of the commonwealth, a new political problem was now in his future.

5. Education. The accelerated educational program was scoring an impact in every home on the island. With less than half the school-age children enrolled in schools at the start of the Popular regime, ninety percent were now receiving formal schooling. The question of teaching English in the schools had been resolved into a policy of making English a language course only. This was partly because of

the belief that Spanish should remain the official language and partly because of a continuing unavailability of English teachers.

The dramatic spearhead of Puerto Rico's educational effort was the University of Puerto Rico. Long stagnant under Spain and during the early years of American colonialization, it was surging ahead now under the leadership of Jaime Benítez, its remarkably competent chief drawn from the ranks of the independence-minded intellectuals who had first joined Muñoz in the 1930's. Benítez, a lithe, dark, intense man, was building one of the largest universities under the American flag. This center of intellectual life in the commonwealth boasted an enrollment of some seventeen thousand students on its campuses in Rio Piedras, San Juan, and Mayagüez. It was an inspiration to the Catholic University in Ponce and the Inter-American University in San Germán.

The university's changing political tone was another manifestation of the success of the government program under the commonwealth. Its students and its international faculty showed an increasing interest in statehood for Puerto Rico. Objective observers understood this tendency in terms of a desire to guarantee the progress that had been made during Puerto Rico's association with the United States, evidence of a determination not to lose the island's gains in a sweep to independence.

Muñoz took a less charitable view of the declarations that were coming out of the university. A coolness crept into his relations with his old friend Benítez. As adherents of each man sought to prove their loyalty by speaking for him, the two were egged into a display of mutual irritation that came close to the breaking point. Leading wasp who stung Muñoz was Thomas S. Hayes, lecturer, teacher, and writer, who told a group of visiting educators in 1957 that Muñoz's power over the dominant party prevented the working of democratic processes on the island. Muñoz's lieutenants, possibly going further than he wished, made efforts to obtain Benítez's retirement. The incident blew over, and the university continued to pour out the well-prepared young men and women needed to implement Puerto Rico's development program.

Perhaps the new restlessness demonstrated in all these phases of Puerto Rican life was part of the pain of growth, part of the price of success in a newly emerging society. It was certainly proof that the people of Puerto Rico had learned Muñoz's lesson of independent thought. The elections of 1956 may well have made Muñoz wonder how to push back into the magic lamp part of the jinn he had brought forth in 1940.

The Populares won again and Muñoz was reelected governor, but there was more warning than encouragement in the results. The Popular party received 433,010 votes, barely 2,000 more than in 1952, an increase below the growth in voter registration. The Indpendentista party fell from its former 126,228 to 86,386 votes. The news was in the surge of the Republican Statehood party—up from 85,591 to 172,838 votes. Representing a new respect for prosperity and the American way of fostering it—with a short memory for the local government program that made it possible—was the Republican party candidate, Luis Alberto Ferré Aguayo.

Luis Ferré, six years younger than Luis Muñoz Marín, was born in Ponce, the son of a rich industrialist and part of a family group whose business operations were extending to Florida and Venezuela. He was a Master of Sciences from the Massachusetts Institute of Technology. As a leading citizen, he had been president of the Lions Club, officer of the Chamber of Commerce, chairman of the YMCA Development Program, member of the Boy Scouts Council of Puerto Rico. He was an articulate speaker and writer, an art collector, and an excellent pianist, fisherman, and fencer. As an industrialist, he was successful and progressive. His employees were paid above the insular averages, and his provision of social benefits gave his workers advantages well beyond those proposed by Muñoz's administration or granted by most other private businesses. As a worshiper, Sr. Ferré was an outstanding layman of the Catholic Church.

Ferré espoused statehood, free enterprise, an end to government guidance of the island's economy. He had led a continuous campaign to undermine the faith of the public in the commonwealth, insisting that it was a transitory step toward independence, that it was unconstitutional, uncertain, and invalid. Ferré's sizable audiences became larger and more enthusiastic when the Hawaiian Islands and Alaska were admitted as states of the Union. Car bumpers appeared carrying "51" signs to enunciate a new Puerto Rican aspiration. A Citizens' Committee for "51" was formed.

Muñoz decided to meet the opposition directly and speedily. As often occurred, he acted with only minimum consultation with others in his party or in the opposition groups. He ordered a bill drawn for congressional approval that would more definitely limit the spheres of federal jurisdiction in Puerto Rico; would allow Puerto Rico, at its own discretion, to initiate contributions to the costs of federal government; and, primarily, would rewrite the Federal Relations Act, supplanting it with "The Articles of Permanent Association of the People of Puerto Rico with the United States."

The bill was killed in committee. Hastily written, it was subject to varied criticism; but its crucial impediment was the word "permanent" in "The Articles of Permanent Association. . . ."

This word "permanent" aroused questions that are still alive. Can one Congress bind its successors? Can any association with the United States other than statehood constitutionally be permanent? Did the commonwealth have the right to enter into a permanent arrangement without a plebiscite on commonwealth, statehood, and independence?

Muñoz contended that a plebiscite should be held only when Puerto Rico would be strong enough economically either to meet the conditions of statehood, including payment of federal taxes and an end to the tax-exemption program that was attracting new industries, or to solve the problem of independence without free access to the American market. In lengthy sessions before the congressional committee, Muñoz also pointed out that "permanent" meant "continuous until both parties should agree on a change—not one party or the other."

His arguments were unavailing. His path up the hill became rockier. The boulder he was shoving toward the top was now heavier. And now, just before the 1960 election, he had suffered this public political defeat.

The towering figure that faced the threat of the 1960 election leaned his bulky shoulders over the governor's desk with undiminished confidence. The life of Puerto Rico bore his mark. He had given his supporters something to cleave to, his adversaries something to challenge. The formless mass that had straggled over the Caribbean island even during the first forty years under the American flag had in the last twenty years become a dynamic example to underdeveloped countries everywhere. And the man who had held stewardship over these two decades now cast his influence well beyond the limits of the island. Muñoz Marín was now an innovator whose ideas touched the problems of the hemisphere and of the world.

The statistics were appearing in scores of studies and reports. In twenty years production had risen three times in constant dollars; personal income had tripled; family income had quadrupled. The changing ownership of wealth in ten years had reduced the percentage of families earning less than $1,000 a year from 46 to 23.9, more than doubled the percentage of families whose earnings were bracketed between $2,000 and $5,000, with an even greater increase in those earning from $5,000 to $10,000. Earners over the $10,000 figure had tripled as a percentage of the population. Wages had increased from an hourly average of 19 cents in manufacturing to a level of 89 cents, in agriculture from 15 to 48 cents, and in the construction industries from 22 to 81 cents. The diet of the people had changed: the consumption of dairy products had nearly tripled, was nearly double for meat, and had more than doubled for eggs.

The island's birth rate, one of the highest in the world, had begun to decline—from 39 per thousand to 31.5—and the average life expectancy had risen from 46 years to an amazing 71. But the great rescue work of the public health services had accelerated the population's growth rate, and an island long ago crowded with 547 persons per square mile now had 683. Even the booming economy and its now 600 new factories could not diminish the high 13 percent of unemployed, although the figure's significance had altered. There was far less child labor, and the unemployed were not left to beg or starve.

This was the work of the political scientist. The philosopher's influence was spelled out in different terms.

Always a dramatic speaker, Muñoz acceded to the increasing requests for talks before groups newly aware that the Caribbean had produced a man of historical importance. His speech-writing methods were as varied and unorganized as most facets of his personal activity. He wrote out some talks, dictated others, often using a team of secretaries and almost simultaneously giving them widely separated parts of a speech, which he would then piece together. He used writers, instructing them as to theme, then editing meticulously and endlessly, often hastily rewriting until half an hour before an address.

One such occasion combined most of these techniques, as Muñoz, writers, and secretaries battled toward completion of a major address over a weekend in the country house in Trujillo Alto. The house bears the unbarbered signs of the natural man who has escaped from his office in the Fortaleza. The garden is half weed, half plant, much of it there by chance. Children, dogs, and farm animals wander about at will. Prominent among this cast of rural characters at the time was an old goat who had been allowed to reach the season of wisdom only because Muñoz could not bear to eat a friend.

It was natural that the animal should take a quiet interest in all proceedings, and on this particular afternoon no one noticed him as he stood in the garden house observing the frenzy of the speech-making process. Coming to his own conclusions, he edged to the desk a secretary had momentarily abandoned and engaged in masticating her part of the speech. This was perhaps Muñoz's finest hour, for even the panic of four secretaries and a junior speech writer did not bring the goat's days to an immediate end.

Muñoz's addresses in Puerto Rico usually outlined his views on political status. On one occasion he declared:

> There seems to be some confusion in Puerto Rico with reference to our political status and its development. . . .
>
> My position is clear. We are not moving toward independence. We are not moving toward statehood. . . . I do not believe in federated statehood. . . . It would result in establishing a priority by the government of the United States as against the elected government of Puerto Rico in the imposition of taxes, thereby impairing considerably the liberty of the people of Puerto Rico. . . .
>
> I do not believe in separate independence. . . . It would destroy all the potentials of the economic growth of Puerto Rico. . . .
>
> I believe in the Commonwealth. . . . It provides our people with more political liberty than federated statehood; it ensures far more economic freedom than separate independence; it sets free our cultural personality. . . .

In concluding the talk, Muñoz struck out at the mounting numbers who based their doubts about commonwealth on the fear that

Muñoz might some day be succeeded by a surge toward independence. Of commonwealth he declared:

> I believe in the moral greatness of the association with the United States, but not because I believe in the moral inferiority of the Puerto Rican . . . not because of slanderous fears as to the capacity of the people of Puerto Rico to create and to develop and to respect their freedom. . . . I would not want to be at the head of people who would follow me because they are afraid of themselves, or because they do not believe in the moral integrity of our people.

At Harvard University's Commencement Day in 1955, the governor discussed Puerto Rico's new Operation Serenity, designed to preserve its cultural heritage and place philosophical restraints on the approach to the island's abundance. Some listeners may have thought his words were reminiscent of John Kenneth Galbraith. Others may have read Galbraith's acknowledgement of debt to Muñoz in the introduction to *The Affluent Society*. Muñoz said to the graduates:

> . . . Serenity may perhaps be defined as the habit of seeing your world whole, as the living society of men and forces and facts in which you as an individual conduct your life. To see it whole, you must see it simply. And to see it with intelligent simplicity you must see it deeply. A society in which Operation Serenity had been successful would use its economic power increasingly for the extension of freedom, of knowledge, and of the understanding imagination rather than for a rapid multiplication of goods, in hot pursuit of a still more vertiginous multiplication of wants.

Muñoz then applied this concept to the responsibilities of the West toward the world's underdeveloped areas:

> . . . Let the highly developed nations of the West help the underdeveloped areas of Asia, Latin America, Africa; help them to help themselves to defeat hunger, slums, evil living conditions; but let us not persuade them to scrap philosophies of good, de-

cent, modest desires. It is beyond the imagination to conceive
what freedom and happiness, great advances in science, can
produce for a civilization of fine modest wants. . . .

Can a culture be efficient in production and at the same time
wise and modest in consumption? Can it be feverish in output
and serene in intake? I say we are getting to the time in which
it must . . . because of the evident possibility of regearing
high productivity to higher ends.

The following year Muñoz Marín developed the theme of United
States relationships with Latin America in talks to two distinctly con-
trasting audiences: the International Ladies' Garment Workers Union
at its annual convention in Atlantic City and the Associated Harvard Club's annual convention at Coral Gables.

To the former he outlined one of the obstacles confronting our
policy-makers:

. . . In a number of Latin-American countries . . . governments tend not to be representative of the will and aspirations of
their peoples. Since all suspicion of intervention must be
avoided, the United States finds itself in the position of being
friendly to the governments and thereby seemingly unfriendly
to the peoples of such countries. This is a very tough and un-
just situation for the American people. . . .

He then served warning on those who would equate free enterprise with the spiritual principles of democracy: recalling the
"eternal principles for which the American Revolution was fought,"
Muñoz noted "a certain promiscuity between those principles and
the technique of private enterprise. There is nothing wrong with
private enterprise . . . but it is not the only technique that can be
used to conduct business under freedom. . . . Free enterprise, as I
say, is a great tool. It is obvious that the impression should not be
given that free enterprise is compulsory."

In speaking to the Harvard Club group, Muñoz rephrased his
message, drawing heavily on the Puerto Rican story for documenta-
tion. "The Commonwealth government," he said, "pioneered in
building and operating factories when there was need to do so be-

cause private capital was hesitant to do it. It socialistically established and managed industries and then capitalistically sold them to private enterprise."

In applying our concepts to improve conditions in the hemisphere, Muñoz suggested: "Let us encourage government and private initiative to share in a good partnership with a view to better distributive justice for all; and let's not be doctrinaire about it. Let us not be doctrinaire either as to socialism or capitalism, but only as to freedom and human dignity."

When Fidel Castro made the dangers of Communist influences in Latin America more apparent to the American people early in 1959, Muñoz was consulted by the United States Senate Foreign Relations Committee. He advised further development of a concept that finally became the Alliance for Progress. He insisted that we had neglected Latin America and that the little we had done had been too rigidly bound to economic doctrine.

Again he used the example of Puerto Rico, pointing out that the island, without the great natural resources of the other countries, had surpassed them in personal income and a fair distribution of its wealth. He claimed that Puerto Rico's advantages of access to the American market, grants-in-aid, and spiritual energy and drive "do no more than compensate for the lack of fuels and raw materials, the scarcity of land in relation to the population, the insular geography." Finally he asked that the government stop putting the label of "self-interest" on its aid to other nations. "Let us cease to pretend that the American people are extraordinarily hardhearted in order to hide the altogether creditable fact that they are decently kindhearted."

The previous year Richard Nixon, the Vice-President of the United States, was stoned and insulted by crowds in the streets of a number of Latin-American cities. Muñoz cited the incidents to dramatize a proposal for action in an article published in the July 8, 1958, issue of *Look* magazine. He again asked that we offer our neighbors freedom and dignity rather than a business policy. His program had six points:

1. The United States should join wholeheartedly with Latin America in its battle against hunger, disease, illiteracy, industrial backwardness, and agricultural poverty. . . .

2. Wherever possible, the United States should reduce tariffs. . . .
3. The United States should encourage actively the establishment of a common market in Latin America. . . .
4. In its relationships with Latin-American countries, the United States should carefully differentiate between the democracies and the dictatorships. . . .
5. . . . In discussing foreign aid, it would be wise to talk less of self-interest. . . .
6. The United States Information Agency should launch a much stronger drive to explain the United States and its true motives to Latin America.

With the exception of the second point—and that has received much attention—the program became a part of American foreign policy. Muñoz gave it considerably more support before the plan was taken up by Washington. Speaking at a dinner in honor of the justices of the United States Supreme Court in Washington in 1959, Governor Muñoz Marín sketched out a program in specific detail. His proposal included strengthening the Inter-American Development Bank, encouraging a common market, expanded technical assistance, elimination of double taxation to encourage a greater southward flow of private investment, the establishment in conjunction with Latin-American governments of a development corporation, modification of United States tariff policies, and an effort to stabilize commodity prices.

In 1959 Muñoz turned his attention to an even larger problem when he gave the Godkin Lectures at Harvard University. Developing the thesis that we must attain a "post-nationalist world" in order to survive the threat of nuclear extinction, he stated:

The idea of the nation, the sovereign nation-state, is not obsolescent because it is weak. It is far from weak. It has a fearful strength. The obsolescence comes from the measureless changes in the world in which it lives. It is precisely its pertinacity in a world in which it is coming not properly to belong that makes our time so tragic in its potentialities. . . .

Much of what Muñoz said to students, teachers, judges, business-men, senators, and labor leaders was paraphrased in the simpler language he used on his own island. There he had said:

We are still climbing a steep hill. We are far from the top, but already we can see the top in the distance. Let us look at it even from afar. . . .

I see at the top of the symbolic hill a people well housed—very few of them in luxurious palaces and none in wretched huts or slums. I see the opportunity for honest work at a rate of pay moderate but adequate to a good and satisfying life. I see families that are at peace in the thought that their children will be educated. . . . I can see that all of us will work with enthusiasm, freedom, and a sense of duty and respect for the rights of others. I see private initiative for the common good conceived as a duty rather than only as a right. . . .

This was Muñoz's view of the crest. Nor was the vision still a distant one. Already revealed in a broader background was a view of hills beyond.

FOURTEEN

The Hills Beyond

Three acres of garden surround the Muñoz Marín retreat in Trujillo Alto. Around them stretches the ribbon of another acre, between two great wire fences with floodlights: a precaution against attack from Nationalists, Castro agents who may have joined them, or, in former years, hostile Dominicans from Trujillo's oppressed island.

There is beauty in this garden, and peace; but there is the vibrancy of clashing ideas and the growth of prophetic striving.

Don Luis, dressed in pale blue denim slacks, a matching short-sleeved sport shirt, and heavy blue tennis shoes, is being interviewed by a young woman who represents a chain of New England educational radio stations. There is a tape recorder between them, and they are seated in the garden house, a spacious Caribbean *bohío* with hardwood floors, upright logs holding up a thatch roof, and no walls. The breeze that blows gently through the shelter hardly ruffles the few papers on the governor's desk. Muñoz leans forward intently while he listens to the young American's questions and answers them with gestures lost to the whirring machine.

On the veranda of the nearby stone bungalow Doña Inés Mendoza de Muñoz is fondling their thirteenth grandchild as she talks with her daughter Victoria and the biographer who is waiting to see Don Luis. The baby, María, is six weeks old and at the moment is very quiet about it. She is the third child of Victoria and her artist husband, José Antonio Rueño. Another daughter, Vivian, has three small girls. She is a social worker, and so is her husband, in New York. Both live and work in Puerto Rican Harlem, an uncomfortable and dedicated assignment. Munita, the daughter of Muñoz and Muna Lee, is also married to a painter, Rosado del Valle, and has three children. Luis Muñoz Lee, the only son, is married to the daughter of Don Luis' old political enemy, Arjona Siaca, and is editor of the English language weekly, the *Island Times*. Tall, handsome, shy, Luisito is an enigma to those who look for another politician to emerge from the family strain.

Doña Inés, married to the writer who long ago set aside his pen, is the mother-in-law of two painters and the leading patron of Pablo Casals, the great Spanish cellist who has returned to the island of his mother's birth. Inés is the almost militant leader of the defenders of Puerto Rican culture. She says, "I believe with Casals that creative work is time added to your life. God does not count it among the years allowed you, but adds it to them." María coos approvingly, for Doña Inés has a soothing voice. Its timbre is low and strong. It reflects a quiet force. Many of those who are otherwise confused by Muñoz's decisions find an easy answer in attributing them to Inés' sturdy attitudes.

Word arrives from the *bohío* that Muñoz's interview has been interrupted. The tape recorder has broken down. While it is being repaired, if a repairman can be found, he will begin a conversation with his other visitor. On the short walk down to the garden house, the biographer sees the slender trees overhead, the flowering bushes alongside, and the uncut grass under foot as a setting for reflections of the past. But he has learned that Muñoz is usually more concerned about the future.

Muñoz is standing outside the shed, and he starts strolling as he talks. There is a lane of bamboo and other tropical trees. He looks up. "It's beautiful how the light comes through those leaves. They have so much color in them. It's like a cathedral with fine stained-glass windows."

Muñoz's voice has retained its pleasant low tone, its sense of restrained power. At sixty-six the governor's body reflects the youth his mind has preserved. He is heavily, but firmly, built. The famous head of unruly black hair has given way to a more tractable gray, matching his moustache. Most impressive, as always, are the eyes—large, dark, probing, glooming into the background of an idea, then coming alive as it takes shape.

This is a man with all the paraphernalia of peace but bearing the painful prod of unfulfillment, the distress of dissatisfaction. One wonders why the balm of peace does not dispel the goading urge in these autumn years.

He had won the 1960 election. The Popular party had attracted fifty-eight percent of the votes, down from the sixty-two percent of 1956. The Independentista group declined from twelve to three percent of the total vote. The new Christian Action party had won only seven percent. These two parties, having failed to obtain the ten percent necessary to qualify for the ballot in the next elections, were virtually eliminated from the political scene. But the Republican Statehood group, with some 250,000 votes, increased its percentage from twenty-five to thirty-two percent of the total vote. The warning trend, which had first been discerned in 1956, had gathered momentum.

The election had been a disturbing experience. The level of the electioneering had sagged as the Republicans continued to assail the validity of the commonwealth and the allegedly dictatorial aura of the Muñoz Marín regime, with its twenty years in office under the monolithic structure of a party dominated by the personality of one man. The entrance of the Church into direct political action was also an embarrassment, if only because on the mainland a Catholic's candidacy for President of the United States was being debated with a minimum of allusion to religious considerations. In Puerto Rico Archbishop James P. Davis and Bishop James E. McManus displayed less delicacy.

Muñoz turned off the Church challenge with insistent references to the American tradition of keeping Church and state in their separate spheres. His reference to an American principle was then exploited by the Republicans, who continued to argue that the security of American citizenship for Puerto Ricans required a statehood status. As in most political campaigns, the polemic often moved into more emotional than logical areas, especially when Republicans scorned the colonial residue still clinging to the commonwealth format.

None of this was lost on Fidel Castro and other Latin-American Communists, who took up Castro's cry that Puerto Rico was "a perfumed colony" directed by a puppet of the United States.

Muñoz, sensitive to ferment in the Caribbean and farther south, again undertook to defend the commonwealth as an instrument of the Puerto Rican will forged in conjunction with the United States. On the island the heavy weighting of the electorate by new and relatively prosperous voters lessened the effectiveness of Muñoz's descriptions of the Popular party record in fostering social justice and economic development. This new group was tending to associate economic well-being, not with the Bootstrap program that had made it possible, but with the even wealthier United States. Now when Muñoz spoke of the future responsibilities of government in Puerto Rico, listeners were less attentive than in the old days of desperate misery.

The truth was, and is, that Puerto Rico's economic problems were far from solved.

Overpopulation was still the island's curse, going into the decade of the 1960's. In a talk to the Puerto Rican community in New York, Muñoz described it in these terms:

> Think of the United States, with her great size and her great resources.
>
> Now, suppose that all the iron, coal, copper, and other minerals were taken away.
>
> Then, almost all her factories.
>
> And now! Imagine that everybody living in the whole world today moved to the United States.
>
> Then you have a picture of the problems we have faced in Puerto Rico: as many people per square mile as the United States would have if her population included everybody in the entire world; no mines or fuels; and very little industry. This gives us an idea of the picture of Puerto Rico twenty years ago.

Little of that picture has changed, except for the factories. Now the man in the garden in Trujillo Alto would mention the 900 industrial plants, 725 owned by United States firms, with more coming at the rate of three a week. He would point out that the island's rate of increase in net income from manufacturing exceeds that of the European Common Market. He would list among the incentives that foster this growth a record in 1962 of an average twenty-five-per-cent return on investment; availability of man-produced electric power; government financing, design, and construction of plants for new industries to buy or lease; government training of labor; main-

tenance of vocational schools for over fifty-five trades; the first
Foreign Trade Zone authorized by the U.S. government outside the
continental United States, with availabilities for manufacturing;
association with the United States.

To his planners he would indicate the problems this boom contains: the surge to the cities, the need for roads and public works to
distribute new industries throughout the island.

He would be forced to admit, too, and he does, that the high rate
of unemployment, between twelve and fourteen percent, persists.
More and more factories are needed. New agricultural programs are
required to replace the declining sugar industry. Proponents of increased autonomy say that U.S. coastal shipping laws shackle Puerto
Rican industry by forcing its use of expensive, monopolistic United
States shipping facilities. Others, returning to the sugar problem, say
it might be solved if the Jones-Costigan Law, retained in the commonwealth charter, were eliminated to allow unrestricted sugar refining on the island.

Prominent among other problems that await solution is housing.
Despite the spectacular program of new housing construction in cities, and the self-help housing campaign in rural areas, the slums still
fester like spreading sores in the heat of San Juan and smaller cities.

Still lagging behind the needs of a growing and eager population
are facilities for education. The biggest share of the insular budget,
between twenty-five and thirty percent, has been assigned to education, and great advances have been achieved. Literacy is up to eighty
percent, the number of children attending school has nearly doubled
in a decade, accelerating programs of school-building and teacher-
training are strongly supported. But classrooms crowd in from forty
to sixty children, and a large percentage can only be accommodated
in half-day sessions.

It is on these and corollary problems that Muñoz wants to concen-
trate the minds and energies of his people. It is to the concept of
material progress to be shared by all, not to enrich the clever and
leave the impoverished in rags, that he would have his people apply
their talents. And he wants the creative spark for such a mission to
be Puerto Rican, associated with the United States, but springing,
like the plants in his garden, from the island's soil. So the impatient
spirit of Muñoz has not found rest in a political triumph, but pain in

the querulous atmosphere of discord over the political status in which the forward strides must be made.

Ironically, it was just such an atmosphere that he stilled when he emerged as the head of a new political movement in 1938, scoring his first political victory on a campaign platform headed by the statement: "Status is not an issue." Why was Muñoz Marín, twenty years later, forced to engage in the debate on status that had been a sterile plague on his island for forty years before he came to the political scene? Why—when the people had ten years ago given him a mandate for a new solution to the old problem, the solution of commonwealth—was he required to defend that creation in 1960? Why did his adversaries, and even members of the United States Congress, use the same term as Fidel Castro in denominating the commonwealth "a perfumed colony"?

He was forced back twenty years because Congress, after its first flush of pride at having acceded to Puerto Rico's request for commonwealth status, had been unwilling to remove the colonial stain that its juridical defects still carried. This had caused dismay in Puerto Rico and a sense of confusion that an opposing political party could exploit. It had also given Communists in other Latin-American countries a chance to return to their claim that the United States is a colonial power. Lack of a solution would be a continuing embarrassment for Puerto Rico and the United States. The wrong outcome, halting Puerto Rico's self-propelled march toward prosperity, would be a greater failure.

So there is no rest for Muñoz Marín in his sixty-sixth year. That is why he hunches forward in a chair in the garden house, intently describing how he hopes to solve this dilemma today.

On the commonwealth's tenth anniversary, July 25, 1962, Governor Muñoz Marín disclosed an exchange of letters between President John F. Kennedy and himself. Muñoz had written:

. . . The commonwealth relationship was a creation of which both the United States and the people of Puerto Rico may well be proud. It was a new type of arrangement in the constitutional system of the United States; at that time, ten years ago, it was a pioneering effort in the world to terminate colonialism by substituting for it not nationalism or independence, but freedom within the framework of a close and mutually beneficial association between a smaller and a larger community. . . .

Munoz's letter went on to say that at the time of initiating the new relationship, there was a clear understanding that its statutes were subject to correction and improvement. He then proposed that the commonwealth principle be further clarified "so as to eliminate any possible basis for the accusation, which is made by enemies and misguided friends of the United States and Puerto Rico, that the commonwealth was not the free choice of the people of Puerto Rico acting in their sovereign capacity, but merely a different kind of colonial arrangement to which they had consented."

He further proposed that "the governmental power and authority of the commonwealth should be complete and any reservations or exceptions that are not an indispensable part of the arrangements for permanent association with the United States should be eliminated. . . ."

And finally Muñoz's letter entered another proposal:

. . . I believe that the people of Puerto Rico should have an opportunity to indicate their preference clearly and directly for any other form of governmental relationship if they should prefer any such other form.

It is my intention to request the commonwealth legislature to enact a law pursuant to which proposals to perfect the commonwealth within its association with the United States would be submitted to the people of Puerto Rico.

It is my purpose also to recommend that advocates of both independence and of federated statehood for Puerto Rico should be afforded the opportunity in the legislation to present these alternatives to the electorate so that no doubt whatsoever may be entertained in Puerto Rico, the United States, or elsewhere that the basic United States principle of self-determination has been thoroughly carried out. . . .

President Kennedy's acknowledgment opened with the usual courtesies, then stated:

I am aware, however, as you point out, that the commonwealth relationship is not perfected and that it has not realized
its full potential, and I welcome your statement that the people
of Puerto Rico are about to begin the consideration of this with
the purpose of moving towards its maximum development. I am
in full sympathy with this aspiration. I see no reason why the
commonwealth concept, if that is the desire of the people of
Puerto Rico, should not be fully developed as a permanent institution in its association with the United States. I agree that this
is the proper time to recognize the need for growth and, both as
a matter of fairness to all concerned and of establishing an un-
equivocal record, to consult the people of Puerto Rico, as you
propose to do, so that they may express any other preference,
including independence, if that should be their wish.

The announcement of this exchange between Governor Muñoz
and President Kennedy unleashed a deluge of polemic rage that has
become a microcosmic wonder of modern politics, a gathering of
confusion like the mists that surround the roar of a storm. No one
knows whether the twisting mass will reach the destination of
Muñoz's original choice. Events outside the status conflict have
made its final resolution a matter of greater importance than was
originally imagined by two letter writers who already shared an intense appreciation of the danger intrinsic in the half-free, half-sub-
jected commonwealth format.

Muñoz immediately announced that the plebiscite on the three
alternate forms of government—commonwealth, statehood, and independence—would contain a statement of "perfected" commonwealth. The voter would consider, not the present status, but one re-
moving all doubt as to its permanence and irrevocability (except by
free decision of both Congress and the Puerto Rican people). It
would include a further extension of the authority of the island to
manage its own affairs, a clear delimitation of areas of continued
United States government jurisdiction, a means by which islanders
might vote for the President and Vice-President of the United States,
and a formula permitting the island to contribute to the expenses of
the United States government.

The Republican Statehood party fell over itself in its hurry to re-
spond. Its perennial gubernatorial candidate, Luis Ferré, stated that

he favored the plebiscite. But the head of his party, Miguel Angel García Méndez, labeled Ferré's declaration a private rather than a party opinion. The party finally agreed to oppose the plebiscite by threatening to boycott the proposed ballot. It claimed that a plebiscite offering a form of commonwealth that might not be achieved would be a deception. Observers saw considerable logic in their position. Commentators pointed out that the hope of qualifying Puerto Rico for the Presidential vote, when the overpopulated island would outvote twenty-five of the states of the Union, was ridiculous. Inadvertently, they were also underlining a major obstacle to the eventual attainment of statehood for Puerto Rico.

It had been Muñoz's hope to go to Congress with a mandate from his people as expressed in the suggested plebiscite. Before the year was over, he had been forced to compromise with the Republicans. He would go to Congress first to negotiate the terms of commonwealth that he could offer the electorate, and he would attempt to obtain a congressional commitment for statehood in case that should be the choice of the voters. No one really believed that Congress would incur such an obligation, but the Republicans were euphoric. They had won a great victory over Muñoz. For a short while they even forgot to call him a dictator.

The next act was played in Washington. The quality of political maneuvering that preceded and accompanied congressional hearings on the issue was in sad dissonance with the international implications of the question at hand. The statehooders waved the American flag effectively. Their contention was that their goal was to be "more American"; hence, Muñoz, who opposed statehood, wanted to be "less American." Some Republican congressmen seemed to feel that Puerto Rican aspirations toward greater autonomy were an expression of dissatisfaction with their association with the United States. The peril point, which Muñoz and the President had understood, was defined by a competent Puerto Rican reporter, A. W. Maldonado, in his comments in the *San Juan Star*, April 22, 1963:

A number of Puerto Rican leaders, including statehooders and *independentistas*, have consistently maintained that Puerto Rico is still a U.S. territory under unilateral congressional power.

Also some congressional leaders insist that Congress did not really mean to give up its powers over Puerto Rico stated back in 1952. The issue is this: If no "compact" exists—if Congress retained the right to unilaterally (without consulting Puerto Rico) revoke Puerto Rico's status—then it is evident that Puerto Rico is still a U.S. colony.

Not only that, but it would also justify a feeling of gross insecurity among Puerto Ricans, who would be living under the constant threat of having Congress change or revoke their status.

Although Muñoz has systematically insisted that Congress no longer can act unilaterally on Puerto Rican status and that Puerto Rico is not a colony, there has always been the possibility of the "compact" itself being tested in federal courts and declared nonexistent.

The discussion had moved to dangerous ground, and Muñoz, alarmed, sought to avoid the legalistic and political pitfalls that threatened the commonwealth. He scrapped his proposal for congressional approval of a commonwealth status adjusted to the five-point formula that he originally hoped to offer Puerto Rican voters. His decision to shift tactics indicated to reporter Maldonado that "Muñoz, it is strikingly evident, is sparing nothing in his determined drive to culminate his own remarkable political career with a decisive and final chapter to Puerto Rico's 460-year-old political status history."

By agreement with Chairman Wayne N. Aspinall of the House Interior Affairs Committee and Chairman Leo W. O'Brien of the Territories Sub-Committee, on April 27, 1963, Muñoz proposed a resolution for a commission to study the commonwealth concept before a plebiscite should be offered Puerto Rican voters. The resolution contained a number of interesting features. One was the preamble, which stated that Congress, "duly recognizing the inherent right and juridical capacity of the people of Puerto Rico to govern themselves and to establish such relationships with the government of the United States as are freely agreed upon . . ." will establish the commission appropriate to the situation. Approval by Congress would, of course, strengthen the Puerto Rican claim to sovereignty.

Another paragraph, Section 5, stated: "The President is hereby authorized to enter, on behalf of the United States, into a compact with the people of Puerto Rico upon fulfillment of the following conditions. . . ." This was a first step toward replacement of Congress by the executive as the future contact point for the relationship with the commonwealth. The idea was not new to Muñoz and his advisers. They had long seen the difficulties of negotiating with Congress. They had visualized too that this transfer of power to the chief executive might solve the nagging question of how Congress could divest itself of plenary powers over a "territory," so that the territory could become something else, like a commonwealth.

There was nothing more for Muñoz to do in Washington. He returned in the summer of 1963 to the Fortaleza and, as soon as possible, to his garden in Trujillo Alto. Should Congress pass the resolution he had left with its committees, a status commission would be given eighteen months to make its study. This would extend its work beyond the 1964 elections.

Muñoz suggested that the debate on status be suspended until the emergence of the commission report in 1965.

If Puerto Rico's accustomed methods of democratic dispute have failed to win many headlines, the ferment in the surrounding Caribbean has compensated in clamor and in danger. Perhaps it was Castro who both attracted interest in the Caribbean and veiled other areas behind the flamboyance of his performance. His spectacular confrontations with the United States, once joined by Russia in a threat to the peace of the world, have partly masked his incursions into neighboring countries.

Puerto Rico has harbored many of his exiled victims, usually to its own benefit. Cuban experts advise the Puerto Rican government, Cuban doctors augment the pressed public health service, Cuban businessmen are in many Puerto Rican enterprises. Castro agents, too, have attempted to infiltrate and incite the handful of Puerto Rican Nationalists. But with Albizu Campos now protected from his own loss of reason in a mental hospital since his trial for treason in 1951, little has been accomplished beyond attracting Señora Campos to the Cuban United Nations delegation in New York.

Castro's greatest thrust has been toward Venezuela, where an old friend of Muñoz Marín's has warded off repeated attempts to overthrow the government and to assassinate him. Rómulo Betancourt, long a staunch champion of democracy, took refuge in San Juan, Puerto Rico, when he fled from the menacing Venezuelan dictator, Pérez Jiménez. In 1963 Betancourt, now President, after three attempts on his life, visited Washington in triumph; but first he stopped in Puerto Rico for a talk with his old friend in the Fortaleza. As he approached the almost miraculous termination of his regime, Betancourt's Democratic Action Government party nominated Dr. Raúl Leoni, who had helped found the party in 1941, to run for the presidency of Venezuela in a free election.

Other events in the Caribbean and on its shores were marking new dangers, forming new patterns, and building a new force that was spreading democratic concepts against the tide of Castro-like communism. The early 1960's saw successful transitions away from colonialism. Trinidad and Tobago became a nation. Jamaica became independent. But these had been British colonies. Their racial and historical context was not Latin American. The Dutch colonies of Aruba, Curaçao, and Surinam also joined the list of self-governing states in the Caribbean. Geographically eligible for ultimate membership in the Organization of American States, these new entities would drastically change its composition from predominantly Latin American to a mixture of European offshoots. In their midst, Puerto Rico was providing guidelines to progress. The government development corporations in Trinidad and Tobago, in Jamaica, and in Venezuela were patterned on the principles of the Economic Development Administration of Puerto Rico.

Steadfast proponents of democratic thought, never formally organized, were leading other countries away from the despotism of the past and aside from the temptations of communism. Veterans like Muñoz, former President José Figueres of Costa Rica, and Betancourt of Venezuela stood by to endorse the newly elected government of Lleras Camargo in Colombia after that country had ejected its dictator, Rojas Pinilla. They cheered when he completed his term without violence, and was succeeded in a free election by Guillermo León Valencia.

Farther south, Haya de la Torre was closing a long career of protest against oligarchic administrations in Peru. Elected in 1962, Haya was blocked from office by military action. The following year Francisco Belaúnde Terry won the presidency on a platform surprisingly close to Haya's proposals for social reform in Peru.

As the aging stalwarts kept pressing for freedom and a fair share of bread and hope for Latin-American masses, new leaders were, and are, being trained in a remarkable academy operating without fanfare in Costa Rica. This advanced school for political leadership is the International Institute of Political and Social Studies. Its faculty is drawn from the countries of Latin America, from the United States, and heavily from the University of Puerto Rico. Its advisory board includes Rómulo Betancourt, Víctor Haya de la Torre, José Figueres, former President Eduardo Santos of Colombia, and Norman Thomas, perennial head of the American Socialist party. Muñoz Marín has never joined the proceedings of the school, but his representatives maintain a continuous liaison.

It may be a coincidence that the college is located in the same city that so joyfully welcomed President John F. Kennedy in April of 1963 when he joined the presidents of the five Central American countries to celebrate their working plan for a common market. It is less than coincidental that most of these figures belong to the broadening group of liberal leaders that Muñoz calls the "democratic left."

In November, 1961, he had spoken of the importance of this "democratic left" in an address to the Associated Press managing editors. Warning American reporters of the dangers of abbreviated reporting, he said:

I should like to point out the damage newspapers can do if they carelessly paste odious political labels on Latin Americans. . . .

Take Betancourt of Venezuela, for example . . . some U.S. papers went so far as to suggest he was not much different from a Communist. Yet he is one of the stoutest supporters of democracy in the hemisphere. . . .

Much of the new emerging Latin-American leadership is, in a sense, leftist. They want great change because their peoples need great change. The touchstone is: Do they seek that change in terms of political liberty, of human freedom, and of respect for human dignity, or not? Men like Betancourt, Lleras, Haya de la Torre, seek the changes that their people need in the terms that every lover of freedom in the United States respects.

There seems to be the widespread feeling in the United States that communism is the only issue.

But there are other issues in Latin America, issues that go deeper than communism, issues that must be resolved before communism can be banished.

The issues are poverty, ignorance, disease, and tyranny—the four horsemen of the Apocalypse. They must be fought with such weapons as land reform, housing, jobs, education, public works, health measures, and enlightened statesmanship.

. . . A continent laid waste by poverty and hunger can, indeed, become a positive threat to peace and stability.

It makes a revolution inevitable and, in the sense of the way we should understand the word "revolution," desirable.

Moving on to a discussion of the Alliance for Progress and its needed stimulus, Muñoz advised:

Aid must not be only abundant but enlightened. As newspapermen, you will appreciate that it should be something else too: it should be profoundly dramatic—not superficially sensational but profoundly dramatic.

. . . The first task is arousing strong hope by immediate, visible, understandable, sustained action.

. . . In the revolutionary transformation of Puerto Rico from a destitute agrarian society to a thriving industrial complex (consciously destined to become the base, not the end, of a fine civilization), we learned that the essential force that powered our effort was *hope*—hope that through hard work and self-help we could reduce the poverty and misery that plagued us.

Perhaps it was in this paragraph that Muñoz uttered the words that have synthesized the attraction of Puerto Rico for eager new nations and have won the regard of American political scientists and poets.

. . . Hope is the necessary first ingredient of a people's creativeness. Hopeless people cannot help themselves. Hope is the spiritual fuel that moves people who live in misery. . . .

Now the program that Muñoz had long before proposed was taking shape as the Alliance for Progress. In discussing its initial difficulties and its future prospects, Muñoz again returned to this theme. Speaking to the AFL-CIO National Conference on Community Services in Chicago on May 3, 1962, he expressed his concern:

What deeply troubles me is the seeming lack of emotional commitment in Latin America toward this great and historical venture.

. . . The economic body is being gradually nourished, but the heart is not. . . . The problem is political and ideological and the solution can only be political and ideological. . . . I believe that there is only one group in Latin America—or at least one group above all others—that can make the Alliance work in the long run. That group is what I call the democratic left.

I would call the democratic left in Latin America the group that seeks social advances and higher living standards for *all* the people in a framework of freedom and consent. It is not necessarily based on class and often includes important elements of the middle class and even a few enlightened members of the wealthy oligarchies.

One of the prime reasons why I believe that this group is the only one that can make the Alianza work is that I think it is the only group that *wants* it to succeed in its entirety. It is the group that really *believes* in social reform and justice as well as economic development, whereas many of the nominal backers of the Alliance applaud its economic purposes and give only lip-service to the social objectives.

I also believe that the democratic left is the only nontotalitarian element that understands the depth of the revolutionary ferment in Latin America and that can provide responsible leadership to shape this revolution into constructive channels. The well-meaning democratic conservatives, men whom we can often respect, have no real grasp of this revolutionary surge and are therefore powerless to compete with the totalitarians, who have a very lively understanding of it and every intention to capture and pervert it for their own purposes. Only the democratic left has the dynamic ideological base, and the popular grass-roots feeling, to compete with the totalitarian left—the Communists, the Castroites, and the Fascists. . . .

Muñoz terminated this speech by transferring the cash value of the Murray-Green Award bestowed upon him to the Institute of Political and Social Studies founded in Costa Rica by the fiery charter member of the democratic left, former President José Figueres.

Muñoz's support of the democratic left was badly needed by his former lieutenant, Teodoro Moscoso, who was attempting to translate his experience as administrator of the Operation Bootstrap program in Puerto Rico to the task of directing the United States participation in the Alliance for Progress.

Although he may have felt at home with the problem of bestirring the needy of Latin America to fend for themselves, and that of inducing the prosperous and the powerful to give their own people a meaningful pledge of hope, Moscoso found himself in a strange environment: he was striving for people beyond his island, he was struggling with a new bureaucracy, and the backing of the governor's office was now unavailable. But the governor's message was still clearly audible. One writer, describing its application to the slum-ridden sections of Rio de Janeiro, stated: "What is important is that the *favelado* somehow be made to believe in himself. No program, no matter what it builds or changes, will have any real effect on the problems of Latin America's poor unless it also does this."

Moscoso could never have felt far distant, however, from the crusade that Muñoz led in Puerto Rico when he read other evaluations of the currents running against the Alliance. This was the kind of opposition he had become used to in Puerto Rico more than a decade ago.

In *The New York Times*, April 14, 1963, page 4E:

> But, quickly, opposition to this concept of the Alliance began to emerge from conservative Latin-American groups—mainly land-owning and traditional business classes—that feared the reformist ideas of the Kennedy planners in the field of agrarian and taxation changes. From the outset, opposition also arose from United States business interests concerned about the safety of their traditional investments.

From the *Economist*, April 13, 1963, page 130:

> The United States, today, and despite all that it is doing that it never did before, is remarkably friendless in Latin America. The Right, the land-owning aristocracy, some of the business middle class, feel themselves betrayed by the very principles of

the Alliance; the Left is sceptical of the programme's radical execution.

The hardened Moscoso has not quailed before a task so similar, if so much broader and more complex, to the one he shared for two decades with Muñoz Marín. He may at times miss Muñoz's charismatic political persuasion at his side. But the governor's reach has gone even beyond Latin America.

In Nice, France, Muñoz projected his socioeconomic concepts again to an international audience. Speaking to the forty-fifth annual convention of Lions International, on June 21, 1962, he declared:

> . . . One of the great issues of our times is to find how to bridge the enormous gap between the wealthy of this world and the desperately poor. . . . Today this principle is only questioned in most Western European countries and in the United States by those that yearn for anachronistic privileges. . . . A country cannot live in peace with itself with a few very rich and many very poor; neither can the world live at peace with itself . . . with a few countries rich and many countries living . . . subject to the ravages and the social-political consequences of extreme poverty. . . .

And again Muñoz restated the principle on which a solution should, in his opinion, be based. Speaking of the poor, he said:

> The great task is to unleash their creative energies. And the first great step is reached when they join together to work with enthusiasm and purpose, armed with adequate technical tools to achieve their own salvation. . . . The great engines of creative energy in peoples are hope and pride. . . . If people cannot be given hope and pride, what is left to them? The answer is simple: despair and probably violence. . . . Only by reaching people spiritually can the necessary material tasks be undertaken successfully. . . .

Before he returned from Nice to his garden, Muñoz made his first pilgrimage to the home of his ancestors, the village of Villota del Duque, in the province of Palencia, Spain.

Muñoz's face lights up as he tells about the visit to the parched, windswept town on the Spanish plain. "There were about two hundred and fifty people there when the first Muñoz left it during the Napoleonic Wars," he says, "and two hundred and fifty people are there now. We had a fine time with them.

"Now," the governor continues, "the Muñozes of Puerto Rico have offered the town a gift in return for its hospitality to Inés, myself, and our group. We suggested either a scholarship for one of its students or a well for the town. They have just told us that there is an abundance of intellectuals in Palencia but a scarcity of water, so they would prefer the well."

When he returned to the island that summer of 1962, there were reasons enough for Muñoz to consider terminating his career with the least possible turbulence and with a view toward the travel, writing, and rest he had so long postponed. The significance of the Puerto Rican story had been recorded by reporters and students of political and economic history. Recognition of the island's accomplishments had been exemplified by the 9,000 visitors from 132 countries who, since 1952, had joined its technical cooperation program of training in branches of public service, as well as by the 3,000 delegates from 100 countries who came for general observation rather than specialized training.

Puerto Rico's relationship with the United States had changed from that of an impoverished responsibility to a prosperous trading partner. Per capita, it was now the second-largest buyer of American goods, in dollar terms the world's fifth-largest customer of the United States, with purchases totaling nearly one billion dollars annually.

Muñoz Marín too had received more honors than most men in public life. He had been granted decorations by three countries and numerous communities. Harvard, the University of Kansas City, Bates College, and Columbia University had given him the honorary degree of Doctor of Laws. He was among the first group to receive the Presidential Medal of Freedom.

It was conceded that although he had dominated the political scene in Puerto Rico for more than two decades, he had encouraged the development of other men who might replace him with some hope of success. Teodoro Moscoso, U.S. coordinator for the Alliance for Progress; Arturo Morales Carrión, deputy assistant secretary for inter-American affairs; Roberto Sánchez Vilella, Puerto Rico's secretary of state; Dr. Rafael Picó, of the government Development Bank; Senate Vice-President Luis Negrón López; speaker of the House Santiago Polanco Abreu; University Chancellor Jaime Benítez; and the Republican candidate, Luis Ferré—all had shown capacities for political leadership and a hopeful measure of statesmanship. In the insular government new men were replacing the first generation of the Bootstrap team and filling their places effectively.

Why not prepare for retirement? Because although the bellies of his people were no longer churning with hunger, their spirits were uneasy with doubt about the validity of their commonwealth. Still beyond reach was the serenity Muñoz proposed for a people that should have a decent minimum of comfort, a proud association with a nation it respected, and a sense of its own identity. It was still possible for a man within Muñoz's own party to publish a statement including this declaration: "Regardless of how much truth is contained in Castro's propaganda, one thing is positive; Castro has succeeded in using Puerto Rico as a tool to impress Latins, to make them believe that United States imperialism predominates in Puerto Rico and we have sold our souls to the devil for material and economic advantages."

Muñoz committed himself to erasure of this misconception when he engaged in the exchange of letters with President Kennedy that threw the question open to public vote. He later strove to achieve clarification in his proposed wording of a bill by which Congress would establish a commission to study the issue.

On August 13, 1963, the House Territories Subcommittee finally announced its own recommendation for the status commission. In its wording the bill had omitted all mention of Puerto Rico's "inherent right" to govern itself. It also passed over the suggestion that the future relationship of the island be with the President of the United States rather than Congress. It stated that the study commission should consist of seven members and stipulated that Puerto Rico be "invited" to nominate six more members to the commission. Although Puerto Ricans might take comfort in the fact that they were "invited" rather than "directed" to join the commission, no doubt exists that the hard core of the commission was created by congressional unilateral action.

Three days later, in a discussion of the problem of Portugal's colonies in Africa, Secretary of State Dean Rusk said, "It's a very practical notion in the modern world that political arrangements are stable and promising when they clearly rest upon the consent of those directly involved."

Could Muñoz do other than smile wryly and say he was "satisfied"? There was hope that statesmen might man the committee, that it would be "nonpolitical," that it would understand that what Dean Rusk was saying for the benefit of the Portuguese also applies in the Caribbean.

While these thirteen commissioners investigate and confer, while the political parties of Puerto Rico wrangle over the 1964 elections, Muñoz might well look for the cathedral lights flashing through the trees in his garden.

As he strolls from the small house to the far end of the garden and gazes toward the hills beyond, he will tell his companion, the visitor who questions him, "The Puerto Rican people can be characterized by three attributes that spell their role in the future: they have a sense of liberty and association, of freedom in conjunction with, not separate from, other people; they have a talent for developing this idea in peaceful and friendly ways; and they have a genius, historically, for bypassing the particular form of nationalism of the age."

Now he pauses to look at a hibiscus bowing in the mild breeze, and then walks on. One hand is in his pocket, the other is gesticulating with his words. His shoulders droop slightly but his gaze is on some distant mark. "These attributes," he says, "can have an important place in helping to bring the hemisphere together, helping it to reach a common ground. And the countries of the hemisphere will have to do that to survive the nuclear age."

His free hand shoots out. Muñoz turns toward his companion. "I don't mean the military threat. It looks as though we might solve that. I mean the question of people in the peaceful world of nuclear power, with the new problems beyond us."

There is a pause, as though an old anguish were goading him. He begins again. "That's why we have to solve this commonwealth issue now. It has to be understood as a bilateral arrangement, without any taint of colonialism. And it has to be understood that it avoids an urge toward nationalism, that it is a format for growth in a changing world."

There is a note of anxiety as well as urgency in the words, almost an irritation that this mundane matter of the commonwealth tangle should throw its fortress walls around the poet's vision of man's freedom and brotherhood: freedom based on liberation from the fear of want, and brotherhood woven into the fabric of a world physically able to overcome the barriers of space and communication. Muñoz seems to say that a people that has found a means toward well-being under a protector's flag should be allowed to seek its own identity too under that banner, without its status being called in doubt by its own politicians or neighboring enemies of the United States. It is the issue of status, or of doctrine, that he sees as raising a wall around the poet's dream of people everywhere free from poverty, everywhere proud of their own cultures, everywhere ready to join their destinies to those of their neighbors. He has taken the people of his island a long way toward this goal. Its promise has inspired the hopes of others around the world.

BIBLIOGRAPHY

BOOKS

Alegría, José S. *Cinquenta Años de Literatura Puertorriqueña.* San Juan: Biblioteca de Autores Puertorriqueños, Editores de la Academia Puertorriqueña de la Lengua Española, 1955.

Allen, Frederick Lewis. *The Big Change.* New York: Harper & Brothers, 1952.

Babín, María Teresa. *Panorama de la Cultura Puertorriqueña.* New York: Las Americas Publishing Company, 1958.

Benítez, Jaime. *Junto a la Torre: Jornadas de un Programa Universitario (1942–1962).* Rio Piedras: University of Puerto Rico Press, 1962.

Brameld, Theodore. *Remaking of a Culture.* New York: Harper & Brothers, 1959.

Brau, Salvador. *Disquisiciones Sociológicas y Otros Ensayos.* Introduction by E. Fernández Méndez. Rio Piedras: University of Puerto Rico, Ediciones del Instituto de Literatura, 1956.

Brown, Wenzell. *Dynamite on our Doorstep: Puerto Rican Paradox.* New York: Greenberg, Publisher, 1945.

Cadilla, M. *Raíces de la Tierra.* Arecibo: Tip. Hernández, 1941.

Canales, Nemesio. *Paliques.* Rio Piedras: Editorial Universitaria, 1952.

Carreras, Carlos N. *Hombres y Mujeres de Puerto Rico.* Mexico: Editorial Orión, 1957.

Chaves, Antonio F. *La Distribución de la Población en Puerto Rico.* Rio Piedras: Editorial Universitaria, 1949.

Clark, Gerald. *The Coming Explosion in Latin America.* New York: David McKay Company, Inc., 1963.

Clark, Victor S., et al. *Porto Rico and Its Problems.* Washington, D.C.: The Brookings Institution, 1930.

Cochran, Thomas C. *The Puerto Rican Businessman.* Philadelphia: University of Pennsylvania Press, 1959.

Dalmau Canet, Sebastián. *Luis Muñoz Rivera, Su Vida, Su Política, Su Carácter.* Introduction by Luis Muñoz Marín. San Juan: Tip. Boletín Mercantil, 1917.

Diffie, Bailey W. and Justine W. *Porto Rico: A Broken Pledge.* New York: Vanguard Press, 1931.

Ebenstein, William. *Today's Isms.* 3rd ed. Englewood Cliffs, N.J.:
  Prentice-Hall, Inc., 1961.
Fernós-Isern, Antonio. *Puerto Rico Libre y Federado.* San Juan: Biblio-
  teca de Autores Puertorriqueños, 1951.
Fitts, Dudley. *Anthology of Contemporary Latin American Poetry.* Nor-
  folk, Conn.: New Directions, 1942.
Freidel, Frank B. *The Splendid Little War.* Boston: Little, Brown & Co.,
  1958.
Galbraith, John Kenneth. *The Affluent Society.* Boston: Houghton Mifflin
  Company, 1958.
Garver, Earl Simeon, and Ernest B. Fincher. *Puerto Rico, Unsolved
  Problem.* Elgin, Ill.: The Elgin Press, 1945.
Géigel Polanco, Vicente. *Los Ismos en la Década de los Veinte.* San Juan:
  Instituto de Cultura Puertorriqueña, 1960.
Gray, L. C. *History of Agriculture in the Southern United States to 1860.*
  New York: Peter Smith, 1941.
Gruber, Ruth. *Puerto Rico: Island of Promise.* New York: Hill and
  Wang, Inc., Publishers, 1960.
Hancock, Ralph. *Puerto Rico: A Success Story.* Princeton, N.J.: D. Van
  Nostrand Company, Inc., 1960.
Hanson, Earl Parker. *A Land of Wonders.* New York: Alfred A. Knopf,
  Inc., 1960.
————. *Transformation: The Story of Modern Puerto Rico.* New York:
  Simon & Schuster, Inc., 1955.
Haring, C. H. *Las Instituciones Coloniales de Hispanoamérica* (siglos
  XVI a XVIII). San Juan: Instituto de Cultura Puertorriqueña,
  1957.
Huebener, Theodore. *Puerto Rico Today.* New York: Holt, Rinehart &
  Winston, Inc., 1960.
Ickes, Harold Le Claire. *Secret Diary.* 3 vols. New York: Simon &
  Schuster, Inc., 1953.
Iglesias Pantín, Santiago. *Luchas Emancipadoras.* San Juan: Cantero
  Fernández, 1929; 2nd ed., preface by Bolívar Pagán, San Juan:
  Imprenta Venezuela, 1958.
Johnson, Virginia W. *The Unregimented General: A Biography of Nelson
  A. Miles.* Boston: Houghton Mifflin Company, 1963.
Lee, Albert E. *An Island Grows: Memoirs of Albert E. Lee, 1873–1942.*
  Introduction by Waldemar F. Lee. San Juan: Published as a public
  service, on the occasion of its eighty-sixth anniversary, by Albert E.
  Lee and Sons, Inc., 1963.
Lieban Córdova, Olivo de. *7 Años con Muñoz Marín.* San Juan: Edi-
  torial Esther, 1945.
Lloréns, Washington. *El Humorismo, El Epigrama y La Sátira en la
  Literatura Puertorriqueña.* San Juan: Instituto de Cultura Puertor-
  riqueña, 1960.
Maldonado, Teófilo. *Hombres de Primera Plana.* San Juan: Editorial
  Campos, 1958.

Mathews, Thomas G. *Puerto Rican Politics and the New Deal.* Gainesville: University of Florida Press, 1960.

Meléndez, Concha. *De Frente al Sol—Apuntes Sobre la Poesía de Luis Muñoz Rivera.* San Juan: Instituto de Cultura Puertorriqueña, 1960.

Méndez, Eugenio Fernández. *Desarrollo Histórico de la Sociedad Puertorriqueña.* San Juan: Instituto de Cultura Puertorriqueña, 1959.

Millis, Walter, *Martial Spirit.* Boston: Houghton Mifflin Company, 1931.

Monclova, Lidio Cruz, and Antonio J. Colorado. *Noticia y Pulso del Movimiento Político Puertorriqueño (1808–1898–1952).* Mexico, D.F.: Editorial Orión, 1955.

Morales Carrión, Arturo. *Ojeada al Proceso Histórico de Puerto Rico.* San Juan: La Editorial del Departamento de Instrucción, 1950.

———. *Puerto Rico and the Non-Hispanic Caribbean: A Study of the Decline of Spanish Exclusivism.* Rio Piedras: University of Puerto Rico Press, 1952.

Morales Otero, Pablo. *El Jíbaro Americano.* San Juan: Biblioteca de Autores Puertorriqueños, 1947.

Muñoz Rivera, Luis. *Obras Completas (Campañas Políticas, 1890–1916 y Apuntes Para un Libro, 1896–1900).* Four volumes selected and edited by Luis Muñoz Marín. Madrid: Editorial Puerto Rico, 1925; 2nd ed., ed. by Dr. Lidio Cruz Monclova, San Juan: Instituto de Cultura Puertorriqueña, 1960.

Pagán, Bolívar. *Historia de los Partidos Políticos Puertorriqueños* (vols. I–II, 1898–1956). San Juan: Librería Campos, 1959.

Pérez-Marchand, Monelisa Lina. *Historia de las Ideas en Puerto Rico.* San Juan: Instituto de Cultura Puertorriqueña, 1960.

Perloff, Harvey S. *Puerto Rico's Economic Future: A Study in Planned Development.* Chicago: University of Chicago Press, 1950.

Quiñones, Samuel R. *Nemesio R. Canales, el Humorista de Puerto Rico.* San Juan: Publicaciones del Senado de Puerto Rico, 1961.

Ramírez, Rafael W. *Cómo Vivían Nuestros Abuelos.* San Juan: Instituto de Cultura Puertorriqueña, 1957.

Rippy, James Fred. *Latin America: A Modern History.* Ann Arbor: University of Michigan Press, 1958.

Robles de Cardona, Mariana. *El Ensayo en la Generación del Treinta.* San Juan: Instituto de Cultura Puertorriqueña, 1960.

Roosevelt, Theodore, Jr. *Colonial Policies of the United States.* New York: Doubleday, Doran & Company, Inc., 1937.

Ruiz Belvis, Segundo, José Julián Acosta, and Francisco Mariano Quiñones. *Proyecto Para la Abolición de la Esclavitud en Puerto Rico.* Introduction and notes by Luis M. Díaz Soler. San Juan: Instituto de Cultura Puertorriqueña, 1959.

Senior, Clarence. *Strangers, Then Neighbors: From Pilgrims to Puerto Ricans.* New York: Anti-Defamation League of B'nai Brith (Freedom Books), 1961.

Spargo, John. *Applied Socialism.* New York: The Viking Press, Inc., 1912.

Steward, Julian Haynes, et al. *The People of Puerto Rico: A Study in Social Anthropology.* Urbana: University of Illinois Press, 1956.

Todd, Roberto H. *Desfile de Gobernadores.* San Juan: Casa Baldrich, 1943.

Torres Mazzoranna, Rafael. *Luis Muñoz Rivera y el Pacto con Sagasta.* San Juan: Instituto de Cultura Puertorriqueña, 1960.

Tugwell, Rexford Guy. *The Art of Politics.* New York: Doubleday & Company, Inc., 1958.

————. *The Stricken Land.* New York: Doubleday & Company, Inc., 1947.

Ward, Barbara. *The Rich Nations and the Poor Nations.* New York: W. W. Norton & Company, Inc., Publishers, 1962.

White, Trumbull. *Puerto Rico and Its People.* Philadelphia: Frederick A. Stokes Company, 1938.

MAGAZINES AND NEWSPAPERS

Ascoli, Max. "Colonialism in Congress," *The Reporter* (June 20, 1963).

Bagué, Jaime, V. M. D. "Porto Rico—An Interesting Experiment," *Pan American Union Bulletin* (July, 1924).

Beals, Carleton. "The Password Is Progress," *Saturday Review* (September 10, 1960).

Benítez, Jaime. "Caribbean: Our Sea of Troubles," *Saturday Review* (July 13, 1963).

Benner, Thomas E. "American Difficulties in Porto Rico," *Foreign Affairs* (July, 1930).

Berle, A. A. "Latin America's True Voice," *Saturday Review* (July 13, 1963).

————. "Porto Rican Independence," *Survey* (September 24, 1921).

————. "Venezuela: The Achievement of Don Rómulo," *The Reporter* (November 7, 1963).

Cater, Douglass. "Puerto Rico: The Best Answer to Castro," *The Reporter* (January 19, 1961).

Charriéz, Alfonso Lastra. "I Accuse," *La Semana* (June 10, 1922).

Colombán Rosario, José. "Nuestra Herencia Social y el Jíbaro en Puerto Rico," *Brújula* (April, May, June, 1934).

Cousins, Norman. "The Puerto Rican Mixture," *Saturday Review* (December 5, 1959).

Durand, Rafael. "Puerto Rico—Industrial Progress in the Caribbean," *International Trade Review* (May, 1963).

Durand, Rafael, ed. "America's Peaceful Revolution," *The Economist* (April 13, 1963).
———. "Between Americas," *ibid.* (April 13, 1963).
———. "Notes on Latin America," *Monthly Review* (March, 1963).
———. "Profit Hunters in Puerto Rico," *Fortune* (May, 1950).
———. "State or Commonwealth?" *Newsweek* (August 6, 1962).
Fischer, John. "Mystery Island," *Harper's Magazine* (June, 1957).
Font Saldaña, Jorge. "Santiago Iglesias Visto por P. Martínez," *Puerto Rico Ilustrado* (December 16, 1939).
Gervasi, Frank. "Puerto Rico Grows Up," *Collier's* (November 3, 1945).
Greenburg, Jonathan. "Bootstrap Financiers," *Barron's Weekly* (May 6, 1963).
Haverstock, Nathan A. "Profile of a Peace Corpsman," *Saturday Evening Post* (September 8, 1962).
Herring, Hubert. "Forgotten Puerto Rico," *The Christian Century* (December 6, 1933).
———. "Rebellion in Puerto Rico," *The Nation* (November 29, 1933).
Iglesias y Harcher. "La Génesis de la Federación Libre de Puerto Rico," *Puerto Rico Ilustrado* (December 6, 1939).
Krippene, H. P. "Porto Rico's Playful Politics," *The New York Times Current History* (January, 1922).
Lear, John. "The Barefoot Boss," *Saturday Evening Post* (December 11, 1943).
Levine, Ted M. "The New Caribbean—What Is It?" *International Trade Review* (May, 1963).
McEvoy, J. P. "Unhand Me, Uncle!" *Reader's Digest* (August, 1945).
McWilliams, Carey. "Puerto Rico: Plebiscite for Identity," *The Nation* (September 15, 1962).
Maldonado, A. W. "Its People Have Made Puerto Rico First Class," *Puerto Rico Spotlight* (June 17, 1963).
Massolo, Arthur. "Puerto Rico's Muñoz Marín," *The New York Post* (March 9, 1959–March 15, 1959).
May, P. W. "The Porto Rican Jíbaro," *Porto Rico Progress* (December 8, 1923).
Meléndez Muñoz, M. "La Realidad del Jíbaro," *Puerto Rico Ilustrado* (June 5, 1937).
Montañez, Rafael. "La Obra Sociológica de Santiago Iglesias," *Puerto Rico Ilustrado* (December 16, 1939).
Morgenbesser, David. "Bright Puerto Rican Future Seen," *Journal of Commerce* (February 13, 1963).
Moscoso, Teodoro. "Puerto Rico—Up from Poverty," *Challenge* (June, 1960).
Moscoso, Teodoro, and Arlene and Howard Eisenberg. "How Freedom Can Win in Latin America," *This Week Magazine* (September 9, 1962).
Moskin, J. R. "Muñoz, the Practical Revolutionist," *Look* (January 17, 1961).

Muñoz Marín, Luis. "Americanization: Three Cases," *The American Mercury* (September, 1930).
———. "Conversaciones Políticas," *Puerto Rico Ilustrado* (June 23, 1923).
———. "Crisis in Latin America—Operation Seeing Is Believing," *Vital Speeches of the Day* (January 1, 1962).
———. "Moods," poem, *Golden Book* (August, 1926).
———. "A 'Ninety-Eight Percent American' in Porto Rico," *The New Republic* (January 4, 1922).
———. "Porto Rico: The American Colony," *The Nation* (April 8, 1925).
———. "Puerto Rico and the United States, Their Future Together," *Foreign Affairs* (July, 1954).
———. "Queries," poem, *Poetry* (December, 1924).
———. "The Sad Case of Porto Rico," *The American Mercury* (February, 1929).
———. "Song-maker of a Continent," ibid. (March, 1925).
———. "T.R. of P.R." *World's Work* (July, 1931).
———. "Tyranny and Torture in Venezuela," *The Nation* (April 15, 1925).
———. "We've Come a Long Way in a Peaceful Revolution, interview in *U.S. News & World Report* (March 28, 1960).
———. "What Next in Porto Rico?" *The Nation* (November 20, 1929).
Reston, James. "The Population Problem and Foreign Aid," *The New York Times* (February 27, 1963).
Robinson, Donald. "Muñoz Marín—Puerto Rico's 'Poet Leader,'" *Reader's Digest* (November, 1956).
Roca, Gaspar, Jr. "Local Participation—Chapter II in Puerto Rico's 'Operation Bootstrap,'" *International Trade Review* (May, 1963).
Theobald, Robert. "Abundance—Threat or Promise?" *The Nation* (May 11, 1963).
Zingler, Ervin K. "Puerto Rico—51st State?" *Forum*, fall issue (1962).

PAMPHLETS, REVIEWS, DOCUMENTS

Alliance for Progress—A Weekly Report on Activities and Public Opinion. Washington, D.C.: Pan American Union, General Secretariat of the Organization of American States, April, 1963.
Annals of the American Academy of Political and Social Science. Vol.

285. Edited by Millard Hanson and Henry Wells. Philadelphia, 1953.

Anuario Estadístico—Estadísticas Históricas. San Juan: Puerto Rico Planning Board, Bureau of Economics and Statistics, 1959.

Baggs, William C. "Puerto Rico: Showcase of Development," *World Without Want.* Chicago: Britannica Book of the Year, Encyclopaedia Britannica, Inc., 1962.

Baitsell, John M., and John D. Glover. "Hilton Hotels Corporation," *Harvard University Graduate School of Business Administration Study.* Cambridge, Mass., 1961.

Barton, H. C., Jr. "Puerto Rico's Industrial Development Program, 1942–1960," *Bulletin of the Center of International Affairs.* Cambridge: Harvard University Press, October 29, 1959.

Benítez, Jaime. *The University of Puerto Rico.* Rio Piedras: Office of Information, University of Puerto Rico, 1960.

Colombán Rosario, José. "The Peasant and His Historical Antecedents," *Porto Rico and Its Problems,* Appendix A. Washington, D.C.: The Brookings Institution, 1930.

Commonwealth of Puerto Rico. Washington, D.C.: Office of the Commonwealth of Puerto Rico, 1962.

El Desarrollo Económico de Puerto Rico: 1940–1950, 1951–1960. San Juan, January, 1961.

Facts About Puerto Rico. Washington, D.C.: Office of the Commonwealth of Puerto Rico, 1963.

Gatell, Frank Otto. "The Art of the Possible, Luis Muñoz Rivera and the Puerto Rican Jones Bill." Photocopy left for the use of "qualified scholars" in the *Colección Puertorriqueña* of the University of Puerto Rico Library, Rio Piedras. June 2, 1959.

Historia del Partido Popular Democrático. San Juan: Partido Popular, 1960.

Hunter, Robert J. *Puerto Rico—A Survey of Historical Economic and Political Affairs.* Committee Print No. 15, 86th Congress, First Session, Washington, D.C., Committee on Interior and Insular Affairs, House of Representatives. November 25, 1959.

Indices Seleccionados de Progreso Económico y Social—Años 1939–1940, 1946–1947 al 1960–1961. Commonwealth of Puerto Rico, Bureau of Economics and Statistics, Puerto Rico Planning Board, 1962.

Institute of Caribbean Studies. Edited by Thomas G. Mathews. Rio Piedras: University of Puerto Rico, 1962-63.

Latin America: A Positive View. New York: *Visión,* 1963.

MacEoin, Gary, Eugenio Chang-Rodríguez, and Myriam Luz, eds. *The Hemisphere's Present Crisis.* New York: Overseas Press Club, 1963.

Negociado de Planificación Económica y Social. San Juan: Junta de Planificación, 1961.

Puerto Rico—A Report on Its Economic Growth and Development. New York: Economics Department and Overseas Division of First National City Bank, May, 1963.

Puerto Rico Federal Relations Act. Hearing before the Committee on
    Interior and Insular Affairs, 86th Congress, First Session on S.2023.
    Washington, D.C.: United States Senate, 1960.
Stead, William H. *Fomento—The Economic Development of Puerto
    Rico.* Planning Pamphlet No. 103. Washington, D.C.: National
    Planning Association, March, 1958.
United Nations Statistical Abstract. New York: United Nations, 1959.

INDEX

		DATE DUE